KODAK Films
Color & Black-and-White
EASTMAN KODAK COMPANY

KODAK EKTACHROME Film

Modern photographic films are truly remarkable when you consider how effectively they capture the events of our lives. The uses of film in our society are almost endless. Because film is such a vital part of the photographic process and so profoundly affects the quality of your pictures, you need a film that gives results of consistently high quality. Kodak films meet these quality requirements.

Eastman Kodak Company is noted for being in the forefront of the industry and for making remarkable advances in film technology. The company is continually performing research to achieve the ultimate perfection in the manufacture of film to provide the greatest possible benefits and value to customers.

Kodak films are manufactured with a wide variety of characteristics so that you can choose the best film for the type of photographs you want to take. In order for you to select the best film to suit your needs, you should be familiar with the characteristics of the films available. The purpose of this book is to acquaint you with Kodak films for general use.

The book has two sections—a text portion and a section of Data Sheets at the end of the book. The text portion explains what you'll want to know about selecting the right film, how to expose it properly, how to get it processed, and how you should store your films. The Data Sheet section gives you all the details for each film, such as film speeds, recommended filters, flash exposure guide numbers, and processing requirements. The information presented in this book will help you make photographs that you will be proud to show to your friends.

For data books on professional roll and sheet films, you may want to purchase *KODAK Color Films for Professional Use* (E-77) and *KODAK Professional Black-and-White Films* (F-5). These books are available at stores that sell photographic products. In most countries outside the United States, Kodak books are sold mainly in bookstores.

Caroline Grimes, *Editor*

KODAK EKTACHROME 200 Film (Daylight)

GARY WHELPLEY

CONTENTS

Book Design: D. J. Malczewski
Picture on front cover
KODACHROME 64 Film (Daylight)
NEIL MONTANUS and BOB CLEMENS

*The Kodak materials described in this book are
available from those dealers normally supplying
Kodak products. Other materials may be used, but
equivalent results may not be obtained.*

KODAK Publication No. AF-1
© Eastman Kodak Company, 1985

Library of Congress
Catalog Card Number 85-081346
ISBN 0-87985-356-5

GARY WHELPLEY

Choosing a Film

Your first consideration in selecting a film is the kind of camera you have—traditional or instant. If you have one of the KODAK Instant Cameras, Kodak makes a film for use in these cameras which gives you instant color prints. If you have a traditional camera, your next consideration is the type of pictures you want—color prints, color slides, or black-and-white prints. Kodak makes several films with different characteristics for each type of picture for use in traditional cameras. Kodak makes one film for disc cameras; it's for color prints. The information in this book will help you select the best film for your needs.

You'll also want to know what films are available in the size that your camera accepts. Kodak films for general photographic use are manufactured in five general forms—135 magazines; disc; 110 and 126 cartridges; rolls; and 144 instant film packs.

The 135 films are rolled on spools in magazines. These films are 35 mm wide and have no backing paper. They are available in 12-, 24-, or 36-exposure lengths, depending on the kind of film.

A 135 magazine. The illustration on the right is a cross-section view of a magazine loaded with film.

Disc film has a light-sensitive flat disc of film supplied in a thin, lighttight plastic disc-enclosure. The enclosure has a dark slide that automatically opens and closes inside the camera to protect the film from light outside of the camera. Disc film has 15 exposures per disc.

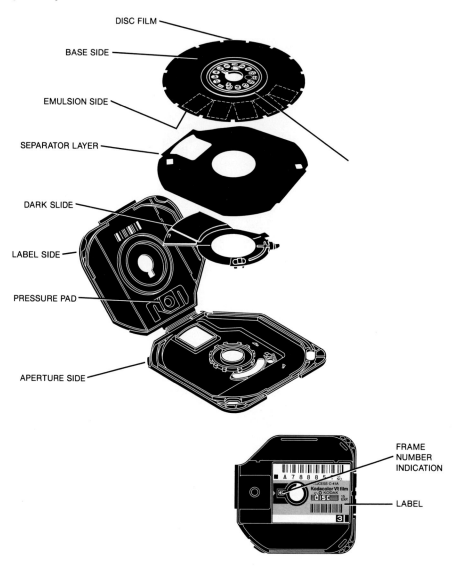

DISC FILM

BASE SIDE

EMULSION SIDE

SEPARATOR LAYER

DARK SLIDE

LABEL SIDE

PRESSURE PAD

APERTURE SIDE

FRAME NUMBER INDICATION

LABEL

Disc film has the exposures arranged in a circular pattern on a flat, circular disc of film. The camera mechanism opens a dark slide and rotates the disc for each exposure.

Cartridge films have a backing paper to protect the film from light and are supplied in plastic cartridges designed for drop-in loading of KODAK EKTRALITE and INSTAMATIC® Cameras and similar cameras. Cartridge film is identified by the number 110 or 126. Some 110- and 126-size films come in 12-exposure lengths, others come in 20- or 24-exposure lengths, and some are available in both 12- and 24-exposure lengths. See pages 146 and 148.

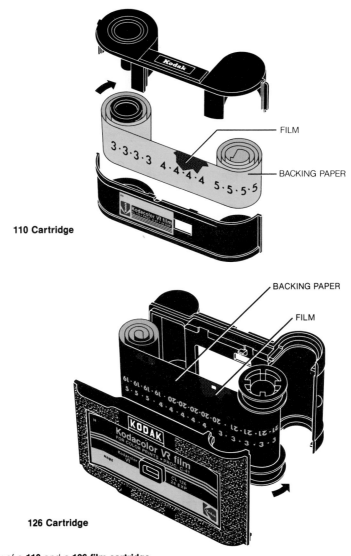

FILM

BACKING PAPER

110 Cartridge

BACKING PAPER

FILM

126 Cartridge

An inside view of a **110** and a **126 film cartridge**. Do not break open the cartridge unless you process the film yourself. Otherwise the film will be ruined by light-fogging.

Roll films also have a backing paper and are rolled on spools. They are available in a variety of sizes and are designated by such numbers as 120, 127, and 620. The number of exposures is determined by the camera format; there are 8 to 16 exposures for rectangular pictures, depending on the camera, and usually 12 exposures for square pictures.

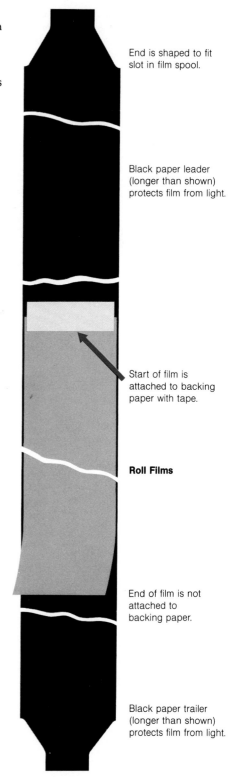

End is shaped to fit slot in film spool.

Black paper leader (longer than shown) protects film from light.

Start of film is attached to backing paper with tape.

Roll Films

End of film is not attached to backing paper.

Roll Films

Film is protected from exposure to light by black paper.

Black paper trailer (longer than shown) protects film from light.

10

KODAK Instant Film packs each hold 10 instant color picture units. The pack is disposable plastic and includes a film cover to protect the film from light before the pack is loaded in the camera.

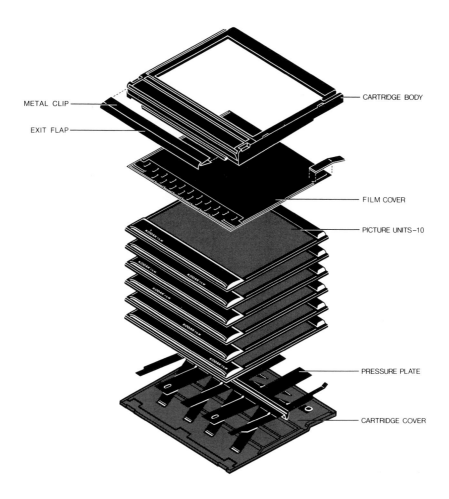

METAL CLIP

EXIT FLAP

CARTRIDGE BODY

FILM COVER

PICTURE UNITS–10

PRESSURE PLATE

CARTRIDGE COVER

An exploded view of a **KODAK TRIMPRINT Instant Color Film Pack HS144-10**

11

DX ELECTRONIC FILM CODING

All popular Kodak 35 mm films and magazines have electronically readable codes known as DX coding. These codes enable appropriately designed 35 mm cameras to automatically perform certain functions. These cameras can sense the speed of the film and set the camera exposure system accordingly. The cameras may also sense the length of each roll and signal the user to rewind the film after the last exposure or even trigger the camera to rewind automatically. They may be able to adjust the exposure system for over- and underexposure tolerances, depending on the exposure latitude of the film that's loaded in the camera—wide exposure latitude for color negative film and narrow latitude for color reversal (slide) film, for example. The information can be displayed in the viewfinder or in a display on the camera body.

In addition, a carefully positioned line of print on the film magazine—identifying film type, film speed, and number of exposures—allows the camera manufacturer to build a window into a 35 mm camera back. Users can then look through the window to determine whether the camera is loaded with film, and determine film information for the type of film in the camera.

Electronic coding of the 35 mm film magazine is called "camera auto sensing" or CAS. This code looks like an abbreviated checkerboard and acts like a miniature electronic circuit board. It appears on the magazine surface as two rows of bright metal or insulated patches that line up with electrical probes in the camera.

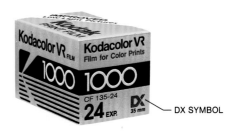

DX SYMBOL

What any particular camera does with the information depends on what the camera manufacturer designs the camera to do. See your camera manual.

Other codes in the form of a bar code on the film magazine, and latent-image bar codes visible on the film after processing are designed to help the photofinisher. These codes make it easier for photofinishers to perform their sorting, processing, and printing procedures. This helps to shorten handling time, minimize errors, and improve finished picture quality resulting in increased productivity and better service to customers.

Film cartons and magazines for the coded film have the designation "DX," which is identified by a special symbol. All popular Kodak 35 mm films are DX encoded.

You can use DX encoded 35 mm film in 35 mm cameras that do not have DX sensing cababilities in the same conventional way as film without DX coding.

ELECTRONICALLY READABLE CODES
FOR *KODAK* 35mm FILM AND MAGAZINES

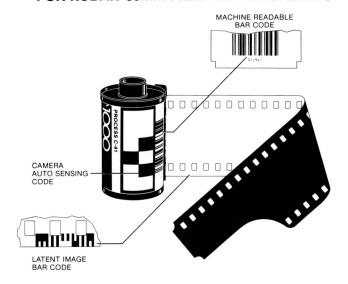

MACHINE READABLE
BAR CODE

PROCESS C-41

CAMERA
AUTO SENSING
CODE

LATENT IMAGE
BAR CODE

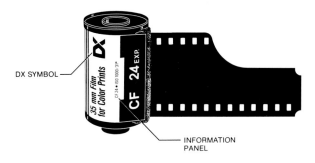

DX SYMBOL

35 mm Film
for Color Prints

CF 24 ● ISO 1000/31°

CF 24 EXP.

INFORMATION
PANEL

The checkerboard pattern and the striped bar
code on the film magazine are part of a series of
electronically readable codes that are included on
popular Kodak 135-size films. Another code used
on the film is a bar code for each image that will
become visible when the film is processed. Film
with the codes are packaged in boxes bearing the
symbol "DX."

CHOOSING A FILM

Each kind of Kodak film is designed primarily to produce only one of these four kinds of pictures. Most film cartons tell you the kind of pictures that particular film makes. For the sizes available in each kind of Kodak film, see pages 146–148. Processing services are available so that you can also obtain other kinds of pictures from your negatives, slides, or prints. See page 69.

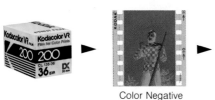

Color Negative

Color Print

BRUCE NETT

KODACOLOR VR 100, 200, 400, 1000 and **KODACOLOR VR Disc Films** are for COLOR PRINTS.

Color Negatives

Color Print

NEIL MONTANUS

14

KODACHROME 25, 40, and **64 Films,** and **KODAK EKTACHROME 64, 100, 160, 200, 400** and **P800/1600 Films** are for COLOR SLIDES.

Color Slide

Black-and-White Negative

KODAK VERICHROME Pan, PLUS-X Pan, TRI-X Pan and **PANATOMIC-X Films** are for BLACK-AND-WHITE PRINTS. Other black-and-white films for special purposes are described on page 69.

Black-and-White Print

KODAK TRIMPRINT™ Instant Color Film, HS144-10 and **KODAK Instant Color Film, PR144-10** with TRIMPRINT Feature is for INSTANT COLOR PRINTS.

Color Print

KODACHROME 64 Film (Daylight)

NEIL MONTANUS

To choose a color film, you'll want to know, in addition to the kind of pictures it makes and the film sizes available, the film speed and the light sources recommended for the film. Also, you'll want to have some idea of the color quality and the definition (see page 63) of the pictures it produces. If you do your own darkroom work, you'll want to know if you can process the film yourself.

To choose a black-and-white film is simpler than selecting a color film. Unless you need one of the few films particularly designed for special purposes, the main considerations for general-use black-and-white films are film speed and the quality of definition you'll get in your pictures. Definition is explained on page 88.

Nonadjustable cameras and some basic automatic cameras will not expose high-speed films correctly. See your camera manual or write to the camera manufacturer for the films recommended for these cameras.

ELIZABETH A. MARSH, KINSA

KODAK PANATOMIC-X Film

KODAK Color Films

While the color of the setting sun and a picturesque opportunity will last only a short time, taking a photograph on color film will capture a visual experience to relive what would be only a fleeting memory. Holland. KODAK EKTACHROME 400 Film (Daylight)

Color films for still cameras are available in three general kinds. One kind produces color negatives which are primarily used to make color prints; another kind of film produces color slides; and the third kind produces instant color prints.

In color negatives, all the tones and colors of the original scene are reversed: Light tones are recorded dark, dark tones are recorded light, and the colors are the complements of the colors you saw when you took the picture. Kodak color negative films have built-in masks that help improve the quality of prints made from them. These masks give the negatives an overall color cast of light orange-tan. All the color relationships are properly reproduced when the negatives are printed on color photographic paper. You can also have color slides made from your color negatives; see "Getting Prints or Slides Made—from Your Negatives, Prints, or Slides" on page 69.

The second kind of color film gives you color slides directly. During processing, the image on the film is reversed from a negative to a postive, resulting in a color slide or transparency that you can either project onto a screen or look at with a viewer. The same film that was exposed in your camera is processed, mounted, and returned to you as slides (or as unmounted transparencies if you prefer). You can order prints or duplicate slides from your slides or transparencies; see page 69.

The third kind of color film, instant color film for use in instant cameras, produces finished color prints in a matter of minutes. There is no usable negative. You can have additional color prints or color slides made from both instant and traditional, finished original color prints.

17

Kodak color negative films, Kodak color slide films, and Kodak Instant Films are available in films designed for general use and in films designed for professional use. The films for general use are manufactured for the needs of photographers who take pictures for recreation, such as photo hobbyists and people who take only casual snapshots. These photographers may have the film in their cameras for longer periods of time at varying temperatures and may have longer delays before the film is processed than professional photographers. Casual photographers usually buy film in smaller amounts; therefore storage conditions are not as much of a factor as for the professional. General-use films produce excellent quality when temperature conditions and delays before the film is exposed and processed are not extreme. See the section on storage of Kodak films beginning on page 128.

Kodak color films for professional use have "professional" or "commercial" in their names or descriptions. Professional films are made for the needs and working habits of professional photographers. Professionals require greater precision for commercial photography, normally process their film soon after taking the pictures, and usually purchase film in large quantities. To achieve this precision and meet these needs, professional films require refrigerated storage, prompt exposure, and prompt processing.

Therefore, the most important difference for the nonprofessional photographer between film for general use and those for professional use is the more rigid requirements recommended for storing and handling professional films to maintain precision when the film leaves the factory.

You'll find a comprehensive table of condensed information for Kodak color films on page 146.

FILMS FOR COLOR PRINTS

The most important considerations in selecting a film for color prints, other than whether the film is for a traditional camera or for an instant camera, are film speed and the film's definition quality. Film speed refers to the film's sensitivity to light and is described in greater detail on page 105. Definition refers to a film's sharpness and graininess characteristics and is discussed beginning on page 63.

There are four Kodak color negative films for color prints for general use in conventional cameras. This family of KODACOLOR VR Films presents dramatic improvements from earlier films in speed, grain, and sharpness. The four films incorporate their ISO speeds in their name—KODACOLOR VR 100, KODACOLOR VR 200, KODACOLOR VR 400, and KODACOLOR VR 1000 Films.

Collectively, these films can expand picture-taking opportunities. Individually, they offer exceptional means of creative expression for camera owners lookng for new worlds to conquer.

For owners of disc cameras, Kodak manufactures KODACOLOR VR Disc Film to exacting specifications using the emulsion technology breakthroughs accomplished in 35 mm KODACOLOR VR Films.

Kodak makes two films for use in KODAK Instant Cameras and similar cameras that accept KODAK Instant Film. One film, KODAK TRIMPRINT™ Instant Color Film, is for newer instant cameras; the other, KODAK Instant Color Film, is for older instant cameras. Both films provide the extraordinary TRIMPRINT™ Feature which lets you separate the slim instant print from the bulky picture unit.

KODACOLOR VR 100 Film is the sharpest color negative film in the family of KODACOLOR VR Films. This film features very high sharpness and extremely fine grain which provides exquisite detail in prints. These qualities are superb for high degrees of enlargement. VR 100 film is excellent for general picture-taking when you want maximum image quality.

Color rendition and contrast are excellent with rich saturated colors. This film has a medium speed of ISO 100, and is intended for exposure to daylight and electronic flash. The speed of VR 100 film is well suited for general lighting conditions as well as for beach and snow scenes in sunlight. The film has wide exposure latitude that produces satisfactory results when moderate exposure errors are made. VR 100 film is sold in 135 and 120 sizes.

NORM KERR

When you want color prints and plan to make big enlargements, choose **KODACOLOR VR 100 Film** for your camera.

CAROLINE GRIMES

KODACOLOR VR 100 Film is a general-purpose color negative film that has the highest image quality of Kodak films for color prints. Its speed of ISO 100 is adequate for many bright daylight and flash picture subjects.

19

BRUCE NETT

The additional speed of **KODACOLOR VR 200 Film** helps you use the high shutter speeds necessary to stop action. 1/500 second f/16

KODACOLOR VR 200 Film with a speed of ISO 200 is a color negative film that offers most of the qualities of KODACOLOR VR 100 Film but with twice the speed, making VR 200 film very versatile. In addition to its faster speed, the film has high sharpness and extremely fine grain. Its superb color rendition and contrast are similar to KODACOLOR VR 100 Film. The film is designed for daylight, electronic flash, and blue flashbulbs. You can also use it for some existing-light scenes that aren't too dimly lighted.

VR 200 film is the ideal general-purpose film with excellent photographic characteristics plus speed. Use this versatile film for general lighting conditions, and when you want to stop some subject movement, use zoom or telephoto lenses, or require more depth of field, such as in close-ups. It's also ideal for extending flash distances for flash pictures and for photographing subjects in less than optimum lighting. The film features wide exposure latitude. It's sold in 135, roll, and cartridge sizes.

KODACOLOR VR 200 Film, supplied in cartridges for 110- and 126-size cameras replaces 100 speed KODACOLOR II Film. Since a more limited exposure capability is generally associated with most 110 and 126 cameras, the wide exposure latitude of VR 200 film expands the range of lighting conditions which will produce good pictures in these cameras. VR 200 film will give a greater yield of good prints especially in situations where underexposure is a problem with these cameras with 100 speed film due to marginal lighting conditions or excessive flash distance.

NORM KERR

KODACOLOR VR 200 Film is an excellent general-purpose film for color prints. It has high quality with a speed of ISO 200 which is ideal for most picture-taking situations when you want color prints.

When the light intensity is less than ideal, such as on an overcast day, you want to use a telephoto lens to get in close to your subject, and you want color prints, an excellent high-speed film—**KODACOLOR VR 400 Film**—lets you capture the picture superbly.

KODACOLOR VR 400 Film is a high-speed color negative film for photographing fast-action or low-light situations. VR 400 film features extremely fine grain and good sharpness with a speed of ISO 400. This film is designed for daylight, electronic flash, blue flash, and existing light.

KODACOLOR VR 400 Film is primarily for picture-taking situations where you need high film speed and where you may also want enlargements. VR 400 film is intended for photographing fast action; subjects requiring good depth of field and high shutter speeds; subjects in dim lighting, such as early or late in the day or existing light; and for extending the flash distance range. This film extends your picture-taking opportunities; it lets you take pictures you couldn't get with slower-speed film. For

example, you can use it to photograph subjects without flash utilizing the natural qualities of the existing lighting, to stop action, or to use zoom or telephoto lenses that do not have much lens speed, in reduced light levels.

VR 400 film has great versatility because you can take pictures under lighting conditions ranging from bright sunlight to dim light like household room lighting, depending on your camera. The film's high speed gives you greater exposure capability in dim illumination, lets you use higher shutter speeds or smaller lens openings, and lets you take flash pictures at greater distances. Higher shutter speeds reduce the effects of camera motion and let you handhold your camera in dim light, and help stop action. Smaller lens openings

In order to use a high shutter speed to stop motion with a telephoto lens and maintain some depth of field, you need a high film speed. **KODACOLOR VR 400 Film,** with a speed of ISO 400, gives you the necessary film speed. 1/1000 second *f*/16

increase depth of field, which is especially helpful for scene elements at different distances and for close-ups.

VR 400 film provides excellent flesh tones and rich color saturation. Special sensitizing characteristics let you obtain pleasing pictures under a variety of other light sources, such as tungsten household light bulbs and fluorescent lamps, without using camera filters. The film can handle mixed light sources without using filters, as well. For critical use, such as for portraits with photolamps where optimum color rendition is important, you should use the recommended filter. See pages 62 and D 6. As with all KODACOLOR Films, this film offers wide exposure latitude. VR 400 film is available in 135, 120, and 110 sizes.

KODACOLOR VR 400 Film in 110 cartridges is intended for cameras that can sense high-speed film. See your camera manual. For simple, non-adjustable cameras, VR 400 film can extend the exposure range to include heavy overcast and open shade in addition to bright sunlight, and can extend the flash distance range.

KODACOLOR VR 1000 Film is a very high-speed color negative film with a speed of ISO 1000 which is 10 times faster than KODACOLOR VR 100 Film. VR 1000 film is the fastest color negative film Kodak has ever produced. Kodak accomplished a major breakthrough in emulsion technology for this film that gives significantly higher speed with excellent grain and sharpness.

The new innovation incorporates KODAK T-GRAIN Emulsion which is a more efficient way to form silver halides, the light-sensitive element in the film. This permits Kodak to manufacture a true 1000 speed film for color prints with a balance of speed, grain, and sharpness which was previously unattainable. In addition, other emulsion improvements have been incorporated to produce excellent color rendition as well. The film is available in 135 size.

VR 1000 film has received further refinements in finer grain, improved sharpness, and improved sensitivity in low-light indoor scenes with tungsten illumination from when the film was first introduced.

This film is color-balanced for daylight and electronic flash. Additionally, the film has special sensitization to reduce the photographic differences between a varity of light sources, such as those in existing light, eliminating the need for filtration in all but the most critical situations involving the use of photolamps where optimum color rendition is important.

An elegant night out can be vividly remembered when you capture the realism of the existing lighting on **KODACOLOR VR 1000 Film.**

KODACOLOR VR 1000 Film is the film to use when you want color prints under demanding conditions when the lighting is poor or the action is fast and you need the benefits of maximum film speed. VR 1000 film provides many of the qualities of KODACOLOR VR 400 but with 2.5 times higher film speed.

VR 1000 film provides photographers greater freedom to take pleasing pictures under low-light situations while offering a choice of higher shutter speeds for stopping action, or smaller lens openings for

JOHN FISH, JR.

KODACOLOR VR 1000 Film with its very high speed gives you the extra depth of field so desirable when you use telephoto lenses to photograph fast action. 1/1000 second f/16

increased depth of field, and more flexibility with zoom or telephoto lenses in marginal light. The film's very high speed also allows for greater flash distance coverage than can be achieved with slower speed films.

Its very high speed makes VR 1000 film the logical choice when you want to take existing-light pictures and handhold your camera in dim lighting when flash would spoil the natural appearance of the lighting or would be inappropriate for the subject. The film is also great for sports photography where the lighting is less than optimum and high shutter speeds are required to stop action.

This film is intended for moderately low degrees of enlargement, such as 8 x 10-inch prints or somewhat larger from properly exposed 35 mm negatives. VR 1000 film is quite tolerant of moderate errors in exposure, so you'll get excellent prints even

CAROLINE GRIMES

To take existing-light pictures while handholding your camera in dim lighting, like that often found in museums, you need a very high-speed film. **KODACOLOR VR 1000 Film** provides the speed—ISO 1000—and the qualities designed for existing-light photography. 1/30 second f/2.8

if your camera settings are a bit off, such as when slight or medium exposure errors are made or when your camera exposure meter system does not properly read the illumination of scenes.

23

SAM CAMPANARO

KODACOLOR VR Disc Film, for use in disc cameras, has the excellent combination of an ISO 200 film speed, micro-fine grain, and very high sharpness. This film has finer grain, improved sharpness, and improved contrast compared with the film when it was originally introduced. VR disc film incorporates the refinements and benefits featured in 35 mm KODACOLOR VR Films, including KODAK T-GRAIN Emulsion to achieve its fine grain.

Many of the film's characteristics are similar to KODACOLOR VR 200 Film; color rendition is superb. VR disc film is color-balanced for daylight, electronic flash, and blue flash. The film's ISO 200 speed together with the fast shutter speeds and relatively fast lenses that many disc cameras offer reduce the effects of camera and subject motion, and produce good exposure under a range of illumination from bright sunlight to some existing-light scenes that have ample lighting.

You can send KODACOLOR Films to Kodak or other photofinishing labs for processing and printing; or if you're a darkroom enthusiast, you can process these films and print the negatives yourself. KODACOLOR VR Disc Film is an exception and is not recommended for processing in home darkrooms. The disc film is designed for machine processing by photofinishers. Home processing of this film would produce poor results because of low-contrast negatives and color mismatches from inadequate agitation.

KODACOLOR VR Disc Film is manufactured to produce pleasing, natural colors of your subjects with both flash and daylight.

BOB CLEMENS

The fine quality of **KODACOLOR VR Disc Film** lets you enjoy the convenient, decision-free picture-taking that disc cameras feature. The high definition characteristics built into the film combined with a fast speed of ISO 200 and wide exposure latitude fully utilize the capabilities of the remarkable disc camera.

You can enjoy the fun and instant satisfaction of color prints when you use **KODAK TRIMPRINT™ Instant Color Film** or **KODAK Instant Color Film** with exclusive TRIMPRINT™ Feature.

KODAK TRIMPRINT™ Instant Color Film and KODAK Instant Color Film (with exclusive TRIMPRINT™ Feature) are for use in instant cameras and instant film backs that take KODAK Instant Film. Both of these films produce brilliant, rectangular color prints directly from the camera. You can compose the picture for either a horizontal or vertical format. KODAK TRIMPRINT Pictures have an elegant, textured KODAK SATINLUXE Finish which gives a pleasing appearance and helps protect the surface from smudges and fingerprints.

KODAK TRIMPRINT Instant Color Film, HS144, has a speed of ISO 320 and is for use in newer instant cameras that take HS144, KODAK Instant Film. KODAK Instant Color Film, PR144, has a speed of ISO 160 and is for use in older instant cameras that accept PR144, KODAK Instant Film. See the instruction manual for your camera for the film to use. Both films have the TRIMPRINT Feature.

Cameras designed for the higher speed HS144 TRIMPRINT Instant Film can produce sharper photos by permitting higher shutter speeds which reduce the effects of camera and subject motion and/or smaller lens openings which increase depth of field. Indoors the higher-speed film lets you take flash pictures at greater distances.

These films are designed for taking pictures in daylight or with electronic flash or blue flash. The films produce beautiful color rendition—brilliant colors by Kodak with sharp detail.

After you take the picture, the development process starts as the print is ejected from the camera. The picture develops right before your eyes without timing. An image begins to appear in about 35 seconds at room temperature 72°F (22°C). You can judge expression and composition in about 90 seconds and exposure in 2 to 3 minutes. The color picture is essentially complete in about 6 minutes under normal temperature conditions. If you want to take additional pictures, you can concentrate on photographing your subject while other exposures are developing. You don't have to wait to take successive pictures because they develop fully by themselves.

You can take sharp, brilliant instant pictures with color by Kodak. Both **KODAK Instant Color Films** give you beautiful TRIMPRINT™ Color Prints with the elegant KODAK SATINLUXE® Finish.

A TRIMPRINT Picture is the most versatile instant color print ever from Kodak. With both KODAK TRIMPRINT Instant Color Film and KODAK Instant Color Film, you have the option of separating and removing the finished color print from the backing material needed to record the image and develop the film. Any time after one hour you can lift off the slim color print or you can leave the backing material on for regular-size instant prints. Across the bottom border of the picture unit, after it has emerged from the camera, is a slit that allows you to separate the print from its backing. The separated prints resemble traditional color prints, and are far easier to mail, carry, cut, and insert in albums, frames, and wallets. You don't have to separate the print from the backing if you choose not to.

Separated prints take up less than half the space and weigh less than half as much as the unseparated instant prints. The advantage is obvious when you compare a stack of separated prints with instant prints retaining all of the backing materials. You can cut separated TRIMPRINT Pictures, mount them in an album, or display them in any way you would a traditional print.

A professional version of KODAK TRIMPRINT Instant Color Film named KODAK INSTAGRAPHIC Color Print Film is available. This film is discussed on page 47.

Anytime after an hour, you can separate the picture from the backing—for a 3 1/2 x 4-inch super-thin, flexible TRIMPRINT Picture. You can cut it, crop it, or put it in your photo album with your other traditional pictures.

FILMS FOR COLOR SLIDES

Kodak offers a variety of color slide films, each with different characteristics so that you can select the film that most closely matches your photographic requirements for the type of subjects and pictures you want to take. The most obvious differences in film characteristics are color balance and film speed. Color balance refers to the color quality of the light source the film is designed for. A discussion on color balance is given on page 48. Some of the other characteristics, such as color rendition, sharpness, and graininess, are more subtle—a critical comparison would be required to see the differences between films. Color balance, film speed, and personal preference are usually the most dominant factors in selecting a color slide film. The following descriptions will help you choose a film to suit your needs.

KODACHROME 25 Film (Daylight) is a popular color slide film noted for extremely high sharpness and extremely fine grain. The film features excellent color quality— pleasing flesh tones, clean whites and yellows, bright reds, greens, and blues, and realistic sky reproduction. KODACHROME 25 Film has good exposure latitude and tone reproduction. It retains good detail in highlights and shadow areas.

This film with a speed of ISO 25 is for use with daylight and electronic flash. We recommend the film for bright-light situations where you want the best possible image quality. KODACHROME 25 Film is available in 135 size only. A professional version of this film, KODACHROME 25 Professional Film (Daylight) in 135 size, is also available. Refer to page 47.

ROBERT KRETZER

KODACHROME 25 Film (Daylight) is an excellent general-purpose film for color slides. It is well known for its superb sharpness and extremely fine grain. 1/125 sec f/8

Choosing a color film by the way it records various colors is a matter of personal taste. The flesh tones produced by **KODACHROME 25 Film (Daylight)** make it a favorite film for many people.

KODACHROME 64 Film (Daylight) is a good choice for all-round picture-taking when you want color slides. Its ISO 64 speed lets you use higher shutter speeds or smaller lens openings under normal lighting conditions and extends picture-taking capability on overcast days, in the shade, or in somewhat subdued lighting. The film produces excellent color rendition with crisp, saturated colors—bright reds, greens, and blues, clean whites and yellows; good blue skies; and pleasant flesh tones. In addition, the film shows adequate detail in both highlight and shadow areas. It has good exposure latitude that helps yield pleasing results even with moderate underexposure or overexposure.

KODACHROME 64 Film is almost as sharp and fine-grained as KODACHROME 25 Film. At normal screen viewing distances, most viewers can't see any difference in sharpness or graininess. KODACHROME 64 Film is for use in daylight or with electronic flash or blue flash. It comes in sizes 135, 110, and 126. For professional use, KODACHROME 64 Professional Film (Daylight) in 135 size, is sold by photo dealers. See page 47.

Have your KODACHROME Films processed by Kodak or another commercial lab. You can't process these films in your own darkroom because the process is highly complex and requires commercial photofinishing equipment.

GARY WHELPLEY

The delicate colors and intricate detail of Indian jewelry have been superbly reproduced by **KODACHROME 64 Film (Daylight).** The additional speed of the film—ISO 64—compared with that of KODACHROME 25 Film is especially helpful when the light level is reduced, as it was in this picture made in the shade.

NEIL MONTANUS

KODACHROME 64 Film (Daylight) has many of the same fine qualities as
KODACHROME 25 Film (Daylight) but more than twice as much speed—ISO 64. The
high-quality definition and color rendition of KODACHROME 64 Film help make it a great
film for general picture-taking.

KODACHROME 40 Film 5070 (Type A)
is a color slide film designed for taking
pictures with 3400 K photolamps. It has a
speed of ISO 40 with this illumination. This
film is valued for its high-definition
characteristics and its excellent color
rendition.

The color balance of KODACHROME
40 Film for photolamp lighting together
with its snap, brilliance, and color fidelity
make it an excellent film for informal
portraits, close-ups, title slides, and for
copying color originals. The film's extremely
high sharpness, extremely fine grain, and
ability to record fine detail will provide high-
quality color slides. You can also take
pictures in daylight when you use a No. 85
filter over your camera lens with a film
speed of ISO 25. You can purchase this
film in 135 size.

KODACHROME 40 Film is processed in the
same commercial process as KODACHROME
25 and 64 Films (Daylight).

BOB CLEMENS

KODACHROME 40 Film 5070 (Type A) is an excellent
color slide film to use for informal portraits of
subjects lighted by 3400 K photolamps.

BOB CLEMENS

JOHN HOOD

If you use title slides, they will help make your slide
shows more effective and enjoyable. **KODACHROME
40 Film 5070 (Type A)** is a good choice for making
your title slides. It produces outstanding results
with 3400 K photolamp lighting, which is easy to
control.

KODAK EKTACHROME 100 Film (Daylight) features outstanding color accuracy and saturation with excellent definition characteristics. This is a superb film for general photography when you want color slides.

An excellent choice for your slide shows is **EKTACHROME 100 Film (Daylight).** It provides clean highlights, good contrast, very high sharpness, and very fine grain.

KODAK EKTACHROME 100 Film

(Daylight) is an excellent general-purpose color slide film with a speed of ISO 100. It's outstanding for color slides outdoors or indoors with flash. This film is a replacement for KODAK EKTACHROME 64 Film (Daylight) in 135 size. (The professional version of the 64 speed film in 135 size continues to be available. See below and page 47.) EKTACHROME 100 Film features improved flesh tones, excellent reproduction of neutral colors, and warmer shadows. Color reproduction is superb with vivid blue skies, bright reds and yellows, clean highlights, and good shadow detail. The film distinguishes well between similar colors.

EKTACHROME 100 Film has 2/3 stop higher speed than 64 speed films to give you a speed advantage while retaining very high sharpness and very fine grain for

high image quality. Compared with KODACHROME 64 Film, the KODACHROME Film is slightly sharper and finer grained, but it's difficult to see the difference on the projection screen. EKTACHROME 100 Film is a daylight-type film. For flash pictures, you can use electronic flash. The film is made for use in 35 mm cameras. EKTACHROME 100 Professional Film (Daylight) is available in 135 and 120 sizes. See the professional films on page 48.

A similar film with a speed of ISO 64, **KODAK EKTACHROME 64 Film (Daylight)** is sold in 110 and 126 sizes. KODAK EKTACHROME 64 Professional Film (Daylight) is available in 135, 120, and 220 sizes.

An additional feature of all KODAK EKTACHROME Films is that you can process these films in your own darkroom if you want to process them yourself.

32

In this picture, the high fidelity of **KODAK EKTACHROME 64 Film (Daylight)** gives you the feeling that you can almost reach out and touch the blossom.

33

KODAK EKTACHROME 200 Film

(Daylight) is a general-purpose color slide film with extra speed. It's excellent for photographing subjects that require high shutter speeds and good depth of field; fast action; existing light; and for extending the flash distance range. This film is a good choice for lengthening your photographic day—from dawn to dusk and outdoors at night. The film has a speed of ISO 200. It is designed for use with daylight and electronic flash. You can also use it to photograph subjects illuminated by carbon-arc spotlights. This is a versatile color slide film which lets you photograph in a large range of lighting conditions from bright sunlight to existing light, depending on your camera.

EKTACHROME 200 Film is the film to use when you need a color slide film with additional speed and very fine grain. The film is a good choice when you want to use a zoom or telephoto lens with high shutter speeds where you need good depth of field, or when you want to capture action on a dull, overcast day. EKTACHROME 200 Film's excellent graininess characteristics are quite significant for its speed because it has nearly as fine grain as that of EKTACHROME 100 Film and has twice as much speed. The difference in graininess between the two films is usually not evident in projected slides viewed from a normal viewing distance.

EKTACHROME 200 Film produces fine color quality with clean color separation between similar hues. In comparison with the 100 speed film, colors are slightly less saturated with the 200 speed film. EKTACHROME 200 Film is available in 135 size. A professional version of this film is sold in 135, 120, and 220 sizes. It's described on page 48.

DON MAGGIO

KODAK EKTACHROME 200 Film (Daylight) with its generous speed of ISO 200 is a versatile film. You can take pictures in light ranging from sunlight to existing light. It's a good choice for taking color slides in the home by existing daylight. This film gives you very fine grain and pleasing color rendition as well as a fast film speed.

KODAK EKTACHROME 200 Film (Daylight) is an excellent film to use when you need versatility, and want to take pictures both outdoors in daylight conditions and indoors with existing daylight, such as in the Air and Space Museum, Washington, D.C. The Daylight film produces a natural appearance in this scene illuminated by the daylight coming through the windows.

When you want to photograph action in color slides and perhaps use a telephoto lens, a film with additional speed will allow you to use the high shutter speeds you'll need. **KODAK EKTACHROME 200 Film (Daylight)** has the speed—ISO 200—and high quality to give you excellent results.

KODAK EKTACHROME 400 Film (Daylight) is a great film for taking color slides under the existing lighting conditions where you often need a high-speed film. The high-wire act at the Damascus Temple Shrine Circus was illuminated by carbon-arc spotlights.

KODAK EKTACHROME 400 Film

(Daylight) is a high-speed color slide film for use when you need higher film speed for difficult lighting conditions, such as existing light or early or late in the day when subjects are often dimly lighted; for subjects where you want both good depth of field and high shutter speeds; and for stopping fast action in your pictures, such as in sports photos.

This film has a speed of ISO 400. Its high speed means that you can get handheld shots where the lighting is dim with a camera that has an $f/2$ or faster lens. The film is good for pictures with long telephoto lenses which don't have large lens openings and where you'll want to use high shutter speeds to avoid camera-motion effects or stop action. For example, you can freeze action at 1/1000 second with medium-aperture telephoto lenses, depending on the lighting. This 400-speed film lets you take flash pictures at greater distances than Kodak color slide films with less speed.

EKTACHROME 400 Film produces attractive color rendition—saturated colors with full tonal values. The film is color-balanced for daylight and electronic flash. You can also photograph subjects lighted by carbon-arc spotlights with this film.

EKTACHROME 400 Film has good sharpness for a high-speed film, and it has fine grain although the grain is not quite as fine as that of EKTACHROME 200 Film. The difference in graininess is not readily discernable under normal projection conditions.

This film offers the versatile feature of push processing to a very high speed of ISO 800 with high quality. This lets you shoot pictures under more difficult lighting conditions. You can also have other EKTACHROME Films push-processed for increased speed. See page 42.

When you need a color slide film with more speed for tungsten illumination, for example in low-light conditions, you can use EKTACHROME 400 Film without using a light-balancing filter. This will produce warm or yellow-red results. Many people find such slides acceptable because tungsten lighting has a natural warm appearance.

This film is sold in 135 and 120 sizes.

KEITH BOAS

This interesting hotel lobby, lighted by a combination of daylight and tungsten light, was realistically recorded on **KODAK EKTACHROME 400 Film (Daylight).**

RICH FREEMAN

The high speed of **KODAK EKTACHROME 400 Film (Daylight)** was beneficial for photographing this low-light scene. The high film speed—ISO 400—let the photographer use a small lens opening for good depth of field without putting the camera on a tripod even though the lighting was dim. With this film you can usually take pictures under adverse lighting conditions while handholding your camera.

Here the photographer needed good depth of field with a handheld camera in a museum dimly lighted by daylight. Exposing at EI 800 on **EKTACHROME P800/1600 Professional Film (Daylight),** which permitted a small lens opening, gave the desired sharpness.

This London bus was stopped sharply on **KODAK EKTACHROME P800/1600 Professional Film (Daylight)** under the demanding conditions of stopping action in the dim lighting of late afternoon shadows. The film was exposed and processed at EI 1600.

KODAK EKTACHROME P800/1600 Professional Film (Daylight) is a color slide film specifically designed for push-processing to a very high speed of EI 800 or EI 1600 depending on how you have the film processed. Although recommended for exposure at these speeds for best picture quality, you can obtain acceptable results using the film at an even higher speed of EI 3200 or at a slower speed of EI 400 but with some loss of quality. Exposing the film at EI 400 requires a KODAK Color Compensating Filter CC10Y.

EKTACHROME P800/1600 Film is an excellent choice whenever you need maximum speed in a color slide film. It provides high sharpness and satisfactory graininess. Color rendition is similar to EKTACHROME 400 Film but with slightly higher contrast. This film is color-balanced for daylight and electronic flash. You can also obtain good color rendition in slides taken of subjects illuminated by carbon-arc spotlights. In addition, P800/1600 film produces acceptable results for noncritical purposes when exposed to tungsten lighting conditions, such as outdoors at night. Color slides made with tungsten illumination will appear yellow-red but are satisfactory to many people.

CAROLINE GRIMES

The very high speeds you can use with **Kodak Ektachrome P800/1600 Professional Film (Daylight)** make this film outstanding for candid photography in dim existing lighting when you want color slides. A film speed of EI 800 was used to take the picture.

When you want to take color slides in public places lighted by tungsten lighting, you need a tungsten film with added speed. **KODAK EKTACHROME 160 Film (Tungsten)** is well-suited for this purpose. Museum of Science and Industry, Chicago, Illinois.

EKTACHROME P800/1600 Film is an excellent choice for action and sports photography; for dimly lighted subjects in existing light; when photographing with long focal length lenses, such as zoom or telephoto lenses, that have small maximum apertures; or when you want to use the smallest possible aperture for maximum possible depth of field and highest possible shutter speed for maximum action-stopping capability. This film is also a good choice when you need to take flash pictures at extended subject distances,

Because P800/1600 film is manufactured specifically for push processing, it provides significantly better quality at EI 800 and EI 1600 than is possible from push-processing EKTACHROME 400 Film to extreme speeds. Maximum density (degree of blackness) with P800/1600 film is higher, avoiding the "smoky" shadow areas that may be seen when other films are push-processed.

Like other Kodak professional color films, EKTACHROME P800/1600 Film requires refrigerated storage before use and prompt processing after exposure. To make it easier for photographers to tell labs how much to push-process each roll, the 35 mm magazines include a write-on section that you can circle to indicate the speed you used—EI 400, 800, 1600, or 3200. A photo of the film magazine is on page 68. All the pictures on the entire roll must be exposed at the same speed. If you plan to use the film at EI 3200, you should expose a test roll to see if the quality meets your requirements. You can purchase this film in 135 size for 35 mm cameras.

KODAK EKTACHROME 160 Film (Tungsten) is a color slide film designed for use with 3200 K tungsten lamps without using filters. It's excellent with existing tungsten light, such as the light from household lamps and other general-purpose lamps. This film has a speed of ISO 160, and excellent color rendition and sharpness.

EKTACHROME 160 Film distinguishes well between similar colors. Its color quality and sharpness are similar to those of EKTACHROME 200 Film (Daylight). You can also take pictures in daylight with the Tungsten film when you use a No. 85B filter over your camera lens, reducing the effective film speed to ISO 100.

For taking pictures under dim tungsten existing-light conditions where you may need more film speed, you can have this film push-processed to increase its speed by 2 times to ISO 320. See page 42. The film is sold in 135 size. It's also available as a professional film in 135 and 120 sizes. Consult page 48.

BOB CLEMENS

For taking the most natural-looking pictures at home, use the existing lighting. When the lighting is provided by tungsten household lamps, and you want color slides, you can use **KODAK EKTACHROME 160 Film (Tungsten),** which is designed for this kind of picture-taking. It has a speed of ISO 160.

CAROLINE GRIMES

KODAK EKTACHROME 160 Film (Tungsten), is a splendid color slide film for night scenes. This view captures the exciting lighting of signs in Las Vegas, Nevada. 1/30 sec f/4

Original slide · DON MAGGIO

Duplicate slide

KODAK EKTACHROME Slide Duplicating Film 5071 (Process E-6) is a superb film for making duplicate color slides from original color slides. Sometimes you can make the duplicate slide better than the original. Here the duplicate was cropped for improved composition.

KODAK EKTACHROME
Slide Duplicating Film 5071
(Process E-6) is a color slide film for copying original color slides. The contrast and color reproduction characteristics and the very high sharpness and extremely fine grain make this an outstanding film for making excellent duplicates which are difficult to distinguish from the original slides.

The film is for use with slow exposure times of about 1 second with tungsten illumination. You can also use the 5071 film with sunlight at the same slow exposure times. There is another similar version of this film—KODAK EKTACHROME SE Duplicating Film SO-366, CAT NO. 159 0223—which is designed for short exposure times with electronic flash at 1/1000-second flash duration. This film has the same color and definition characteristics as the 5071 film. You can also use the SO-366 film with sunlight at exposure times of 1/10 second or shorter.

With both of these films, you expose them using color filters, like those used for color printing, to balance the light source to each new film emulsion. See pages D 27 and D 28.

Sometimes when the original slides are less than ideal, you may be able to make improvements when you make the duplicates, such as cropping for better composition, correcting for exposure, correcting or changing color, and combining two or more images in one duplicate slide. The potential for creating new interpretations from your original slides is considerable.

These films are sold in 135 magazines, 36 exposures. The films are not intended for general, pictorial photography. Unexposed film should be stored in your refrigerator at 55°F (13°C) or lower.

Increased Film Speed with KODAK EKTACHROME P800/1600, 400, 200, and 160 Films. An exceptional feature of these films (and of EKTACHROME 200 and 160 Professional Films) is that you can expose them at higher-than-normal speeds when you obtain special processing. Kodak in the U.S.A. offers a special push-processing service for these films, in 135 and 120 sizes, which increases the effective speed 2 times the normal speed (1 stop). This process is referred to as KODAK Special Processing, ESP-1 (Push 1). The speeds are increased to ISO 800 for EKTACHROME 400 Film (Daylight), ISO 400 for EKTACHROME 200 Film (Daylight), and ISO 320 for EKTACHROME 160 Film (Tungsten). Since

EKTACHROME P800/1600 Professional Film (Daylight) is designed for push processing, its speed is EI 800 with the Push 1 special processing and EI 1600 with Push 2 special processing. Both processing services are available from Kodak at additional cost.

When necessary, such as when exposure errors are made, you can specify the Push 1 special processing for KODAK EKTACHROME 100 Film (Daylight) [also KODAK EKTACHROME 100 and 64 Professional (Daylight) and KODAK EKTACHROME 50 Professional (Tungsten) Films]. The speed of EKTACHROME 100 Film is increased to ISO 200, the speed of EKTACHROME 64 Film is increased to ISO 125, and the speed of EKTACHROME 50 Film is increased to ISO 100. However, since quality is reduced slightly with special processing, it's seldom practical to pay the additional cost of the special processing for these films when you can use EKTACHROME P800/1600, 400, 200, and 160 Films at their normal speeds or intended speeds.

The processing section on page 66 tells how you can obtain special processing of your film.

CAROLINE GRIMES

EKTACHROME 400 Film (Daylight) with ESP-1 Processing offers a very high speed of ISO 800 to help you stop action in low-light pictures. Damascus Temple Shrine Circus, 1/250 sec f/2.8

CAROLINE GRIMES

EKTACHROME P800/1600, 400, 200, and 160 Films have an exceptional feature. You can expose the 135- and 120-size films at 2 times their normal speeds (the intended speed of EI 800 with P800/1600 film) when you have the film specially processed. EKTACHROME 200 Film (Daylight) with ESP-1 Processing—ISO 400, 1/125 sec f/4. Damascus Temple Shrine Circus

MARTIN TAYLOR

To record the majestic beauty of Niagara Falls at night, it helps to have a very high film speed. EKTACHROME 400 Film (Daylight) with ESP-1 Processing for a film speed of ISO 800.

ROBERT KRETZER

Home lighting at night is relatively dim so you need a high film speed for handholding your camera. Otherwise, with films that have less speed, you may have to use slower shutter speeds and use a camera support, such as a tripod. EKTACHROME 160 Film (Tungsten) with special processing—ISO 320, 1/30 sec f/2

You'll obtain the best quality with EKTACHROME 400, 200, and 160 Films when you expose the films at their normal speeds and have the films processed normally. However, the high film speeds and high quality of these films with special push processing make possible many opportunities for color pictures that would be impossible or impractical with slower-speed films. The increased speed is very helpful under dim lighting conditions—in existing light, for example. It's also helpful when you want to use higher shutter speeds to stop action and smaller lens openings to increase depth of field.

Push processing increases contrast and graininess to some extent. These changes,

BRUCE NETT

Taking pictures by the existing lighting is an excellent technique for photographing interesting interiors, like this cathedral. But since the existing illumination is usually dim, it's beneficial to use a film with very high speed so you can use a smaller lens opening, for example, to obtain better sharpness and greater depth of field for this kind of subject. EKTACHROME P800/1600 Professional Film with special processing (push 2) to EI 1600.

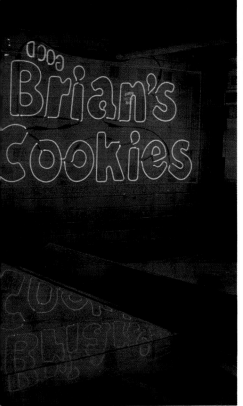

CAROLINE GRIMES

To photograph subjects of opportunity in existing light with a handheld camera often requires a very high-speed film. This colorful design was captured on EKTACHROME P800/1600 Professional Film with special processing (push 1) to EI 800.

though, are not too noticeable on the projection screen. The overall quality is very good.

Keep in mind that push-processing to EI 800 or EI 1600 is the intended process for EKTACHROME P800/1600 Film, and produces excellent quality with this film.

When you take pictures with KODAK EKTACHROME P800/1600, 400, 200, and 160 Films at high shutter speeds combined with small lens openings, there is an additional exposure factor to be aware of in determining exposure for some cameras. This is discussed on page 122.

OTHER *KODAK* COLOR FILMS

The following films are designed for the professional; therefore, only brief descriptions are given in this book. If you have questions about these films, write to Eastman Kodak Company, Photo Information, Department 841, 343 State Street, Rochester, New York 14650. In countries outside the United States, contact the normal source for Kodak products in that country. The book *KODAK Color Films for Professional Use* (E-77) and *SLIDES—Planning and Producing Slide Programs* (S-30), available from photo dealers and bookstores—mainly bookstores in most other countries, include technical data and other information for many of the films described here.

Since these films are intended for critical photography by professional photographers, they are manufactured with more rigid requirements for storage and handling than Kodak color films for general use. Store unexposed professional color films under refrigeraton—55°F (13°C) or lower, unless different storage recommendations are given on the film carton or film instructions. After exposure, have these films processed promptly. See "Storage and Care of KODAK Films," page 128.

These films are sold by photo dealers who sell professional photographic products.

KODAK VERICOLOR III Professional Film, Type S, is an improved color negative film intended primarily for professional use and professional photofinishing equipment and procedures. This film replaces KODAK VERICOLOR II Professional Film, Type S. The new film is designed for portraiture, wedding photography, school pictures, and other commercial purposes. The film has increased sharpness compared with the former version of the film. Its better sharpness provides significant benefits for making larger prints. The film has improved color rendition in yellows, greens, and neutrals—blacks, grays, and whites—with excellent reproduction of flesh tones and hair colors which make it a superb film for portraits. It has higher film speed for increased versatility and greater picture-taking range with flash; greater exposure latitude which permits more negatives to be printed in cases of moderate exposure error; and improved dye stability for improved dark storage of image-forming dyes for longer useful life for negatives.

VERICOLOR III Professional Film is designed with lower contrast, softer tone reproduction, and a more subtle level of color enhancement technology. These features enable photographers to retain better shadow detail, and reproduce the more subtle lighting relationships and tonal values involved in portrait and similar professional applications compared with general pictorial photography.

The lower contrast and softer tone reproduction of VERICOLOR III Film allow greater retention of shadow detail including hair reproduction, black flesh tones, and dark clothing. The lower contrast also enables greater retention of highlight and shadow detail within the same scene, such as white wedding gowns together with black tuxedos, and gives the photographer greater control in lighting.

VERICOLOR III Film has a speed of ISO 160 and excellent graininess characteristics. This Type S film is designed for short exposure times of 1/10 second to 1/10,000 second and is balanced for exposure to daylight and electronic flash. It's available in 135, 120, and 220 sizes and in sheet-film sizes.

KODAK VERICOLOR II Commercial Film, Type S, is a color negative film similar to KODAK VERICOLOR III Professional Film, Type S, except that the Commercial Film has about 15 percent higher contrast. Commercial Film, Type S, has the same daylight color balance as VERICOLOR III Film, Type S.

The Commercial Film's higher contrast is beneficial for pictures when you want more snap in the prints, such as outdoor portraits photographed under low-contrast lighting conditons as on cloudy days or in the shade. The film is excellent for commercial, industrial, and aerial photography, and for copy work where increased contrast is desirable. Commercial, Type S, Film has contrast approximately equal to that of KODAK VERICOLOR II Professional Film, Type L.

VERICOLOR II Commercial Film has a speed of ISO 100. Use this film with exposure times of 1/10 second or less. For flash pictures you can use electronic flash without filters. The film is sold in 120 size and sheet-film sizes.

KODAK VERICOLOR II Professional Film, Type L, is the tungsten-light version of VERICOLOR Film. The Type L Film has higher contrast than VERICOLOR III Professional Film, Type S, which is desirable for still lifes, product photography, and other industrial and commercial applications. The Type L Film is available in 120 size and in sheet-film sizes. This professional film is designed for exposures of 1/50 second to 60 seconds with tungsten lamps 3200 K. Its speed at 1/50 second under these conditions is ISO 100. You can also use the film in daylight with a No. 85B filter at a speed of ISO 64.

KODAK INSTAGRAPHIC Color Print Film is the professional version of KODAK TRIMPRINT Instant Color Film, for professional photographers. INSTAGRAPHIC Film has the TRIMPRINT Feature which allows you the option of separating and discarding the film backing materials after development, leaving a thin traditional-appearing color print which you can cut, store, or mount. INSTAGRAPHIC Film is manufactured to narrow professional standards which require storage at 45°F (7°C) before use. Refrigerated storage maintains the film's photographic qualities and allows for long storage life before exposure. This film has the same ISO 320 speed and other photographic characteristics as TRIMPRINT Instant Color Film. INSTAGRAPHIC Film is sold by dealers in professional or audiovisual products.

KODAK VERICOLOR Slide Film 5072 is a special-purpose color film for printing color slides—positives—directly from color negatives or for photographing artwork to make reverse-text title slides.

To make color slides from your color negatives, you can use the film with contact printing techniques in the darkroom or use the film in your 35 mm camera with slide duplicating equipment to photograph your color negatives. To make reverse-text title slides, you can photograph black text or artwork on a white background with a color filter over the camera lens or photograph it on a color background. Because VERICOLOR

Slide Film is used normally for making positive transparencies from color negatives, it reverses the tones and produces colors complementary to the original negative. You can create a wide range of background colors in slides by photographing simple black lettering or line art on a white background. This gives you color title slides with white printing or white line art on a color background. Such slides are relatively easy to make.

The film is intended for exposure to tungsten enlarger-lamp illumination using exposure times from 1/4 to 8 seconds. It is sold in 35 mm 100-foot long rolls and in 135-36 exposure magazines. In the 135 size, the film is identified as KODAK VERICOLOR Slide Film SO-279. If your photo dealer doesn't have the SO-279 film in 135 magazines, the dealer can order it for you using CAT No. 162 2364.

KODACHROME 25 Professional Film (Daylight) and **KODACHROME 64 Professional Film (Daylight)** feature extremely fine grain, extremely high sharpness, and high resolving power. These professional color slide films' color rendition and color balance to daylight and electronic flash, and other photographic characteristics are comparable to the general-use films—KODACHROME 25 Film (Daylight) and KODACHROME 64 Film (Daylight). The professional films have the same speeds as the general-use films, ISO 25 and ISO 64, respectively.

KODACHROME Professional Films are manufactured to tighter tolerances for speed and color balance than the general-use films to meet the most critical professional photographic demands. To maintain these tolerances, these films like other Kodak professional color films require refrigeration before use and prompt processing after exposure. You can purchase both KODACHROME 25 Professional Film and KODACHROME 64 Professional Film in 135 size.

KODAK EKTACHROME 64 Professional Film (Daylight) is a high-quality color slide film for general photography. It has a speed of ISO 64. This film is the professional version of EKTACHROME 64 Film (Daylight) in cartridge sizes. EKTACHROME 64 Professional Film offers excellent color reproduction for pleasing flesh tones, vivid blue skies, rich reds and yellows, clean highlights, and neutral shadows with good detail. The film also provides realistic rendition of wood tones and fabric hues.

EKTACHROME 64 Professional Film has an excellent speed-to-grain ratio—very high sharpness and very fine grain which give high image quality. The film is sold in 135, 120, and 220 sizes and in sheet film sizes.

For increased accuracy for professional use, the effective speed of a specific emulsion for KODAK EKTACHROME Professional Films is printed on the instruction sheet packaged with the film. The effective speed may be the same as, or plus 1/3 stop, or minus 1/3 stop from the nominal speed. For example, for the 64 speed film, the effective speed can be ISO 64, 80, or 50.

KODAK EKTACHROME 100 Professional Film (Daylight) offers outstanding color accuracy for both hue and color saturation. The film is optimized for the professional photographer. Its characteristics are similar to the general-use EKTACHROME 100 Film (Daylight)—both films have a speed of ISO 100. The film produces excellent highlight detail, realistic neutrals, and excellent rendition of flesh tones. EKTACHROME 100 Professional Film also features very fine grain, very high sharpness, and high resolving power. The film, with its modified color sensitivity, easily handles certain fabrics (azo-dyed) and colors that have been difficult to photograph. Good neutral shadow reproduction, such as in open shade conditions, are another of the film's features.

The professional film requires the same storage and handling as other KODAK EKTACHROME Professional Films—cold storage before being used and no extended delay after exposure before processing. EKTACHROME 100 Professional Film is sold in 135, 120, and sheet film sizes.

KODAK EKTACHROME 200 Professional Film (Daylight) is the professional version of EKTACHROME 200 Film (Daylight). The professional film is designed for critical photography requiring professional handling techniques. It has the same speed and other characteristics which are similar to the general-use film. The professional

film comes in 135, 120, and 220 sizes and in sheet film sizes.

KODAK EKTACHROME 160 Professional Film (Tungsten) has the same ISO 160 speed as the general-use EKTACHROME 160 Film (Tungsten). Both films are similar in most other respects. The professional film is available in 135 and 120 sizes.

KODAK EKTACHROME 50 Professional Film (Tungsten) is a color slide film designed for taking pictures with 3200 K tungsten lamps. It has a film speed of ISO 50 with this illumination. The fine color quality of this Tungsten film makes it an excellent film for informal portraits, close-ups, title slides, and for copying color originals. You can also use this film to take pictures in daylight by using a No. 85B filter over your camera lens, reducing the film speed to ISO 32. You can purchase this film in 135 and 120 sizes.

COLOR BALANCE

Color balance refers to the ability of a film to reproduce the colors of a scene approximately as the eye sees them. Color films are balanced in manufacture for exposure to light of a certain color quality, such as daylight, 3400 K photolamps, or 3200 K tungsten lamps.

You'll get the best results when you use a film with the kind of illumination for which it's balanced. Usually under these conditions you don't need a filter to obtain correct color rendition. If you use a light source with a color quality different from that for which the film is balanced, you'll need to use the conversion filter recommended in this book or on the film instructions. You can get good results with filters, but most of them absorb light and reduce the effective speed of the film.

Since the film in a slide or transparency is usually the original film you expose in your camera, the color rendition depends primarily on the light source and the filter you use when you take the picture. The color balance of prints made from color negatives exposed with the wrong light source usually can be improved somewhat when the prints are made. But if the film was exposed with light sources significantly different from that for which the film is balanced, satisfactory corrections may not be possible.

When you want to take pictures outdoors with a film balanced for tungsten light, use the recommended conversion filter to obtain proper color balance. EKTACHROME 160 Film (Tungsten) with a No. 85B filter.

If you don't use the recommended filter with Tungsten film outdoors, this is the kind of bluish result you'll get.

FLASH PICTURES WITH COLOR FILMS

Electronic flash, blue flashbulbs, flashcubes, magicubes, and flipflash are recommended for taking flash pictures with daylight-type Kodak color films.

The color quality of these flash light sources is similar to that of daylight, and you don't normally need a filter. Electronic flash units do vary, though, and some flash units may produce pictures that are too bluish. If your pictures are consistently too blue, use a No. 81B yellowish filter and increase exposure by 1/3 stop. If you prefer to use clear flashbulbs with daylight film, you'll need a blue conversion filter; see the table on the next page.

When you want to take flash pictures on EKTACHROME 160 Film (Tungsten) or KODACHROME 40 Film 5070 (Type A), you can use electronic flash, blue flashbulbs, or flashcubes with the proper conversion filter. See the table. If you prefer, you can use clear flashbulbs with the proper filter.

Electronic flash, blue flashbulbs, flashcubes, magicubes, and flipflash are recommended for taking flash pictures with most Kodak films for general use.

49

Color Film	Electronic Flash	Blue Flashbulbs, Flashcubes, Magicubes, Flipflash	Clear Flashbulbs	
			25, 26	AF-1, M-3
KODAK Daylight Color Films*	None†	None	80C	80D
KODAK EKTACHROME 160 (Tungsten)	85B	85B	81EF	85C
KODACHROME 40 5070 (Type A)	85	85	81C	81EF

*Includes KODACOLOR Films.
†If your pictures are consistently too blue, us a No. 81B filter.

FILMS FOR EXISTING-LIGHT PHOTOGRAPHY

Existing light, sometimes called available light, includes artificial light which naturally exists in the scene, the lighting indoors or outdoors at night, daylight indoors, and twilight outdoors. Technically, daylight lighting conditions outdoors, including bright sunlight, are existing light. But in defining existing light for photography, we are referring to lighting that is characterized by lower light levels than you would encounter in most daylight conditions outdoors. Outdoor scenes after dark or at twilight are considered to be existing-light situations.

Actually you can use all Kodak color films for general use for taking pictures by existing light if you don't mind putting your camera on a tripod or some other firm support and using slow shutter speeds or time exposures in some situations. But your picture-taking will be made much more versatile and convenient if you can handhold your camera and use shutter speeds of 1/30 second or higher. This requires an f/2.8 or faster lens and a high-speed film for most subjects, because existing lighting is often quite dim.

This is the modern way to take existing-light pictures—take advantage of today's high-speed lenses and high-speed films by taking candid pictures while handholding your camera. Excellent high-speed films to use are KODACOLOR VR 1000 and VR 400 Films for color prints and KODAK EKTACHROME P800/1600, 400, 200, and 160 Films for color slides.

PETE CULROSS

Usually you don't need a filter for taking color pictures with electronic flash. But, if your pictures are consistently too blue, use a No. 81B filter on your camera lens or over the flash reflector to improve the color rendition.

For taking existing-light color slides with daylight illumination or with carbon-arc spotlights, such as those illuminating this scene at the Ice Follies, use a film balanced for daylight. EKTACHROME 200 Film (Daylight) is excellent for well-lighted existing-light scenes because of its superb quality and fast speed.

JOHN MENIHAN, JR.

CAROLINE GRIMES

EKTACHROME 400 Film (Daylight) with its high speed of ISO 400 is a high-quality color slide film for existing-light photography. Here it was used to record these antique airplanes illuminated mainly by existing daylight with some fluorescent illumination from the overhead lights. Movieland of the Air, Santa Ana, California

A good choice for outdoor night pictures when you want color prints is KODACOLOR VR 400 Film. Its high speed—ISO 400—came in handy for photographing this eye-catching ferris wheel while there was still some twilight in the sky.

Since KODACOLOR VR 1000 and VR 400 Films have special sensitizing characteristics and color rendition can be partially controlled when the prints are made, you can take pictures of good quality in various kinds of existing light without using filters. If your're using color slide films, such as EKTACHROME Films, the choice between the Daylight film and the Tungsten film depends on the type of lighting, the amount of film speed required, and your personal taste.

The Daylight film, of course, is better for indoor scenes illuminated by existing daylight. You can also use it to photograph performers illuminated by carbon-arc spotlights. When you're photographing subjects indoors with fluorescent lighting, Daylight film will give the best results; however, the color rendition of the slides will usually be greenish, depending on the type of fluorescent lamps used. See "Filters for Fluorescent Illumination" on page 58.

You can use the Daylight film for existing-light photography outdoors at night, too. The results will be warmer or more yellow-red than if the pictures were made on the Tungsten film. With mercury-vapor lamps used at some sports stadiums and for some street lighting, you'll get the best results on Daylight film. However, your pictures will have a blue-green appearance because mercury-vapor lamps are deficient in red. You can usually identify mercury-vapor lighting by its slightly blue-green appearance in comparison with tungsten light.

Some large sports stadiums have Multi-Vapor lamps for illuminating the playing area. These lamps provide improved color quality suitable for color television and photography. Color rendition is good in pictures taken on daylight film without filters under this illumination for noncritical purposes. You can identify this lighting at sports stadiums by its more neutral appearance compared with the slightly blue-green color of mercury vapor lamps.

Another type of lighting commonly used for street lighting is sodium vapor lamps. These lights are easy to identify by their strong amber color. Pictures on daylight

KODACOLOR VR 1000 Film, with a very high film speed of ISO 1000, is an outstanding film for existing-light pictures when you want color prints. The extra margin of speed that this film provides, helped the photographer get sharp results in a close-in view by using a telephoto lens while handholding his camera. Photograph taken at a college opera.

When you use KODACOLOR VR 1000 Film, you can get pleasing results in your color prints without using camera filters in a variety of existing-light conditions, such as tungsten household lighting (regular light bulbs), fluorescent illumination, and daylight indoors. The illumination for this gathering of friends in a home was a mixture of tungsten and daylight.

film will look similar to the way the lighting appears—yellow amber. Tungsten film will produce photos more neutral in appearance with this lighting.

The various types of vapor lamps are also referred to as high-intensity discharge lamps. If there is sufficient light provided by the vapor lamps for the camera settings required by the picture-taking situation, you can use camera filters to improve the color rendition in your photos. See the recommendations in the table "Filters for High-Intensity Discharge Lamps" on page 60.

EKTACHROME 160 Film (Tungsten) is excellent for existing tungsten light, such as the light from household light bulbs and other general-purpose tungsten lamps, when you want color slides. Outdoors at night you can use the Tungsten film for pictures of illuminated buildings, fountains, statues, signs, street scenes, and similar subjects. Slides of such subjects taken on Tungsten film may look more natural than those taken on Daylight film. The type of color slide film you use for outdoor pictures at night is a matter of personal taste as far as color rendition is concerned. Both types produce pleasing results. If you need higher speed with Tungsten film, you can have EKTACHROME 160 Film push-processed to double the speed to ISO 320.

Sometimes you'll find more than one kind of illumination in the same scene. If one type of light source is predominant, use color slide film balanced for that light source. For example, in an indoor scene which includes both daylight and tungsten light, daylight is usually the predominant light source and Daylight film would give more pleasing results. If the kinds of illumination in the scene are about equal in intensity and distribution, the choice of color slide film is a matter of personal taste. If you like warmer-looking pictures, or more in the yellow-red direction, use Daylight film; if you prefer colder-looking pictures, or more in the blue direction, use Tungsten film. Of course, in many situations the choice depends on the type of film that happens to be in your camera.

Since most existing light is dim, you'll often need all the film speed you can get. With KODACOLOR VR 1000 and EKTACHROME P800/1600 Films you have very high film speeds of ISO 1000 and

EI800 or EI1600 respectively which are very helpful in existing-light photography. When you are using EKTACHROME 400, 200, or 160 Films and you need more speed, you can use the special processing service for increasing the speed of EKTACHROME Film which was mentioned earlier. See pages 42 and 66 for more information on special processing.

In brighter levels of existing light, such as existing daylight indoors, you can use a medium-speed film—KODACOLOR VR 200, KODAK EKTACHROME 100, or KODACHROME 64 Film.

KODACOLOR VR 1000 Film with its very high speed of ISO 1000 and fine quality is a superb film for taking stop-action sports pictures. 1/500 sec f/2.8.

JOHN MENIHAN, JR.

NORM KERR

When you want to stop action in color slides, you can choose EKTACHROME P800/1600 Professional Film (Daylight) for exposure and processing to EI 1600. 1/1000 sec f/2.8

The lighting for museum displays can be dramatic but is often dim. Here's where a very high-speed film is required for taking pictures with a handheld camera. EKTACHROME P800/1600 Professional Film (Daylight) exposed and processed to EI 800. 1/30 sec f/2

EKTACHROME P800/1600 Professional Film (Daylight) is an exceptional film for candid existing-light photography for color slides. Its very high speed combined with high quality lets you take pictures freely without being encumbered by a camera support, depending on your camera. EI 800

STEVE KELLY

Since existing daylight is usually brighter than other kinds of existing light, you can use a medium-speed film, such as KODACHROME 64 Film (Daylight), depending on the capabilities of your camera.

CAROLINE GRIMES

BOB CLEMENS

With an adjustable camera, you can take pictures in existing daylight on KODACOLOR VR 200 Film.

When the existing lighting is provided predominantly by tungsten lamps, you'll get more natural-looking color slides by using film balanced for tungsten light. EKTACHROME 160 Film (Tungsten) at Water Tower Place, Chicago, Illinois.

CAROLINE GRIMES

For photographing scenes illuminated by existing tungsten light on color slide film, it's often helpful to have a film with high speed. An excellent film to choose is EKTACHROME 160 Film (Tungsten) with KODAK Special Processing, ESP-1, ISO 320. Heritage Plantation of Sandwich, Massachusetts

Filters for Fluorescent Illumination

Pictures made on daylight-type film without a filter in fluorescent light may be acceptable, although the pictures sometimes have a greenish cast depending on the film and the type of fluorescent tubes in use. Tungsten film without filters usually produces pictures that are much too blue. Generally speaking, it's often not practical to use filters in existing-light photography because they absorb too much light and reduce the effective speed of the film. However, when the reduced film speed is acceptable for the type of pictures you want to take, you can improve the color quality of pictures taken under fluorescent illumination by using filters over your camera lens.

Selecting filters for fluorescent illumination is sometimes difficult because the lamps are often inaccessible and therefore hard to identify. There are several kinds of fluorescent lamps, and each kind produces light of a slightly different color. If optimum color rendition is important and you can find out the kind of lamps in use, you can improve the color in your pictures by using the filters recommended in the table on the next page. These filters are available from photo dealers.

Since you may have difficulty finding out what kind of fluorescent lamps are in use, you can use a compromise filter. The most common fluorescent lamps sold are cool white, white, or warm white. Therefore, you can reasonably assume that the lamps in use are one of these three kinds. Recommendations for compromise filters are given in the table for unknown, or average, fluorescent light. These filters are for emergency use when you don't know what type of fluorescent lamp is in use and you can't find out.

For taking color pictures under fluorescent illumination without using a filter, you'll get the best results on daylight film. Although the pictures are usually acceptable, they may have an overall color cast depending on the kind of lamps. EKTACHROME 200 Film (Daylight), no filter.

For better color rendition in photographs of subjects brightly illuminated by fluorescent light, use the filters recommended in the table on the next page. With cool white deluxe fluorescent lamps and EKTACHROME 200 Film (Daylight), the recommended filters are CC20C + CC10M.

DON MAGGIO

FILTERS FOR FLUORESCENT LIGHT
Kodak Color Film

Fluorescent Lamp	KODACOLOR VR 100, VR 200, VR 400,* VR 1000* KODACHROME 25 (Daylight) EKTACHROME 100 and 200 (Daylight)	KODACHROME 64 (Daylight) EKTACHROME 64 (Daylight) EKTACHROME 400 (Daylight) EKTACHROME P800/1600 Professional (Daylight)	EKTACHROME 160 (Tungsten)	KODACHROME 40 5070 (Type A)
Daylight	40M + 40Y + 1 stop	50M + 50Y + 1⅓ stops	No. 85B + 40M + 30Y + 1⅔ stops	No. 85 + 40R + 1⅓ stops
White	20C + 30M + 1 stop	40M + ⅔ stop	60M + 50Y + 1⅔ stops	40M + 30Y + 1 stop
Warm White	40C + 40M + 1⅓ stops	20C + 40M + 1 stop	50M + 40Y + 1 stop	30M + 20Y + 1 stop
Warm White Deluxe	60C + 30M + 2 stops	60C + 30M + 2 stops	10M + 10Y + ⅔ stop	No Filer None
Cool White	30M + ⅔ stop	40M + 10Y + 1 stop	60R + 1⅓ stops	50M + 50Y + 1⅓ stops
Cool White Deluxe	20C + 10M + ⅔ stop	20C + 10M + ⅔ stop	20M + 40Y + ⅔ stop	10M + 30Y + ⅔ stop
Unknown Fluorescent†	10C + 20M + ⅔ stop	30M + ⅔ stop	50M + 50Y + 1⅓ stops	40M + 40Y + 1 stop

Except for the No. 85 and No. 85B filters, the filters suggested for fluorescent illumination are KODAK Color Compensating Filters (CC), sold by photo dealers.

Note: Increase exposure by amount shown in table.

*For critical use.

†These filters are for emergency use only, when it's not possible to determine the type of fluorescent lamp in use. Color rendition in pictures taken with these filters will be less than optimum.

For critical work with color slide film, you should take test pictures exposing your film with the filters recommended in the table for each type of lamp, and with filters that vary at least plus and minus CC10M and CC10Y from the filters listed. Color negative film such as KODACOLOR Film, is a good choice for taking pictures under fluorescent illumination because color rendition can usually be improved when your negatives are printed. KODACOLOR VR 1000 and VR 400 Films with their special sensitizing characteristics are especially good for fluorescent lighting. With these films you do not normally need to use filters with fluorescent light unless the results are for critical use.

In general with fluorescent lamps, use a shutter speed slower than 1/60 second to avoid uneven exposure or underexposure due to the flicker in brightness of the lamps. This is caused by the 60-cycle alternating current, and is not apparent to the eye.

Filters for High-Intensity Discharge Lamps

As explained earlier, daylight film is the best choice for mercury vapor and Multi-Vapor lighting. The bluish-green cast in pictures taken under mercury vapor illumination without using filters is acceptable for noncritical photos by some people, and the reasonably good color rendition in pictures exposed with Multi-Vapor lighting without filters is acceptable to most people. However, for more demanding color quality you should use the filters suggested in the table below.

With high-intensity discharge lamps as with fluorescent lamps, it's often difficult to find out what kind of lamps are in use. If possible, make some test pictures in advance with the suggested filters and with filters that vary at least a plus and minus CC10 filter. Preferably use a color negative film where color rendition can usually be improved in printing.

Taking pictures under illumination provided by high-intensity discharge lamps with high shutter speeds may cause unevenness or underexposure effects. This is caused by the lamps pulsating with the 60-cycle electrical current which is too rapid for the eye to detect. These exposure problems are most evident when you use shutter speeds higher than 1/125 second. The effects, however, are unpredictable and depend on the lighting installation. An area illuminated by a large number of lamps may not show any adverse effects in photographs.

For more information on taking pictures by existing light, you can purchase the Kodak book *Existing-Light Photography*, (KW-17), from your photo dealer or bookstore.

FILTERS FOR HIGH-INTENSITY DISCHARGE LAMPS
KODAK Color Film

High-Intensity Discharge Lamp	KODACOLOR VR 100, VR 200 VR 400, VR 1000 KODACHROME 25 (Daylight) EKTACHROME 100 and 200 (Daylight)	KODACHROME 64 (Daylight) EKTACHROME 64 (Daylight) EKTACHROME 400 (Daylight) EKTACHROME P800/1600 Professional (Daylight)	EKTACHROME 160 (Tungsten)	KODACHROME 40 5070 (Type A)
General Electric LUCALOX	70B + 50C + 3 stops	80B + 20C + 2⅓ stops	50M + 20C + 1 stop	55M + 50C + 2 stops
General Electric MULTI-VAPOR	30M + 10Y + 1 stop	40M + 20Y + 1 stop	60R + 20Y + 1⅔ stops	50R + 10Y + 1⅓ stops
Deluxe White Mercury	40M + 20Y + 1 stop	60M + 30Y + 1⅓ stops	70R + 10Y + 1⅔ stops	50R + 10Y + 1⅓ stops
Clear Mercury	80R + 1⅔ stops	70R* + 1⅓ stops	90R + 40Y + 2 stops	90R + 40Y + 2 stops

Note: The filters in the table are KODAK Color Compensating Filters (CC). Increase exposure by the amount shown in the table.
Sodium vapor lamps are not recommended for critical use.

*For EKTACHROME 400 Film (Daylight) and EKTACHROME P800/1600 Professional Film (Daylight), use CC25M + CC40Y filters and increase exposure 1 stop.

Photolamps let you see the lighting and adjust the light before you take the picture, so it's easier to obtain high-quality results. KODACHROME 40 Film 5070 (Type A) with 3400 K photolamps

WALTER LEE

FILMS FOR PHOTOLAMP ILLUMINATION

You may want to take some indoor portraits of your family or friends, photograph small objects close up, or make title slides for your slide shows. Excellent light sources for these subjects are the various types of photolamps sold by photo dealers. Generally, lamps are available in two color temperatures designated 3400 K and 3200 K. The advantage of using photolamps is that it's so easy to control the light. You can see the lighting and make corrections before you take the picture and you can use your exposure meter to determine exposure.

When you want the highest quality and you don't need much film speed, KODACHROME 40 Film 5070 (Type A) is the best choice for color slides. You can use this slide film with 3400 K photolamps without a filter. To use 3200 K tungsten lamps with the Type A film, see the table on the next page for the recommended filter and film speed.

If you need a color slide film with more speed, an excellent choice is KODAK EKTACHROME 160 Film (Tungsten), which requires no filter when you expose it by 3200 K illumination. You can also take pictures using 3400 K lamps when you use the proper filter; see the table.

You can take pictures on Daylight color slide film under photolamp illumination, but the conversion filters absorb a lot of light and reduce the speed of the film considerably, as shown by the table. So when you want color slides, it's better to use Type A or Tungsten film under these conditions. If you want color prints of subjects lighted by photolamps, KODACOLOR VR 100, VR 200, and VR 400 Films exposed with the filter recommended in the table will give you excellent results.

Even though KODACOLOR Films are recommended for exposure to various existing-light sources without camera filters, you should use the recommended filter when exposing these films with photolamp 3400 K or tungsten 3200 K illumination. The 3400 K and 3200 K lamps used for photography are brighter than normal tungsten lamps, so therefore it's easier to use filters with the lamps intended for picture-taking. In addition, viewers of the photographs expect accurate color rendition because of the professional appearance of the lighting and because of the type of pictures taken with these light sources, such as portraits of people.

FILTERS AND ISO FILM SPEEDS FOR PHOTOLAMPS

KODAK Color Film	3400 K Photolamps	3200 K Tungsten Lamps
KODACHROME 40 5070 (Type A)	None **40**	No. 82A **32**
EKTACHROME 160 (Tungsten	No. 81A **125**	None **160**
KODACOLOR VR 100	No. 80B **32**	No. 80A **25**
KODACOLOR VR 400	No. 80B* **125**	No. 80A* **100**
KODACHROME 25 (Daylight)	No. 80B **8**	No. 80A **6**
KODACHROME 64 (Daylight)	No. 80B **20**	No. 80A **16**
EKTACHROME 64 (Daylight)	No. 80B **20**	No. 80A **16**
EKTACHROME 100 (Daylight)	No. 80B **32**	No. 80A **25**
EKTACHROME 200 (Daylight)	No. 80B **64**	No. 80A **50**
EKTACHROME 400 (Daylight)	No. 80B **125**	No. 80A **100**

*Filter recommendations for critical use.

Note: Numbers in heavy type are film speeds. If your camera has a built-in exposure meter that makes the reading through a filter used over the lens, see your camera manual for instructions on exposure with filters. Also, see page 119.

FILMS FOR COPYING

For copying originals such as photographs (prints), drawings, documents, and paintings, choosing a color film is much the same as for conventional subjects. The choice depends on whether you want prints or slides and on the type of illumination.

You can use any of the light sources recommended for the film, such as daylight, flash (used off the camera if there are reflecting surfaces), or photolamps. However, since most copies are close-ups, photolamps are usually the best choice because they make it easier to control the illumination, and you can use your exposure meter to determine exposure. See "Using Exposure Meters in Copying" page 123. If you use photolamp illumination, film recommendations for copying are the same as those under "Films for Photolamp Illumination."

If your original is black-and-white, you can obtain good copies on color film. However, if you want a monochromatic image that is a more accurate reproduction of the original or if you have many copies to make, it may be better or more economical to use black-and-white film. See page 95. Also, see the note about copyrighted material on page 96.

Copying is a specialized application of photography, and can require different techniques than general photography depending on your copying needs. If you would like an in-depth discussion on the subject, you may want to obtain the Kodak book *Copying and Duplicating*, (M-1), sold by photo dealers.

KODACHROME Films are well known for their outstanding definition characteristics.
KODACHROME 64 Film (Daylight). 1/125 sec f/8

FILMS FOR DUPLICATING COLOR SLIDES

When you want to make duplicate slides of color slide originals made on such films as KODACHROME and KODAK EKTACHROME Films, you'll usually get the best results when you use a film specifically designed for duplicating. KODAK EKTACHROME Slide Duplicating Film 5071 (Process E-6) and KODAK EKTACHROME SE Duplicating Film SO-366 are made for this purpose. These films have low contrast and color-rendition characteristics suitable for producing excellent slide duplicates.

You can use conventional color slide films for making duplicate slides, but the duplicates made with such films are generally less than satisfactory due to contrast that's too high, some loss in color saturation that may be evident, and possible loss of image sharpness. Sometimes if you have an original slide that would be better with increased contrast, you can duplicate it on a conventional color slide film, such as KODACHROME 25 Film (Daylight), and get good results. A duplicate slide made on this film will usually have increased contrast.

DEFINITION

Definition is the clarity of detail seen by a person when viewing a photograph. Several factors give you the impression of definition. The degree of graininess, resolving power, and sharpness are usually used to describe a film's definition characteristics. Classifications for each of these definition factors have been assigned to Kodak films for general use. See the Definition Tables in the Data Sheets. A more thorough discussion of definition is given on page 88 in the chapter "KODAK Black-and-White Films."

Since the "Degree of Enlargement" classification described on page 91 applies to prints, this classification is not given in the Data Sheets for color slide films. When color prints are made from color slides, the degree of enlargement depends on the method used to made the prints; i.e., through internegatives or directly on reversal color printing paper. Definition classifications are not provided for Kodak instant films because they would not be meaningful for comparing these films with a negative or slide film.

RECIPROCITY CHARACTERISTICS

Most color films are designed for the typical short exposure times used in general picture-taking. At exposure times of 1 second or longer, the speed of most films will begin to decrease and color rendition will shift away from normal. These changes are referred to as the "reciprocity characteristics" of the film.

You can correct for the reciprocity effect by using filters and increasing the exposure. Recommended corrections for critical work are given on the Data Sheet for each Kodak color film. In most existing-light situations it's not practical or essential to use filters, but you can increase exposure to compensate for the decrease in film speed. You can avoid the effect simply by using shutter speeds shorter than 1 second when it's practical. Kodak instant films are exceptions to this guideline. See the reciprocity recommendations in the Data Sheet section.

Generally, when applying the exposure compensation to correct for reciprocity effect, it's better to use a larger lens opening to increase exposure rather than use a longer exposure time. Making the exposure time even longer would compound the reciprocity problem. If necessary for large corrections, you can apply part of the exposure compensation to the lens opening and the rest to the exposure time.

PROCESSING

Have your film processed promptly after exposure. Return Kodak color film to your photo dealer for processing by Kodak or another laboratory, or mail it directly to Kodak in the appropriate KODAK Processing Mailer for prepaid processing. See page 68 for specific recommendations for having KODAK EKTACHROME P800/1600 Professional Film processed. The processing comments made here do not, of course, apply to Kodak instant films. For developing these films, see page D 11.

When you have taken some unusually important and irreplaceable pictures, and you're concerned about the remote possibility that they could be misplaced or lost during processing, you may want to

EASTMAN KODAK COMPANY

KODAK Processing Mailers are convenient to use because you can mail your Kodak color film directly to Kodak for processing. The mailers are sold only in the U.S.A. After your pictures are processed, they are mailed to any address you specify.

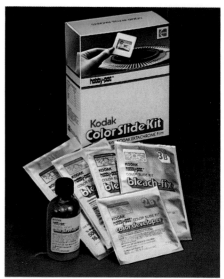

DON BUCK

Kodak chemicals for processing KODAK EKTACHROME Films and KODACOLOR Films are available from photo dealers in handy kit form. Each kit contains the chemicals you need plus complete instructions. Shown above is the KODAK HOBBY-PAC™ Color Slide Kit for processing KODAK EKTACHROME Film (Process E-6).

take special precautions in identifying your film. You can photograph a piece of paper or a piece of cardboard with your name and address printed on it, on one frame of the film to identify you as the owner. For extra assurance in the mails, it's also a good idea to attach a name and address sticker or band directly to the film container in case the film becomes separated from the mailing package.

You can process KODACOLOR and KODAK EKTACHROME Films yourself in processing kits sold by photo dealers. All the necessary chemicals and instructions for processing the film are included in the kits. KODACOLOR VR Disc Film is an exception and is not recommended for processing in the home darkroom.

See pages 96–100 in the black-and-white film section for information on film tanks and agitation procedures for film processing. For additional information on processing and printing Kodak color films, see your photo dealer or write to Eastman Kodak Company, Photo Information, Department 841, 343 State Street, Rochester, New York 14650, and request the pamphlet *Introduction to Processing and Printing KODAK Color Films* (AE-12). For prompt delivery of the pamphlet, please send a self-addressed business-size envelope with the publication title and number written on the back. We'll pay the postage. This applies only to the U.S.A. In other countries contact the normal source for Kodak products in that country.

Processing KODACOLOR VR 100, VR 200, VR 400, and VR 1000 Films. To process these films, you can use the KODAK HOBBY-PAC™ Color Negative Film Kit for processing KODACOLOR and KODAK VERICOLOR Films, or you can use KODAK FLEXICOLOR Chemicals (Process C-41). The HOBBY-PAC™ Kit features snip'n'pour foil packs of concentrated chemicals that make 500 mL (16.9 fluidounces) of each of the four solutions. Just snip, pour into water, mix, and process; it's that easy.

The processing steps given here are to familiarize you with processing KODACOLOR and VERICOLOR Film. Complete instructions come with the processing chemicals.

Both processes require 7 steps that take 24 1/4 minutes, not including the time it

takes for your film to dry. The temperature of the developer for the first step must be 100°F ± 1/4 (37.8°C ± 0.15). The other solutions and the wash water should be within a range of 75 to 105°F (24 to 41°C). The processing steps and the time in each solution in minutes are as follows:

1. Developer—3 1/4*
2. Bleach—6 1/2
3. Wash, running water—3 1/4
4. Fixer—6 1/2
5. Wash, running water—3 1/4
6. Stabilizer—1 1/2
7. Dry

*Increase development time after processing the specified quantity of film as recommended in the processing chemical instructions.

After your color negatives are processed, you can have prints made through your photo dealer or you can make them yourself in your own darkroom. If you want to make your own color prints and have questions about the procedure, write to Kodak at the address given above. You can purchase Kodak books on making color prints— *Color Printing Techniques* (KW-16) and *Basic Developing, Printing, Enlarging in Color* (AE-13)—from your photo dealer and bookstores.

Processing KODAK EKTACHROME 64, 100, 160, 200, 400, and P800/1600 Films and EKTACHROME Slide Duplicating Film 5071 and EKTACHROME SE Duplicating Film SO-366. To process these films, you can use the KODAK HOBBY-PAC™ Color Slide Kit for KODAK EKTACHROME Films for Process E-6.

The process for the HOBBY-PAC™ Kit has 8 steps and takes approximately 30 minutes at a temperature of 100°F (38°C), not including the time it takes for your film to dry. You can use processing temperatures between 70°F (21°C) and 110°F (43.5°C). You'll obtain best results, though, with solution temperatures between 96°F (35.5°C) and 110°F (43.5°C). The higher temperatures require a recirculating water bath to keep the containers of solutions at the proper temperature. Maintaining the water bath within ± 0.5° F (0.3° C) is ideal for controlling the temperature of the processing solutions. The temperature of the first developer and the processing time in this solution are the most critical.

Instructions are provided in the processing kit. The steps in the process and the time in each solution in minutes at 100°F (38°C) are as follows:

1. First Developer—6 1/2*
2. Wash—1 to 3
3. Color Developer—6
4. Wash—1 to 3
5. Bleach-Fix—10
6. Final Wash—4
7. Stabilizer—1
8. Dry

*Increase the time in the first developer after processing the specified quantity of film as recommended in the processing kit instructions. Different processing times in the first developer are required for processing EKTACHROME P800/1600 Film. See the discussion below.

Processing times vary depending on the solution temperatures you use. Refer to the instructions that come with the processing kit for other temperatures.

To process EKTACHROME P800/1600 Professional Film, extend the time in the first developer at 100°F (38°C) to 10 1/2 minutes for a speed of EI 800, Push 1, or to 13 minutes for a speed of EI 1600, Push 2. The times for the other steps in the process remain the same. For other temperatures and film speeds, see the processing kit instructions.

You can also process EKTACHROME Films for Process E-6 in the KODAK EKTACHROME Film Processing Kit, Process E-6, which is available in a larger one-gallon size. This process has 11 steps and requires 37 minutes, not including the time for your film to dry. Instructions are provided in the processing kit.

With both of these processes for EKTACHROME Film, you can increase the effective speed of the film by as much as three stops with push processing or decrease the speed of the film by as much as two stops with pull processing. Push processing is accomplished by increasing the time in the first developer and pull processing is achieved by decreasing the first developer time. See the discussion on this page, the table on page 67, and the processing kit instructions.

Handling color film during processing is much the same as handling black-and-white

film (see page 96). The main differences are that different processing chemicals are required for color, there is a greater number of steps in the color process, and some of the processing solutions must be very close to the recommended temperature. Color processing has to be precise and consistent for satisfactory results, so carefully follow the instructions that come with the chemicals. The Kodak book *Basic Developing, Printing, Enlarging in Color*, (AE-13), mentioned previously, provides information on how to process Kodak color films.

Special Processing for Increased Speeds

When lighting conditions are dim, as in many exisitng-light scenes, you may need higher film speed for taking pictures while handholding your camera, stopping action, using a telephoto lens, or using a small lens opening to gain greater depth of field. You can increase the speed of KODAK EKTACHROME 400, 200, and 160 Films (or KODAK EKTACHROME 100 Film when necessary) by obtaining special processing from Kodak, by sending your film to another processing lab, or by extending the development if you process the film yourself. The effective speeds of the films are increased to 2 times the normal speeds. The speed of EKTACHROME 400 Film (Daylight) is increased to ISO 800, the speed of EKTACHROME 200 Film (Daylight) to ISO 400, and the speed of EKTACHROME 160 Film (Tungsten) to ISO 320. The speed of EKTACHROME 100 Film (Daylight) is increased to ISO 200.

This special processing service by Kodak is not available in most countries outside the United States. Other processing labs may offer the service.

To obtain the special processing from Kodak, purchase a KODAK Special Processing Envelope, ESP-1, sold only in the United States, for *each* roll of EKTACHROME 400, 200, or 160 Film (or EKTACHROME 100 Film), 135 and 120 sizes. The charge for special processing is in addition to the regular cost of processing KODAK EKTACHROME Film. Expose the entire roll of film according to the instructions that come with the ESP-1

PROCESSING ADJUSTMENTS FOR DIFFERENT SPEEDS WITH *KODAK EKTACHROME* FILMS, PROCESS E-6

ISO Film Speed						*KODAK EKTACHROME* FILM CHEMICALS, PROCESS E-6		*KODAK HOBBY-PAC* ™ COLOR SLIDE KIT
EKTACHROME P800/1600 Professional (Daylight)	EKTACHROME 400 (Daylight)	EKTACHROME 200 (Daylight)	EKTACHROME 160 (Tungsten)	EKTACHROME 64 (Daylight)	EKTACHROME 100 (Daylight)	Change the time in the first developer by	Or change the temperature of the first developer by	Change the time in the first developer at 100°F (38°C) by
EI 200	200	100	80	32	50	− 2 minutes	− 6°F (− 3.3°C)	− 1¼ minutes
EI 400	400	200	160	64	100	Normal time	Normal temperature	Normal time
EI 800	800	400	320	125	200	+ 2 minutes	+ 8°F (+ 4.4°C)	+ 4 minutes
EI 1600	1600	800	640	250	400	+ 5 minutes	+ 12°F (+ 6.7°C)	+ 6½ minutes
EI 3200*	—	—	—	—	—	+ 10 minutes	+ 16°F (+ 8.9°C)	+ 9½ minutes†

Processing for film speeds different from the normal or Kodak's design speed results in some loss in quality compared with normal exposure and processing, but can enable you to obtain photographs under otherwise unsuitable conditions, or salvage a roll of film exposed at the wrong film speed.

Refer to the processing instructions that come with the chemicals for more complete information. Additional corrections for salvaging films exposed at wrong film speeds are given in the processing instructions.

*Because of loss of quality at this high film speed, test the procedure before using.

†For push processing to EI 3200, the color developer must be diluted and the time increased to 14 minutes in this solution.

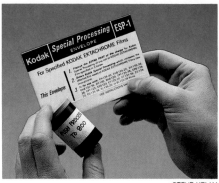

You can increase the speed of most KODAK EKTACHROME Films by 1 stop when you have them push processed. To obtain this service from Kodak, purchase a KODAK Special Processing Envelope, ESP-1, from your photo dealer for each roll you want to have push processed.

The film magazine for KODAK EKTACHROME P800/1600 Professional Film (Daylight) has a writable surface so that you can indicate the speed for which the film should be processed. Circle the speed you used to expose the film. See discussion below.

Envelope. Put the roll of exposed film into the ESP-1 Envelope, and then either take the film to your photo dealer for processing by Kodak, or mail it in the appropriate KODAK Processing Mailer to a Kodak Processing Lab in the United States.

EKTACHROME P800/1600 Professional Film is designed for special processing to attain its very high speeds. Kodak Processing Labs offer a 1-stop push processing service for processing this film to a speed of EI 800 and a 2-stop push-processing service to a speed of EI 1600. For the Push 1 processing service, EI 800, you can use an ESP-1 Envelope with a KODAK Processing Mailer for prepaid processing or take the film to your photo dealer and ask for this service. For Push 2 processing, EI 1600, from Kodak, request this service from your photo dealer—don't use the ESP-1 Envelope. If you want the film processed to EI 400, have the film processed normally without push processing. Push 3 processing to 3 stops, EI 3200, is not available from Kodak but is offered by other processing labs as well as Push 1 and Push 2 processing services. Push 2 processing for other EKTACHROME Films is also not available from Kodak.

Expose the whole roll of EKTACHROME P800/1600 Film at the same speed. Circle the speed you used to expose the film on the writeable surface of the film magazine.

An indelible felt-tip pen works best. This will indicate to the processing lab the speed you want the film processed to.

If you want to process the film yourself to obtain increased speed, simply increase the normal first-development time by the amount given in the table on the preceding page. For all the other steps, follow the normal processing times given in the instructions that come with the chemicals. Also, see page 65. When you process your own films, you can change their effective speeds over a wide range, as shown in the table. Exposing and processing the film at speeds other than the normal or Kodak's design speed will result in some reduction in photographic quality. The more the speed of the film is varied from normal, the greater the reduction in quality.

Push processing is not recommended for KODACHROME Films or for Kodak color negative films, such as KODACOLOR VR Films. Overdevelopment of color negative film does not significantly increase the speed of the film, but does cause adverse photographic results. A high fog level is produced which diminishes shadow detail, contrast is increased, and color rendition errors are generated which cannot be corrected during printing. Push processing KODACHROME Film can cause color casts in highlights and shadows along with increased contrast and graininess.

GETTING PRINTS OR SLIDES MADE—FROM YOUR NEGATIVES, PRINTS, OR SLIDES

Color Prints

When you want color prints or enlargements made from your color negatives, see your photo dealer. The dealer can order the prints for you. When they're made by a Kodak Processing Lab, the color prints from these negatives are called KODAK Color Prints, and the enlargements are called KODAK Color Enlargements. From 35 mm color negatives, you can obtain 4 x 6-inch color prints which are larger than the standard size. When these prints are made by Kodak, the service is called MAGNAPRINT35™ Service.

You can also have color prints and enlargements made directly from finished color prints. This service is especially suitable for obtaining extra prints from instant color prints. (Note: TRIMPRINT Pictures can be separated or unseparated from their backing materials for obtaining copies.)

Your photo dealer can have color prints or enlargements made from your color slides, too. Extra large color enlargements, 20 x 30 inches, referred to as Poster Prints by Kodak are available from 35 mm color negatives, 35 mm color slides, or color prints. Cropping is not available for these prints.

Color Slides

When you want duplicates of your slides or transparencies, you can have them made by Kodak or another laboratory. You can have color slides made from your Kodak color negatives, except for size 110 and disc. You can also have color slides made from your color prints. See your photo dealer.

Color negatives from Color Slides or Color Prints

If you do your own darkroom work and you want color prints from color slides or additional color prints from original color prints when you don't have the original negatives, you can make color prints from color negatives made from the slides or prints. Kodak Processing Labs and other labs can produce these color negatives for you (except from 110-size slides from Kodak Processing Labs) so that you can then make your own prints.

You can also produce your own color negatives from color slides or from color prints, or you can print color slides directly onto color photographic paper manufactured for this purpose. See the Kodak address on page 65 if you want information on these techniques.

JOHN FISH

When you want to make your own black-and-white prints from your color negatives, you can print them on KODAK PANALURE Papers. This picture was taken on KODACOLOR Film.

Black-and-White Prints from Color Negatives or Color Slides

If you want black-and-white prints from your color negatives, you can make them on KODAK PANALURE Papers, which are specially designed for this purpose. Instructions are included with the paper. To make black-and-white prints from color slides, you'll need to make a black-and-white negative from each slide first. If you have questions about this procedure, write to the address given on page 65.

Some processing labs also offer these services for making black-and-white prints from color negatives or slides.

For processing services for Kodak black-and-white films, see page 96.

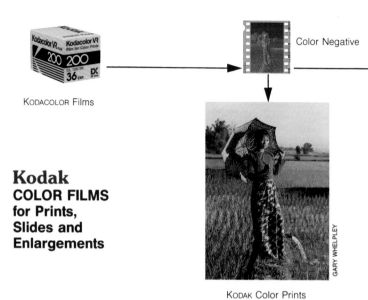

Color Negative

KODACOLOR Films

Kodak
**COLOR FILMS
for Prints,
Slides and
Enlargements**

GARY WHELPLEY

KODAK Color Prints
and Enlargements
(made by Kodak)

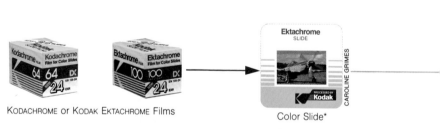

CAROLINE GRIMES

KODACHROME or KODAK EKTACHROME Films

Color Slide*

*"KODACHROME Slide" for KODACHROME Film

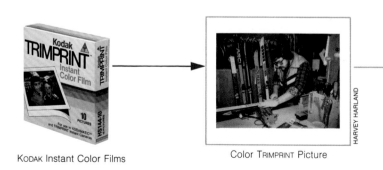

HARVEY HARLAND

KODAK Instant Color Films

Color TRIMPRINT Picture

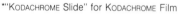

KODACOLOR Slides (made by Kodak)*
*Not available from disc and
110-size KODACOLOR Film

Black-and-white prints
and enlargements on
KODAK PANALURE Paper

Prints and enlargements
on KODAK EKTACOLOR Paper

KODAK Color Prints and Enlargements
(made by Kodak)

Prints and enlargements
on KODAK EKTACHROME Paper

KODAK Color Slide Duplicates
(made by Kodak)

KODAK Color
Copyprints and
Copy Enlargements
(made by Kodak)

KODAK Color Copy Slides
(made by Kodak)

Kodak Plus-X Pan Film

KODAK PLUS-X Pan Film
ERIC J. LINGER, KINSA

KODAK Black-and-White Films

The most important considerations in selecting a black-and-white film for conventional photography, as mentioned before, are the film speed that's best for the kind of pictures you want to take, and the definition quality you'll obtain. A few films are designed for special purposes, such as recording infrared radiation and copying printed material.

A table listing Kodak black-and-white films is given on page 148.

FILMS FOR GENERAL USE

KODAK VERICHROME Pan Film is a medium-speed, all-purpose film which performs beautifully indoors or out, in good light and on overcast days. This panchromatic film has extremely fine grain and very high sharpness. It has a speed of ISO 125, which is just right for most situations, and superb exposure latitude.

VERICHROME Pan Film is a good choice for general picture-taking with cartridge and 120-size roll-film cameras ranging from simple, nonadjustable cameras to the most advanced models. Most other Kodak black-and-white films require an adjustable camera for proper exposure. The film comes in 110, 126, and 120 sizes. For 35 mm cameras, a very similar film is available—KODAK PLUS-X Pan Film.

KODAK PLUS-X Pan Film is a general-purpose panchromatic film featuring extremely fine grain, very high sharpness, and high enlargeability—definition almost as good as KODAK PANATOMIC-X Film. PLUS-X Pan Film has medium speed—ISO 125—which makes it suitable for use in most lighting conditions except poor light. The film has excellent latitude so it's forgiving when exposure is less than optimum. It has finer grain than KODAK TRI-X Pan Film. PLUS-X Pan Film's combination of medium speed, excellent definition, and beautiful tonal qualities makes it a good choice for all-around picture-taking. The film is available in 135 size. A professional version of this film is available in 120 and 220 sizes. It's described more fully on page 83.

MICHAEL J. LACWITA, KINSA

LOUIS MANCUSO, SKPA*

KODAK VERICHROME Pan Film, with a speed of ISO 125 and extremely fine grain, is an excellent general-purpose film. It will suit your needs ideally for most black-and-white pictures.

*Courtesy Scholastic/Kodak Photography Awards

DON MAGGIO

KODAK PLUS-X Pan Film has many of the same fine characteristics as KODAK VERICHROME Pan Film. PLUS-X Pan Film is for use in 35 mm cameras.

KODAK PANATOMIC-X Film combines extremely fine grain with very high sharpness and very high resolution with film emulsion characteristics designed for a very high degree of enlargement. Its film speed of ISO 32 is sufficient for many picture-taking situations. It has panchromatic sensitizing. This film is a good choice when image definition quality for high magnification is the main consideration.

With special reversal processing, the 135-size film will produce black-and-white positive slides. In 120 size, the film is called KODAK PANATOMIC-X Professional Film; see page 83.

KODAK PANATOMIC-X Film. This film has excellent definition characteristics, and is designed for making prints with a very high degree of enlargement.

VICTOR ROGELIO DIAZ BALLESTEROS, KINSA

KODAK TRI-X Pan Film is well known as a top-notch film of excellent quality for existing-light pictures. Its high speed of ISO 400 is especially helpful in the comparatively dim illumination encountered in natural lighting conditions.

KODAK TRI-X Pan Film is a high-speed panchromatic film with fine grain and excellent sharpness. The combination of high speed—ISO 400, very good definition characteristics, and wide exposure latitude makes TRI-X Pan Film an excellent choice for photographing dimly lighted subjects, fast action, and subjects requiring good depth of field and high shutter speeds. It also extends the distance range for flash pictures. This film has great flexibility because it lets you take pictures under a wide range of subject and lighting conditions from bright sunlight to dim existing light, depending on your camera. TRI-X Pan Film is sold in 135 and 120 sizes.

JOHN O. KAPLAN, KINSA

KODAK TRI-X Pan Film features excellent tone reproduction—tonal separation is superb, highlights are brilliant—and high-quality definition in addition to its high speed. These qualities make it a very popular and outstanding film.

KODAK TRI-X Pan Film is a great film for photographing sports. Its high speed lets you use the high shutter speeds necessary to stop motion in existing-light pictures. 1/250 sec f/1.8

KODAK ROYAL-X Pan Film is a very high-speed panchromatic film. This film, for 120-size cameras, is designed for situations in which you need the highest film speed, as in taking action photographs by existing light or taking pictures when the light is very poor. ROYAL-X Pan Film with its very high speed—ISO 1250—has medium grain and good sharpness. The film is intended for moderately low degrees of enlargement. It's medium grain is usually acceptable for the type of pictures for which the film is designed—those taken under poor lighting conditions. Since negatives on 120-size film are larger than those from smaller film sizes, the negatives don't have to be enlarged as much for printing which minimizes the impression of graininess.

KODAK ROYAL-X Pan Film with its extremely high speed is a good choice for stopping action in sports photography at night. 1/250 sec f/4

MARK CHRISTIAN PEDERSON, SKPA

JOHN MENIHAN, JR.

Here's a picture-taking situation with adverse conditions—fast action photographed with a telephoto lens at night. These conditions require a very high-speed film such as KODAK ROYAL-X Pan Film or KODAK Recording Film 2475. The choice between these two films depends on the size of film your camera accepts. Photographed on **KODAK Recording Film 2475,** 1/250 sec f/2.5.

KODAK Recording Film 2475 is a very high-speed panchromatic film with extended red sensitivity (see page 84). This film is designed for taking pictures in low-light levels with higher than normal shutter speeds or with wide-angle, telephoto, or zoom lenses that do not have high lens speed. Recording Film 2475 is for 35 mm cameras. You can use it for the same purposes as ROYAL-X Pan Film. It has coarse grain because of its very high speed—1000. Use this film for picture-taking situations where the extra speed is more important than fine grain.

80

KODAK Technical Pan Film 2415 and 6415 is a multi-purpose, panchromatic film with extended red sensitivity, micro fine grain, and extremely high resolving power. You can vary the contrast of the film from normal pictorial contrast, to moderately high, to high by the choice of developer and development time. The speed of the film varies depending on the type of photographs you use it for and the development.

This film is superb for making impressive, giant-size enlargements with a minimum of grain and extreme sharpness for pictorial photography. To use the film for this application, it must be developed in a special low-contrast developer, such as KODAK TECHNIDOL Liquid Developer or KODAK TECHNIDOL LC Developer, to achieve normal contrast and sufficient exposure latitude. Conventional developers produce negative contrast that's too high

KODAK Technical Pan Film has extraordinary definition characteristics that let you make giant enlargements of 25X to 50X from high-quality negatives. In addition to its micro-fine grain and extremely high sharpness, Technical Pan Film provides a long tonal range when developed in low-contrast developers for pictorial photographs.

with this film for pictorial photographs. The speed of the film for this purpose is EI 25. See page D 45 for recommendations and limitations for using TECHNIDOL Developer, depending on the size of the film you use.

Technical Pan Film developed in TECHNIDOL Developer provides the finest grain and highest resolving power of any black-and-white pictorial film ever offered by Kodak. The film's extremely high sharpness and micro fine grain provide enlargements of excellent quality at magnifications of 25X and even 50X, equivalent to a 4 x 6-foot enlargement from a frame of 35 mm film. The film and developer combination produces a full tonal range ideally suited to pictorial photography, exhibition prints, and similar premium-quality applications of black-and-white photography.

Technical Pan Film's variable contrast feature and excellent definition characteristics make it very useful for copying purposes or for making black-and-white

reverse text slides. You can use the film to copy black-and-white or color originals and printed matter which may include both illustrations and type, such as books, magazines, and documents. See the discussion about photographing copyrighted material on page 96.

This is an excellent film to use for personal microfilming—for record-keeping purposes, for example. Or when you need black-and-white title slides, you can make them with this film by photographing artwork composed of black type on a white background. Technical Pan Film has a tungsten speed of 320 when you use it as a high-contrast material.

The film is sold in 135, 120, and sheet film sizes. The film name in 135 size and sheet film is KODAK Technical Pan Film 2415, and in 120 size, KODAK Technical Pan Film 6415. The sheet film is not recommended for pictorial photography; it's intended mainly for technical photography applications.

For an eerie, abstract quality in architectural or landscape photographs, take your pictures on **Kodak High Speed Infrared Film 2481** with a No. 25 filter. 1/60 sec *f*/16

PETER GALES

Conventional rendering on Kodak Plus-X Pan Film, no filter. 1/125 sec *f*/16

Normal appearance

Kodak High Speed Infrared Film 2481

is a fast, moderately high-contrast film that's sensitive to infrared radiation. With this film and the recommended filter, you can create some striking and unusual photographs of subjects such as landscapes and architecture. In infrared photographs the sky appears almost black; shadows are dark, but usually show adequate detail; live grass and leaves appear very light, as though covered by snow; and distant details obscured by haze in the original scene show up with remarkable clarity. By using a flash unit with the proper filter you can photograph subjects in the dark without their being aware of it. This film has many applications for technical and scientific photographs.

You can take pictures on High Speed Infrared Film with daylight, electronic flash, clear flashbulbs, and photolamps with the recommended filter. See pages D 42 and D 43.

The film has an approximate tungsten speed of 125 and an approximate daylight speed of 50, both with a No. 25 red filter. This film has fine grain, but it is not intended for high degrees of enlargement. The negatives can be printed on conventional black-and-white photographic papers.

Camera lenses do not focus infrared rays in the same plane as visible light rays. Some camera lenses have index marks on their focusing scales for infrared focus. If your lens does not have an infrared focusing mark, focus on the near side of the main subject and use a small lens opening. See page D 42.

Because of the sensitivity of High Speed Infrared Film, cameras must be loaded and unloaded in total darkness; a safelight cannot be used. Also see page D 42. Store 135 magazines of this film in the tightly closed film cans or in total darkness. Unexposed film requires refrigerated storage at 55°F (13°C) or lower. The film is sold in 135 size. A sheet film is also available—Kodak High Speed Infrared Film 4143 (Estar Thick Base).

OTHER *KODAK* BLACK-AND-WHITE FILMS

There are several black-and-white 35 mm and roll films designed for professional or special use. Descriptions of the more popular of these films are given here; if you have questions on these films, write to Kodak at the address given on page 46. For complete information on professional films, see the books KODAK *Professional Black-and-White Films* (F-5) and *SLIDES—Planning and Producing Slide Programs* (S-30), available from photo dealers and bookstores.

These films are sold by photo dealers who sell professional or audiovisual photographic products.

KODAK PLUS-X Pan Professional Film is a medium-speed panchromatic film with extremely fine grain and very high sharpness. It has a speed of ISO 125. The emulsion side of the roll film has a retouching surface; both sides of the sheet film have retouching surfaces. This film, which is available in 120 and 220 sizes, is the roll-film counterpart of 135-size KODAK PLUS-X Pan Film. This is an excellent general-purpose film with characteristics much the same as those of KODAK VERICHROME Pan Film. Sheet film with a similar name, KODAK PLUS-X Pan Professional Film 4147 (ESTAR Thick Base), but with different photographic characteristics, is also available. The sheet film is suitable for studio use where added highlight separation is desirable.

KODAK TRI-X Pan Professional Film is a high-speed panchromatic film with fine grain and very high sharpness. It is the roll-film version of KODAK TRI-X Pan Professional Film 4164 (ESTAR Thick Base) in sheets, and it has a speed of ISO 320. This film, which has photographic characteristics different from TRI-X Pan Film described on page 78, has been designed to produce both excellent shadow gradation and brilliant highlights, in photographs taken under artificial light, such as portraits made in studios. Both sides of the film have surfaces designed for retouching. The roll film is available in 120 and 220 sizes.

KODAK PANATOMIC-X Professional Film is the 120-size roll version of KODAK PANATOMIC-X Film in 135 size. The professional film has the same ISO 32 speed, panchromatic sensitizing, and the same excellent definition characteristics as the 135 film—extremely fine grain, very high sharpness, and very high resolving power—for making enlargements with high magnification.

KODAK Direct Positive Panchromatic Film 5246 is a medium-speed reversal film with extremely fine grain and high sharpness. It is designed for making black-and-white positive slides of high quality directly from the camera exposure. Its reversal processing is faster and simpler than using a negative film and then making separate positives. Develop the film in the KODAK Direct Positive Film Developing Outfit available from photo dealers.

You can make 35 mm slides with this film by photographing other slides, photographs, and outdoor and indoor subjects. It has a speed of 80 for daylight and 64 for tungsten. Direct Positive Panchromatic Film is sold only in 35 mm 100-foot-long rolls and must be loaded into 135 magazines for use in 35 mm still cameras. KODAK SNAP-CAP 135 Magazines are available from photo dealers for this purpose.

KODAK EKTAGRAPHIC HC Slide Film is an extremely high-contrast orthochromatic film intended primarily for making reverse-text, black-and-white title slides. It produces clear images on a black background when you use it to photograph black-on-white text or artwork. You can then color the clear image areas of the transparency with water-soluble dyes or water colors, or you can "sandwich" a color filter with the transparency made on this film to produce a title slide with colored lettering.

EKTAGRAPHIC HC Slide Film is the 135 magazine version of KODALITH Ortho Film 6556, Type 3. The speed of the film varies depending on the developer used. It has a tungsten speed of EI 8 when developed in KODALITH Developers. Development recommendations are provided on the instructions packaged with the film.

With panchromatic film, you can darken the gray-tone rendering of a color in a photograph by using a filter with a color complementary to the color you want to darken. You can use a No. 15 deep-yellow filter to darken the blue sky in the picture and to make the sky and clouds appear more natural. This filter has a filter factor of 2.5, so increase exposure by 2.5 times or 1 1/3 stops.

EASTMAN Fine Grain Release Positive Film 5302 is a low-speed blue-sensitive film with extremely fine grain and high sharpness for printing black-and-white slides—positives—from continuous-tone or line negatives. This film is not recommended for general use in your camera. It's sold in 35 mm 100-foot-long rolls.

COLOR SENSITIVITY

The color sensitivity of a film, also referred to as spectral sensitivity, describes its response to light of various wavelengths or colors. While the average normal eye is sensitive to all colors, the same is not necessarily true of films. Silver bromide, the fundamental light-sensitive element in all emulsions, is sensitive only to blue and ultraviolet. Sensitizing dyes incorporated in panchromatic, orthochromatic, and infrared emulsions make these classes of films sensitive to certain other colors or wavelengths of light or other radiation. The type of sensitizing is one of the most important photographic characteristics of a black-and-white film because it affects both the monochromatic rendition of colors in the photographs you obtain and the handling of the film in the darkroom.

Kodak black-and-white films are divided into several spectral sensitivity classes. Except for certain special sensitizings, there are four general classes. Professional films are available in all four classes; films for general use are available in only two of them—panchromatic and infrared. The spectral sensitivity of each black-and-white film is given on the Data Sheets in this book. The four spectral sensitivity classes are as follows:

Noncolor-sensitized or blue-sensitive films are sensitive only to ultraviolet and blue-violet; this characteristic is inherent in silver halides—the light-sensitive element in the emulsion.

Orthochromatic films are sensitive to green light in addition to ultraviolet and blue-violet.

Panchromatic films are sensitive to all visible colors, including red, as well as to invisible ultraviolet radiation. Some panchromatic films have extended red sensitivity.

Infrared films are sensitive to ultraviolet, and all visible colors, including deep red, as well as to the invisible infrared radiation.

Color Sensitivity of a Black-and-White Film Determines the Following

Gray-Tone Rendition of Colored Objects. A film that's not sensitized to green or red light will reproduce these colors as tones of gray that are too dark in the print. Panchromatic films for general use will record colors as gray tones in the print in approximately the same relative brightness as they appear to the eye. For critical work you can obtain gray-tone rendition in a photograph that's very close to the visual brightness of the original scene by using the proper correction filter. See the filter recommendations in the Film Data Sheets.

A few panchromatic films that have extended, or increased, red sensitivity will reproduce red objects as tones of gray that appear lighter in the print than the brightness of the objects themselves appears to the eye, and lighter than in prints made with conventional panchromatic films.

Caucasian flesh tones in photographs obtained from films with extended red sensitivity may look lighter than normal. This characteristic may be desirable for some circumstances because it helps mask the appearance of some types of skin blemishes.

You can reduce the effects of extended red sensitivity by using a No. 38 light-blue filter or, for a more moderate reduction, a KODAK Color Compensating Filter CC40C over the camera lens. With the No. 38 filter try exposure increases of 1 stop in tungsten light and 2 stops in daylight or with electronic flash to compensate for the light absorbed by the filter. No exposure increase should be necessary with the CC40C filter. Because of variations in conditions with different films, experiment to find the technique you like best.

Filters and Filter Factors. The filters that you can use depend on the color sensitivity of your film. For example, a red filter should be used only with a film sensitive to red light, such as panchromatic film. Since filters absorb light, their use requires an exposure increase. This increase in exposure is specified by the filter factor, which depends on the color sensitivity of the film and the color quality of the light source. For example, a film with a large portion of its sensitivity in the blue-violet requires a much greater relative exposure through a yellow filter, which eliminates most of the blue light, than a panchromatic film requires. Panchromatic film is sensitive to all colors and therefore can record the red and green light transmitted by the yellow filter.

How to apply the filter factor for proper exposure is explained beginning on page 119.

If you want to make an object appear darker in the print than it appears to the eye, use a filter that has a color complementary to the color of the object. For example, a yellow filter darkens a blue sky. To lighten the gray-tone rendering of an object, use a filter similar in color to the object. You can also use filters to increase the contrast between colored objects that would normally photograph as nearly the same shade of gray.

Filter Designations. Filter designations, such as K2, A, and G, that were used to identify different filters in the past have been replaced with the present numbering system. Since published literature sometimes makes reference to the older designations, both designations are given here.

Current Designations	Discontinued Designations	Color
No. 6	K1	Light Yellow
No. 8	K2	Yellow
No. 11	X1	Yellowish Green
No. 13	X2	Dark Yellowish Green
No. 15	G	Deep Yellow
No. 25	A	Red
No. 29	F	Deep Red
No. 47	C5	Blue
No. 58	B	Green
No. 61	N	Deep Green

Recommended filters and filter factors for each black-and-white film are given in the Data Sheets in this book. There is more information on filters in the KODAK Photo Book *Using Filters* (KW-13), available from photo dealers and bookstores.

Graphical Representation of Typical Black-and-White Photographic Tone Reproduction

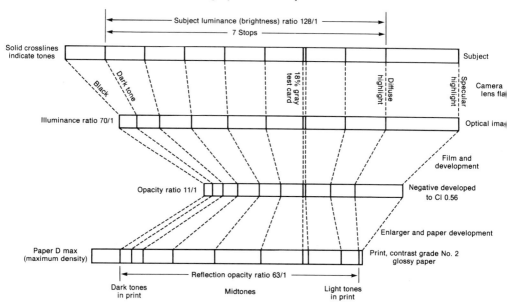

Excellent tone reproduction means: delicate gradation in the highlights, with diffuse highlights separated tonally from specular highlights, which are reproduced as white paper; good separation throughout the middletones; and a range of shadow tones that provide enough detail but still have some areas of deepest black to provide a tonal foundation reference. The contrast and overall brightness should be appropriate for the subject. KODAK Technical Pan Film 2415 developed in KODAK TECHNIDOL LC Developer.

BOB CLEMENS

Safelight Filters. The function of a safelight filter is to provide maximum visibility in the darkroom without fogging the film. For some films, this is achieved by selecting a filter which transmits light in the region to which the film is least sensitive. For example, an orthochromatic film is sensitive only to blue-violet, blue, and green light. You can safely handle this kind of film under a safelight filter transmitting only red light, such as the KODAK 1A Safelight Filter (light red).

Since panchromatic films are sensitive to all colors of visible light, you must normally handle them in total darkness. With some restrictions, you can use a dark-green safelight filter. A filter of this color, because it transmits light to which the eye is most sensitive, provides maximum visibility with a minimum amount of light.

Safelight recommendations for each Kodak black-and-white film are given in the Film Data Sheets in this book.

TONE REPRODUCTION

In photography, the variations in brightness of the subject and the image are called *tones*. Tone reproduction is the means in the photographic process by which the various brightness elements of the subject are reproduced to form an image in the photograph. In color photographs, variations in brightness, hue, and saturation are all evident. This discussion on tone reproduction, however, will be limited to black-and-white, because altering tone reproduction in color photographs can also affect color reproduction, and is not usually done for general photography. Tone reproduction for color materials is predetermined by the manufacturer in order to produce optimum color rendition. The ability to alter tone reproduction in color photographs is more limited than in black-and-white without resorting to complex or exotic methods because of the objective of producing correct color reproduction.

In black-and-white photographs, only the characteristic of brightness is involved in tone reproduction. The neutral and colored tones of the subject are converted to tones of white, gray, and black in the print. How well these tones are reproduced is an important criterion of photographic quality.

The overall brightness range of the typical outdoor frontlighted subject, with the sun at a 45-degree angle to the camera axis, exceeds 1000/1 when the deepest shadows and the specular highlights are included. Typical black-and-white photographic paper can reproduce a brightness range of about 60/1. The brightness range of the paper varies depending on the kind of paper. Photographic paper with a glossy surface usually has the greatest brighness range and is therefore capable of reproducing the greatest range of tones. Since the tonal range of the paper is less than the brightness range of the scene, the tonal scale of the image has to be compressed and/or selectively printed onto photographic paper for reproduction. Since in photographs we don't expect to see detail in the brilliant, specular highlights nor in deep, black shadows, we can eliminate these tones from the brightness scale of the subject when interpreting tone reproduction. This leaves a subject brightness range of about 125/1, extending from the diffuse highlight areas to dark shadow areas. The intention is to reproduce these dark shadows just lighter than black in the print.

When the camera photographs the subject, the camera-lens system introduces some flare light to the optical image which compresses the tonal scale, mainly in the shadows. The optical image is recorded on the film, and the film further compresses all the tones in the tonal scale with the dark tones being compressed more than the others.

When the negative is finally printed onto photographic paper, the tonal scale from the negative is then expanded somewhat but fits within the tonal scale of the paper when properly printed with average conditions. The printing paper expands the midtones from the negative while compressing both highlight-tone and dark-tone areas. The paper compresses the highlight tones more than the dark tones. This means that the overall tone reproduction has about the same amount of compression at both ends of the tonal scale. The tones in the dark regions are compressed by camera flare and the film characteristics, while tones in the highlight region are compressed by the paper. The greater compression of highlights by the paper about equalizes the compression of shadows by flare light and the film.

It helps photographers to have a basic understanding of tone reproduction to obtain high-quality results. A print with high quality will have the type of tone reproduction that has been described when printed on the correct contrast grade of photographic paper from a high-quality negative that has been properly exposed and developed. For most conditions, exposing Kodak black-and-white film at its ISO speed and developing it at the time, temperature, and agitation recommended in the film instructions or in the Data Pages in this book, will generally provide high-quality photographs. You may need to alter the developing time of your film slightly to adjust the contrast of your negatives to your specific darkroom printing equipment. See the discussion under "Degree of Development" on page 100.

Characteristics of a Good Negative

Sharpness: The areas of the negative that are intended to be sharp should be sharp and well-defined when you view the negative through a magnifier.

Density: The overall density—degree of blackness—of the negative should allow reasonably short printing times, such as 10 to 20 seconds for an 8X enlargement. Refer to the center negative in the negative array on page 102 for the appearance of a negative with good tone reproduction.

Density Range (Tonal Scale): The tonal scale of the negative should give good highlight and shadow reproduction with good separation of midtones when printed on grade 2 or 3 or medium grade photographic paper with your enlarger.

Shadows: Deepest shadow areas and black areas should be clear in the negative. Medium shadows should show detail, and should have varying light densities.

Highlights: Diffuse highlights should show gradation and detail, and should have noticeably less density than brilliant white areas and specular highlights in the scene.

Graininess: The print image should not show excessive graininess for the kind of film and degree of enlargement that you used.

Uniformity: The negative should be free from mottle or unevenness caused by improper agitation during development or a short developing time. Unsatisfactory uniformity may result with development times shorter than 5 minutes in a small film tank, depending on the developer.

Physical Defects: The negative should not have physical imperfections, scratches, static markings, scum, water spots or water marks, pinholes caused by dust or improper development, or dried-on dust particles or contaminants from the processing solutions or wash water.

DEFINITION

The terms definition and sharpness are often used interchangeably, but such usage is only partly correct. Definition refers to the overall appearance of detail, while sharpness is one factor affecting definition and describes the appearance of edge sharpness between details in a photograph.

Definition is the composite effect of several factors, among which are sharpness, resolving power, and graininess. Usually resolving power and sharpness increase as graininess decreases, but this is only a general rule, and there are exceptions.

The terms used to describe sharpness, resolving power, and graininess, which are given on the Data Sheets for each film should not be used to compare one class of films, such as black-and-white negative films, with another class of films, such as color negative or color slide films.

These terms are determined by instrument measurements and by looking at pictures by trained observers. Instrument measurements and pictures are affected by factors such as diffusion, spectral sensitivity, halation, and contrast. These effects are less of a factor among films in a class so comparison of definition terms within a class of films is valid. They can be large between films in different classes so that comparision of definition terms between different classes of films is not meaningful nor recommended.

Graininess. This refers to the sandlike or granular appearance in a film, slide, or print, resulting from the clumping of the silver grains, or dye particles in color film or color prints. Graininess is caused by the

When enlargements are made from a grainy negative, objectionable graininess usually becomes the most important definition factor limiting the degree of enlargement.

irregular distribution of the silver grains rather than by the individual grains themselves. Individual grains are not visible under the magnifications used for ordinary enlargements.

For films of a general type, graininess tends to increase with film speed. When a given black-and-white film is developed in different developers to the same contrast index (see page 103), graininess will vary somewhat, depending on the type of developer used. Some fine-grain developers produce less graininess, but at the expense of some loss of film speed. Several Kodak developers are recommended in the Film Data Sheets in this book. To help you select a developer for black-and-white film, descriptions are provided on page D 29 of the Data Sheet section.

Graininess is increased by overexposure or overdevelopment of black-and-white negatives, and by underexposure or overdevelopment of color negatives, and overdevelopment of color reversal (slide) film in the first developer. Overdevelopment results when the temperature of the developer is too high, the development time is extended, or the film receives excessive agitation during development.

The graininess in a print is most apparent in the lighter middle tones, especially in large, uniform areas such as the sky. You can conceal graininess somewhat by softening the focus of your enlarger or by printing on a paper with a rough textured surface, but with some sacrifice in sharpness. The type of enlarger you use affects the graininess of black-and-white prints, and slightly affects the sharpness. An enlarger with a diffuse light source produces images that appear very slightly softer in sharpness, and minimizes graininess from black-and-white silver negatives (or positives). A condenser enlarger, which has a more specular light source, produces images that appear very slightly sharper, but makes graininess more apparent from black-and-white silver images.

The graininess of both negatives and prints increases with increasing contrast. Use the recommended development for your film, and in black-and-white printing, use the contrast grade of paper suitable for the contrast of the negative. Printing paper that's too low in contrast for the negative reduces apparent sharpness while paper too high in contrast increases the appearance of graininess.

Kodak films in the Data Sheets have been assigned graininess classifications, such as *Micro Fine, Extremely Fine, Very Fine, Fine, Medium, Moderately Coarse, Coarse*, or *Very Coarse*.

Resolving Power. The ability of a film or print to record fine detail is referred to as resolving power. In measuring resolving power a parallel-line test chart is photographed at a great reduction in size (see the illustration). The lines of the test chart are separated by spaces of the same width as the lines. The image is examined under a microscope at a specific magnification, and the number of lines per millimetre that can be seen as separate lines is determined. Lines closer together than this number (more lines per millimetre) are indistinct from each other on the film and appear as a gray mass.

The resolving power of a film depends only slightly on the degree of development, but resolution falls off considerably with both overexposure and underexposure.

This is one important reason for exposing negatives correctly. The resolving-power classifications given in the Film Data Sheets are based upon the maximum values determined for recommended exposure and processing.

The maximum resolution which you can obtain in your negatives is limited by the camera lens as well as by the film, and is lower than the resolution of either one alone. To obtain the maximum resolution of which a film is capable, the resolving power of a lens would have to be at least three times the resolving power of the film.

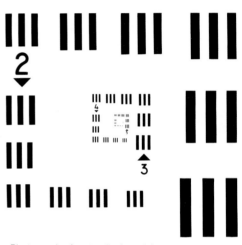

Photograph of a standard resolving-power test object

RESOLVING-POWER CLASSIFICATIONS

Resolving Power	Lines per mm
Ultra High	630 or Above
Extremely High	250 to 500
Very High	160 to 200
High	100 to 125
Medium	63 to 80
Low	50 or Below

Sharpness. The sharpness of a film is the visual impression of good edge sharpness between details in a photograph. The boundary between detail that is dark in a photograph and detail that is light is not a perfectly sharp line. The dark area in the negative tends to bleed over into the light area because of light scatter or diffusion in the emulsion. This effect varies with

This picture shows excellent definition.

JOHN C. HABERSTROH

different types of emulsions, the thickness of the emulsion, and the thickness of the film base, as well as the antihalation properties of the base and its backing. Kodak films have thin emulsion coatings and very efficient antihalation properties, and as a result they produce sharper pictures than many of the films in the past.

Sharpness measurements are made by the manufacturer. The procedure is a complex one beyond the scope of this book; but briefly, a sine-wave test pattern of varying frequencies is photographed. The test pattern recorded on the film is scanned by sensitive measuring equipment. Then the data is plotted graphically and is analyzed to determine the sharpness classification. Kodak films in the Data Sheets have been placed in one of the following sharpness classifications: *Extremely High, Very High, High, Medium, Moderately Low,* or *Low.*

The sharpness of some films can be enhanced when you develop them in certain developers that have been diluted. Some diluted developers produce edge effects that make boundaries between objects appear sharper. Development recommendations for those films that will produce improved sharpness with diluted developers are given in the Data Sheets.

Degree of Enlargement. Graininess, resolving power, and sharpness have a combined influence on definition. However, under certain conditions, any one of these may be more important that the others in controlling the definition of a photograph.

When a negative made on a coarse-grain film is enlarged, graininess usually increases to an objectionable level before the loss of resolution or sharpness becomes unacceptable. In this situation, then, graininess is the limiting factor in definition.

While the resolving power and the sharpness of the film are related, resolving power alone is not a definite indication of ability to produce sharp pictures. In some cases it may be misleading. When viewing a picture at normal reading distance and under the best conditions, the normal eye can resolve about 10 lines per millimetre. If the resolving power of the film is too low to reproduce details about twice as fine as this in the print, definition will be limited by the resolving power. However, when resolving power is adequate and graininess is not noticeable, the sharpness of the image is the most important factor affecting definition. All these factors were taken into consideration in assigning the "Degree of Enlargement Potential" for each negative film in the Data Sheets.

In addition to sharp camera focus, one of the most important factors in obtaining high definition is to hold your camera steady while you press the shutter release. PLUS-X Pan Film, 1/60 sec *f*/4

For high definition in action pictures, you have to use high shutter speeds to freeze the action. This is especially important when you use a telephoto lens which magnifies both the image and the blur from subject motion. PLUS-X Pan Film, 1/1000 sec *f*/5.6

Tips for Good Definition

When a photographer takes pictures, processes the film, and makes prints, the definition may be limited not by the film characteristics but by the way the photographer handles the equipment and materials. To realize the maximum definition the film is capable of producing, observe the following tips:

Picture-Taking Tips

1. Use a high-quality camera lens and make sure it's clean and free of dust and fingerprints.

2. Use a lens hood to reduce flare by blocking the light source from illuminating the front of the lens. Reducing flare increases contrast and detail in the image.

3. Focus carefully, preferably with an accurate rangefinder or ground glass. If your camera doesn't have either of these, estimate the distance as accurately as you can. For close-up pictures, use a tape measure to measure subject distance if your camera does not have ground-glass focusing.

4. When you want sharp images of both near and distant objects in the same picture, consult the depth-of-field scale on your camera lens or a depth-of-field table in your camera manual for the best focus setting and lens opening to use. Most lenses produce the best definition at a lens opening about midway on the lens-opening scale.

5. Hold your camera steady and squeeze the shutter release slowly. When you can, use a shutter speed of 1/125 second or higher to minimize the effects of camera movement. Telephoto lenses, including zoom lenses set on telephoto, require higher shutter speeds than normal or wide-angle lenses for handholding the camera. For maximum steadiness, place your camera on a tripod or other firm support and use a cable release or the self-timer to trip the shutter. A tripod will usually increase sharpness in most cases at all but the very highest shutter speeds. For shutter speeds slower than 1/30 second, a tripod or other support is a necessity for sharp pictures.

6. With a single-lens reflex camera, locking the camera mirror up or using the self-timer will reduce vibration and increase sharpness. These techniques are especially helpful when you're using long focal-length telephoto lenses or close-up equipment with your camera on a tripod and slow shutter speeds.

7. Expose correctly; avoid overexposure and overdevelopment, either of which will produce negatives that are too dense, or dark. Excessive density causes a loss of definition and increased graininess. Use the minimum amount of exposure that will produce an excellent print with good shadow detail. Develop your film using the recommended developer, time, temperature, and agitation.

Printmaking Tips

1. Use a high-quality enlarger lens and check it for cleanliness. The bottom lens surface is especially prone to fingerprints and the top lens surface to dust.

2. If definition is of utmost importance, use a smooth-surface printing paper, such as glossy or smooth lustre.

3. Choose the grade of black-and-white printing paper that will give you a good print with good tone rendition from your negative without either excessive or insufficient contrast.

4. When you make enlargements, be sure that your enlarger is free of vibration and the image is sharply focused on your printing paper.

5. Use the recommended safelight filter and bulb at the proper distance.

RECIPROCITY CHARACTERISTICS

Reciprocity effects are less serious with Kodak black-and-white films for general use than for Kodak color films. You don't have to be concerned with shifts in color balance with black-and-white film. However, film speed and contrast of black-and-white films change when you use long or very short exposure times rather than the typical brief exposure times used in general picture-taking.

Reciprocity characteristics for black-and-white films are given in the Data Sheets. Reciprocity characteristics for color films are described on page 64.

You can correct exposure and development time for the reciprocity effect with black-and-white films according to the tables in the Data Sheets. It's often impractical, though, to correct the development time for a roll of film unless the whole roll was exposed at similar exposure times. Usually varied exposure times are used for taking different pictures on the roll. For this situation, develop the film normally and correct the contrast for the reciprocity effect when you make the prints.

FLASH PICTURES WITH BLACK-AND-WHITE FILM

You can use electronic flash, blue flashbulbs, or clear flashbulbs for flash pictures with black-and-white film. Guide numbers for electronic flash are given on the Data Sheets in this book. Guide numbers for flashbulbs are provided on the bulb cartons. If you use flashbulbs, it's more convenient to use blue ones since they're recommended for both black-and-white and color film. Then you don't have to buy two different kinds of flashbulbs if you switch from black-and-white to color.

FILMS FOR EXISTING-LIGHT PHOTOGRAPHY

The primary requirements in choosing a black-and-white film for photographing existing-light subjects are high speed and good quality. KODAK TRI-X Pan Film has these features; it's a superb film for existing-light photography. If you're photographing subjects in relatively bright existing light,

ROBERT MEYERS, KINSA

Electronic flash effectively stopped the action in this picture made on PLUS-X Pan Film.

94

1/125 sec *f*/1.4

Since the light levels are often low in existing-light photography, you have much more versatility with a high-speed film. KODAK TRI-X Pan Film.

such as existing daylight indoors, or if you don't mind putting your camera on a tripod for subjects in dim light, you can use a film with a lower speed, such as KODAK PLUS-X Pan Film or VERICHROME Pan Film.

If the lighting is extremely poor, or if you want to photograph fast action in existing light or use telephoto lenses, you may need a film even faster than TRI-X Pan Film. For 120-size cameras you can use KODAK ROYAL-X Pan Film; for 35 mm cameras, you can use KODAK Recording Film 2475. Since Recording Film 2475 is so fast and 35 mm negatives are small, prints made from this film have coarse grain. But if you need the very high film speed, you may find the results acceptable. ROYAL-X Pan Film has medium grain and produces good-quality prints.

You can also consider push-processing the film to a higher exposure index but with some loss in quality. Consult the discussion under "Push Processing," page 103.

Existing daylight. 1/60 sec *f*/5.6

FILMS FOR COPYING

For photographing continuous-tone originals—photographs, paintings, or pictures in magazines or books, for example—use one of the films recommended for general picture-taking, such as PLUS-X Pan or VERICHROME Pan Film. The speed of these films is ample for originals lighted by photolamps. If the lighting is dim, such as the existing lighting in an art gallery (ask permission to take pictures first), a better choice would be high-speed TRI-X Pan Film. However, when you can put your camera on a tripod or other firm support, a high-speed film is unnecessary.

If you want to copy printed matter, such as the text portion of documents, magazines, or newspapers, you'll get better results with a high-contrast film suitable for this work. Copies of printed matter made on KODAK Technical Pan Film 2415 or 6415 developed to a high contrast will have a cleaner, whiter background and will look more like the originals than copies made on conventional, general-purpose films.

Copyrighted Material. Although we do not intend this as legal advice, we feel that a note of caution is warranted. By law, the exclusive right to reproduce a copyrighted work in copies belongs to the copyright owner. Limited copying for "fair use" purposes such as criticism, news reporting, teaching, or research is permitted. However, to avoid potential copyright problems, it is always safer, as well as more courteous, to get written permission from the copyright owner before making a copy. As responsibility for complying with the copyright laws must remain with the person making the photographic copy, Eastman Kodak Company can take no responsibility for copyright matters.

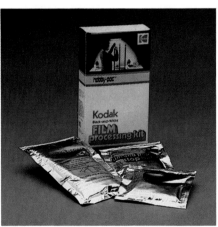

WALTER LEE

The KODAK HOBBY-PAC™ Black-and-White Film Processing Kit provides a convenient means for processing popular Kodak black-and-white films. The kit contains easy-to-use snip'n-pour foil packets of film developer, stop bath, and fixer to make one pint of each solution, and instructions for use.

PROCESSING

After you have exposed a roll of film, you should have it processed promptly for best results. It's easier and more convenient to take your film to your photo dealer for developing and printing by Kodak or another processing lab. Tell the photo dealer the kind of black-and-white film you want to have processed in case it's special-purpose film that should be custom processed.

Prints from KODAK Black-and-White Film

Kodak provides processing and printing services for popular Kodak black-and-white roll films: KODAK PLUS-X Pan, VERICHROME Pan, TRI-X Pan, and PANATOMIC-X Films. The high-quality prints are standard snapshot-size. Other processing labs also offer black-and-white film processing, and prints and enlargements from black-and-white negatives.

It's a good idea to identify unusually important and irreplaceable pictures with your name and address when you send them in for processing, see the suggestions on page 64.

Processing the Film Yourself

When you do your own darkroom work, you'll find it's a lot of fun—and a rewarding and interesting extension of your photo hobby as well. You have much more control over the results when you process the film yourself and make your own prints.

You can process Kodak black-and-white films yourself in processing kits or chemicals sold by photo dealers. Follow the instructions given below, on the Data Sheets in this book, or packaged with the film and chemicals. If you have questions about the procedure or about making black-and-white prints from your negatives, write to Kodak at the address given on page 65.

To process the film, we recommend that you use a film tank. Several different kinds are available from your photo dealer. Be sure that the one you select will accept the size of your film.

Loading your film into the developing tank requires TOTAL DARKNESS.

To open **135 magazines,** hold the magazine with the long end of the spool down, and use a lid lifter or a hook-type

Kodak
BLACK-AND-WHITE
FILMS for Prints and
Enlargements

KODAK PLUS-X Pan,
VERICHROME Pan, TRI-X Pan,
or PANATOMIC-X Films

Black-and-White Negative
KERDALL REMBOLDT, KINSA

KODAK Black-and-White Prints
(made by Kodak)

Prints and Enlargements on KODAK Black-and-
White Paper

97

To process your own 135 film, open the magazine in TOTAL DARKNESS. Hold the magazine with the long end of the spool down, and use a lid lifter or a hook-type bottle opener to remove the upper end cap from the magazine.

To open a 126 or 110 cartridge for processing, break open the cartridge in TOTAL DARKNESS by bending the cylindrical chambers toward the label.

bottle opener to remove the upper end cap from the magazine. Pull the loaded spool out of the magazine, taking care not to let the film unwind. The film is attached to the magazine spool with a strip of tape. Separate the film from the spool and cut off the tongue. Load the film-tank reel according to the film-tank instructions.

To break open an exposed **110 or 126 cartridge,** hold it with the label facing you and your thumbs on the label. Use both hands to bend the two cylindrical chambers toward the label. If it's a 110 cartridge, pull the film, together with its backing paper, from the take-up chamber in a direction so that the *paper* rubs against the inner surface of the cartridge back. This minimizes the likelihood of scratching the film emulsion. If the end of the backing paper (trailer) has been wound into the take-up chamber, you will have to pry open the chamber (after breaking the cartridge) to retrieve the film.

After breaking open a 126 cartridge, remove the film spool from the larger chamber by separating the plastic sections surrounding the spool. Unroll the film and the paper backing. The film is attached to the paper backing in the same way as roll film.

Rip the "Exposed" sticker on **roll film** and carefully unroll and separate the film from the paper backing. Be careful not to cinch or scratch the film. The film is attached to the paper with a strip of tape at the end near the core of the film spool.

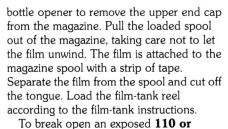

To remove the film after you've opened a 126 cartridge, separate the plastic sections surrounding the spool. If it's a 110 cartridge, pull the paper backing out of the broken cartridge in a direction so that the paper rubs against the cartridge. The film will come out along with the backing paper. Handle the film by the edges only.

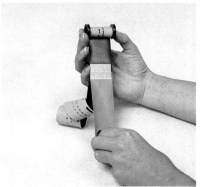

DON BUCK

The film in 126 cartridges is attached to the paper backing with a strip of tape. Detach the film and discard the paper and tape. Handle the film by the edges only.

98

Processing Recommendations

Develop your film for the time given in the development table in the Data Sheet for the film you're using. Be sure to use the recommended agitation procedure. See "Tips on Using Film Developing Tanks."

The developing times given in the Data Sheets for Kodak black-and-white films are for small roll-film tanks. A small tank is defined as one in which the agitation is produced by moving the tank or the reel inside when the reel has a handle. A small tank is for processing roll film of conventional length and size, such as 135, 126, 110, 120, 127, and 620 sizes, with the film held in a reel or apron. The reels are not used in a rack, basket, or on a spindle. The solution volume of a small tank is usually 1 quart (about 1 litre) or less.

Rinse in KODAK HOBBY-PAC™ Black-and-White Film and Paper Stop Bath, KODAK Indicator Stop Bath, or KODAK Stop Bath SB-5 at 65 to 75°F (18 to 24°C) for about 30 seconds with agitation. With most films you can use a water rinse if an acid stop bath is not available. However, an acid stop bath is better because it stops development instantly by neutralizing the developer. See the Data Sheet for your film.

Fix in KODAK HOBBY-PAC™ Black-and-White Film and Paper Fixer, KODAK Fixer, KODAK Fixing Bath F-5, KODAK Rapid Fixer, or KODAFIX Solution at 65 to 75°F (18 to 24°C). *Agitate films frequently during fixing.* See the Data Sheet for your film for the recommended fixing time and other processing recommendations. If the Data Sheets differ from the information given here, follow the Data Sheets.

Wash for 20 to 30 minutes in running water at 65 to 75°F (18 to 24°C). After washing, to minimize drying marks, treat in diluted KODAK PHOTO-FLO Solution for 30 seconds, or wipe surfaces carefully with a KODAK Photo Chamois or a soft viscose sponge.

You can use KODAK Hypo Clearing Agent after fixing to reduce washing time and conserve water. First remove excess fixer, also referred to as hypo, by rinsing the film in water at 65 to 75°F (18 to 24°C) for 30 seconds. Then bathe the film in KODAK Hypo Clearing Agent solution for 1 to 2 minutes at 65 to 70°F (18 to 21°C), with moderate agitation. Then wash it for 5 minutes in running water at 65 to 70°F (18 to 21°C), using a water flow sufficient to give at least one complete change of water in 5 minutes.

For maximum image stability and long-term storage, consult the Kodak book, *Conservation of Photographs,* F-40, sold by photo dealers, for additional processing treatment.

You'll obtain the best results when you keep the temperatures of the rinse, fix, and wash approximately the same as the developer temperature.

Dry in a dust-free place.

Refer to the Film Data Sheets in this book for processing recommendations for the specific film you're using. When the Data Sheets differ from the general guidelines given here, follow the Data Sheets.

Tips on Using Film Developing Tanks

In the dark (see safelight recommendations on the Data Sheets), start the timer and place the loaded film reel or apron into your tank containing the developer. Keep the reel or apron under the surface of the solution, and tap it on the bottom of the tank before you replace the tank cover. This helps dislodge air bells (bubbles). After you replace the cover, tap the tank on the countertop or sink to dislodge any remaining air bells. Then you can carry out the remaining steps in normal room light.

If this procedure is not possible with your tank, begin the process by pouring in the developer with the reel of film inside the tank. Tap the bottom of the tank against the working surface to dislodge air bells.

Recommended Agitation

Proper agitation is as important as the correct temperature and development time. Too little agitation during development will cause mottle and uneven development. Too much agitation can cause overdevelopment and streaks on the film. When you follow the recommended agitation procedures, you'll avoid these undesirable effects.

Methods of Agitation. After the film has been immersed for 30 seconds, agitate the tank for 5 seconds according to the method recommended below for your tank. Repeat this agitation at intervals of 30 seconds for the remainder of the development time.

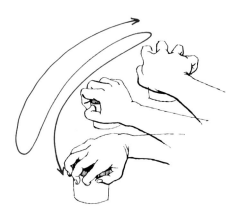

Recommended method of agitation for a film tank that can't be inverted.

1. For a tank that can't be inverted, agitate by sliding the tank back and forth over a distance of about 10 inches at a rate of two cycles per second during the agitation intervals. At the same time, turn or rotate the tank back and forth through about one-half turn (see above).

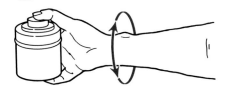

Recommended method of agitation for a film tank that can be inverted.

2. For tanks that you can turn upside down without spilling the solution, invert the tank once per second during the 5-second agitation intervals, ending the agitation cycle with the tank right side up (see above).

3. With tanks that have a handle for turning the reel, rotate the reel back and forth gently through about one-half turn at a rate of one cycle per second during the agitation intervals.

If the method of agitation described in the instructions for your film tank differs from these, agitate the film for 5 seconds at 30-second intervals according to the method recommended in the tank instructions. A special method of film tank agitation is recommended for pictorial results with KODAK Technical Pan Film 2415 and 6415. This is described on the film Data Sheet on page D 46.

Degree of Development

The degree to which you develop your film has an important effect on the quality of your finished pictures. Development determines to a large extent the contrast grade of photographic paper you'll need to make the best possible prints with good tone reproduction from your negatives. The degree of development for a film and developer combination depends on the developing time, the temperature of the developer, and the degree of agitation. Underdevelopment reduces the contrast of the negative and can cause loss of shadow detail. Overdevelopment increases negative contrast and graininess, reduces sharpness, and can block up highlights, making the negatives hard to print. Negatives that have received correct exposure and development should print best on contrast grade No. 2 or No. 3 photographic paper. The development recommendations given in the Data Sheets will produce the proper contrast in prints made with average printing conditions from properly exposed negatives of average subjects.

Since the degree of development depends on time and temperature, several normal development times are given to compensate for changes in temperature. See the development tables in the Data Sheets.

In this picture, detail has been retained in both highlights and shadows for good tone reproduction—the result of normal exposure and normal development of the film.

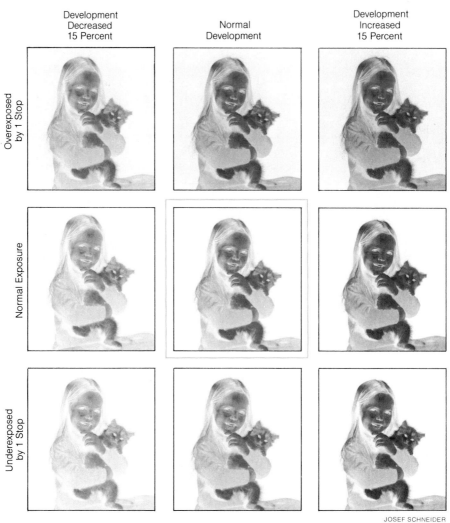

| | Development Decreased 15 Percent | Normal Development | Development Increased 15 Percent |

Overexposed by 1 Stop

Normal Exposure

Underexposed by 1 Stop

JOSEF SCHNEIDER

These negatives show the results of changing camera exposure and the degree of development. The negative in the center received normal exposure and normal development.

These illustrations were made from negative print images for technical reasons. However, each negative print was matched as closely as possible to actual negatives exposed and processed as indicated.

Contrast Index

The degree of development, or development contrast, is specified by contrast-index measurements. Most of the recommended development times given in the Data Sheets are based on a normal contrast index of 0.56. Under average conditions, properly exposed negatives processed to this contrast index should print on medium-contrast photographic paper with good tone reproduction. If your negatives are consistently too contrasty and require low-contrast paper such as grade No. 1, develop your film to a lower contrast by reducing development time by about 30 percent. If your negatives are consistently too low in contrast and print on high-contrast paper, such as grade No. 4, develop your film to a higher contrast by increasing the development time by about 40 percent.

To produce negatives consistent in overall density and quality, you should make an exposure compensation when you adjust development times, particularly with shorter development times. When reducing development times, increase exposure by about ⅓ stop. When increasing development times, reduce exposure by about ⅓ stop.

The effective printing contrast of your negatives is affected by the method you use in making prints. A diffusion-type enlarger produces about the same degree of contrast in the print as a contact printer. A condenser enlarger produces greater contrast than a diffusion enlarger or a contact printer. The difference in contrast may be as much as the contrast difference between No. 2 and No. 3 grades of photographic paper. Complete information on printing papers is given in the book *Quality Enlarging with KODAK B/W Papers* (G-1). If you want to know more about enlarging techniques, a good book on this subject is *Black-and-White Darkroom Techniques* (KW-15). Both of these Kodak books are sold by photo dealers and bookstores.

Push Processing

Push-processing black-and-white film lets you expose the film at a higher film speed number for situations where you need more film speed. As explained earlier, a higher speed film permits you to take pictures in dim existing light while handholding your camera, use high shutter speeds to stop action, use telephoto lenses for larger images, or use small lens openings to gain depth of field, all under poor lighting conditions.

With push processing you can expose your film at twice the film speed. For example, if you're using KODAK TRI-X Pan Film which has a speed of ISO 400, you can expose it at 800 if you push-process the film one stop. This recommendation is for normal-contrast scenes. For low-contrast scenes, for example, scenes with little or no shadow detail to record, you can usually expose the film at 4 times the normal speed with push processing. That's a film-speed number of 1600 with TRI-X Pan Film. By taking advantage of the latitude of the film with low-contrast scenes, you can usually expose the film at 2 times the normal speed and process the film normally. With TRI-X Pan Film that would be a film speed number of 800.

To push-process your film, increase the recommended development time by 50 percent. You can use the developers recommended on the film instructions or on the Data Sheets in this book. Push processing is not recommended, however, with KODAK MICRODOL-X Developer. If the recommendations for extended development on some film instructions differ from those given here, follow the film instructions.

It's important to realize that push-processing black-and-white film does not actually increase the speed of the film by a significant amount. The speed of a negative film is an inherent characteristic determined during manufacture. Increasing the development time will not produce detail on the film where nothing was recorded in the camera, such as in underexposed areas of the image. Push processing does increase the density, or blackness, of exposed areas on the film to make negatives of normal- or low-contrast scenes more printable. Prints from push-processed, underexposed negatives will usually look better than with normal processing. While push-processing film does increase the quality of prints made from underexposed negatives, it does not compensate fully for

Tʀɪ-X Pan Film—ISO 400, 1/15 sec *f*/6.7, normal processing. A tripod would be necessary to hold your camera steady for this slow shutter speed.

TOM BEELMANN

Tʀɪ-X Pan Film—Film Speed Number 800, 1/30 sec *f*/6.7, push-processed 1 stop with a 50-percent increase in development time. Since push processing lets you use less exposure, you could handhold your camera with this shutter speed to take the picture, while maintaining good depth of field with the medium-size lens opening.

underexposure. Push processing will not produce the same level of quality as normally exposed and processed negatives. The most serious change in prints made from push-processed negatives is a loss of shadow detail.

In addition, push processing increases negative contrast and overall graininess. The negatives will require a lower-contrast photographic paper for making the prints and grain will be more apparent in enlargements. Prints from negatives of normal- and low-contrast scenes should be quite acceptable if you're willing to accept a slight loss of shadow detail and an increase in contrast. It's usually not practical to push-process film images of high-contrast scenes because the negatives will be difficult to print and the prints will be too contrasty.

Push-processing black-and-white film is beneficial when it helps you get good pictures that otherwise would be impractical or impossible because of adverse exposure conditions. But you should keep in mind that you'll obtain the highest photographic quality in pictures of normal scenes when you expose your film at its ISO speed and process it normally.

EXPOSURE

FILM SPEEDS

To determine correct exposure, you need to know the speed of the film you're using unless your camera senses the film speed automatically. Knowing the film speed also helps you select the best film to do the job for the specific picture-taking conditions in the scenes you're going to photograph. The film speeds in this book are for cameras with built-in exposure meters or for separate exposure meters marked for ISO or ASA speeds or Exposure Indexes.

Film speed indicates relative sensitivity to light. Film with a high speed number is more light-sensitive, or faster, than a film with a low number. For example, a film with a speed of ISO 200 is twice as fast as a film with a speed of ISO 100. The film speed for each Kodak film is given in the Data Sheets in this book, on the outside of the film carton, and in the instructions packaged with the film, depending on the kind of film.

Some automatic cameras automatically sense the speed of the film or are designed for specific kinds of film, and do not require the photographer to set the film speed on the camera. These cameras include those that feature DX coding when used with DX coded films, and cameras that take disc film, 110- and 126-size cartridges, and instant film. See page 12 and your camera manual. Many of the older 110-size cameras are not designed for use with high-speed film, such as KODACOLOR VR 400 Film. Read your camera instruction manual or write to the manufacturer or the American distributor of your camera to see if you can use such films.

Film speeds are determined according to International Standards and American National Standards and are designated ISO speeds. These speed values replace ASA speeds. Both of these speed values are arithmetic, they are numerically the same, and you use them in the same way. In addition, ISO logarithmic speeds replace DIN speeds which are used on some cameras and exposure meters manufactured outside the United States. ISO logarithmic speed numbers are identified with the degree symbol (°). ISO logarithmic speed values are numerically the same as the DIN speeds. However, both ISO logarithmic speeds and DIN speeds are different from ISO arithmetic speeds and ASA speeds.

Generally, the ISO designation that's printed on Kodak film cartons looks like this, for example: ISO 100/21°. The number after "ISO," 100 in the example, is the ASA equivalent and the number with the degree symbol (°), 21° in the example, is the DIN equivalent.

You should use the speed system that's marked on your equipment. Since most of the photographic equipment sold in the United States uses ISO arithmetic speeds, formerly ASA speeds, this speed system will be used throughout this book.

You use ISO speeds in the same way as the speeds they replace. For example, if the speed of a film is ISO 100, you would set 100 on the ISO/ASA dial of your camera or exposure meter.

If your in-camera exposure meter or separate handheld meter is marked with a different scale of film-speed numbers, you can convert ISO arithmetic speeds to the film-speed numbers used on your meter. See the conversion table above for obtaining equivalent ISO logarithmic or DIN speeds.

You can also obtain the KODAK Customer Service Pamphlet, *Accurate Exposure with Your Meter* (AF-9), which gives equivalent ASA, DIN, BSI, early Weston, and Scheiner film-speed numbers. See your photo dealer for a copy, or write to Kodak at the address given on page 65.

ISO/ASA/DIN Film-Speed Conversions

As mentioned before, the ISO° (DIN) series of speed numbers are different from ISO (ASA) speed numbers. You can use the following table for converting ISO (ASA) speeds to ISO° (DIN) speeds. If your equipment has a ISO°/DIN film speed dial, set the ISO° logarithmic speed of the film on the dial.

ISO (ASA)/ISO° (DIN) FILM SPEEDS

ISO (ASA)	ISO° (DIN)	ISO (ASA)	ISO° (DIN)
6	9°	160	23°
8	10°	200	24°
10	11°	250	25°
12	12°	320	26°
16	13°	400	27°
20	14°	500	28°
25	15°	640	29°
32	16°	800	30°
40	17°	1000	31°
50	18°	1250	32°
64	19°	1600	33°
80	20°	2000	34°
100	21°	2500	35°
125	22°	3200	36°

OPTIMUM EXPOSURE

Optimum exposure is the minimum exposure required to produce a picture of excellent quality. Cameras, exposure meters, and flash equipment that are operating properly and that are used correctly will generally produce optimum exposure when you set the equipment for the recommended film speed provided with the film. Modifying film speeds when necessary is discussed on page 124.

Underexposure results in less density, or blackness, in your negatives or more density, or darker colors, in your slides and loss of shadow detail in both. Color and black-and-white negatives will be too light, or thin, and color negatives will have increased graininess. Prints from underexposed negatives will have milky, gray shadows, flat contrast, and an overall muddy appearance. Underexposed color slides will be too dark.

Overexposure increases negative density or decreases slide density and results in a loss of highlight detail in both. Furthermore, overexposure in negatives increases graininess with conventional black-and-white films, reduces sharpness, increases printing time, and makes focusing the enlarger more difficult. Overexposed color slides will be too light with desaturated colors and loss of detail in highlight areas.

EXPOSURE LATITUDE

The exposure latitude of a film is the range of camera exposures from underexposure to overexposure which will produce pictures of acceptable quality with that particular film. In other words, exposure latitude is the amount you can be off from the ideal exposure and still get acceptable pictures. Exposure latitude depends mainly on the film you're using, the subject brightness range, and your own requirements for picture quality.

Continuous-tone negative films have greater exposure latitude than slide, or reversal, films. However, you obtain the best quality with any film when your pictures are properly exposed.

Film speeds and exposure guides for Kodak negative films are based on the minimum exposure required to record important shadow detail. Because of the latitude of negative films, slight variations in exposure produce no loss of image quality. Generally, negative films have greater latitude for overexposure than they do for underexposure. This is especially true for Kodak color negative films. KODACOLOR VR Films, for example, produce satisfactory prints from negatives overexposed by up to approximately 3 stops, or underexposed by up to 1 stop.

Film speeds and recommended exposures for Kodak color slide films and black-and-white slide films are based upon the exposure that produces the best picture when highlight detail and shadow detail are of equal importance. Slide, or reversal, films have higher contrast than most negative films. In addition, no corrections can be made after you take pictures because no printing step is used. As a result, camera exposure is more critical with reversal films than with continuous-tone negative films. Since reversal films have limited exposure latitude, carefully follow your exposure-meter readings or exposure guides unless results with your equipment consistently indicate the need for an adjustment in the indicated exposure.

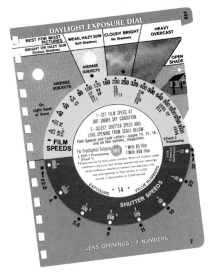

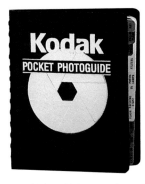

You can obtain a high percentage of properly exposed pictures by following exposure guides. This Daylight Exposure Dial is from the KODAK Pocket Photoguide (AR-21), available from photo dealers.

EXPOSURE GUIDES

Kodak provides exposure tables and dial exposure guides which are based on many practical picture tests and extensive data on illumination, subject brightness, film speed, and printmaking requirements. The exposure recommendations have been confirmed by years of experience. For any picture-taking situation specifically covered by a Kodak exposure guide, the camera settings indicated by the guide will produce a high percentage of properly exposed photos.

Even if you have an exposure meter, exposure guides are useful for verifying that you're using your meter correctly or for providing a backup in case your meter stops working, and for determining exposure for scenes that are difficult to meter. In addition, exposure guides are helpful for planning purposes to indicate in advance what camera settings, film speed, and equipment requirements will be necessary for the pictures you want to take.

The KODAK Pocket Photoguide (AR-21) contains dial exposure calculators covering the use of daylight, flash, photolamps, and existing light with a variety of Kodak films. The text includes information on lighting techniques, filter selection, depth of field, and other essentials. This guide is sold by photo dealers.

Exposure tables are provided in the Data Sheets in this book, in the instructions included with Kodak films, and in many Kodak publications.

EXPOSURE METERS

The big plus of owning a camera with a built-in exposure meter or a separate handheld meter is that you can determine exposure for almost any kind of scene and lighting situation. If you use your exposure meter according to the procedures recommended by the camera or meter manufacturer, you should get a very high percentage of properly exposed pictures.

However, an exposure meter doesn't think for itself. If you use your meter in a purely mechanical fashion, chances are that you will not get consistent results. Study your camera or exposure-meter instruction book and learn how to use your meter properly; familiarize yourself with the flexibility and limitations of the type of exposure meter you have. Then you can use this knowledge to interpret your meter readings and obtain a larger percentage of correctly exposed pictures.

Basically there are two types of exposure meters: reflected-light and incident-light. The exposure meters built into cameras are reflected-light meters. Some meters have attachments that let you measure either reflected light or incident light. A special kind of reflected-light meter is the spot meter. This kind of meter selectively reads the light reflected from one small area in a scene.

JOHN HOOD

LEE HOWICK

For average scenes such as these, it's a simple matter to determine the correct camera settings. Just make an overall meter reading from the camera position.

An exposure meter is invaluable when the lighting or atmospheric conditions are unusual. KODACHROME 25 Film (Daylight), 1/125 sec f/5.6

Reflected-Light Meters

A reflected-light exposure meter measures the light reflected from all the areas included in the meter field of view. One of the main advantages of a reflected-light meter is that you can make the meter reading from the camera position for most scenes. Because the meter is designed to average the overall light reflected from scenes with normal reflectance characteristics, it gives correct exposure for most pictures.

Since the exposure meters built into cameras are reflected-light meters, you can aim and use the meter from the camera position when you are ready to take the picture. The information given here for reflected-light exposure meters also applies to in-camera meters. Some cameras are automatic; that is, you don't have to be concerned with exposure because the built-in meter makes the reading and sets the exposure for you automatically. Built-in exposure meters give very good results for most scenes.

An exposure meter indicates the camera settings necessary to reproduce average subjects as a tone equivalent to a medium gray. This works well for average subjects and average conditions. However, for some scenes an overall exposure-meter reading will result in incorrect exposure. When you

With a reflected-light exposure meter, you point the meter or camera with built-in meter toward the subject to determine the correct exposure.

With an incident-light exposure meter, you point the meter toward the camera position to make the reading.

make an overall meter reading from the camera position, your exposure meter is influenced by any predominant light or dark area if there's one in the scene. Your exposure meter, though, has no way of knowing what part of the scene is the most important part of your picture, such as the main subject. If the scene has light and dark areas of about equal distribution and importance, your meter will usually indicate the correct exposure. However, if the most important part of the picture is surrounded by a large area which is much lighter or darker, your meter will indicate an exposure that would reproduce the large light or dark area as a medium tone which is incorrect for the important part of the photograph.

The way to determine the correct exposure in such situations is to make a selective meter reading of the principal subject. For example, a close-up reading of the subject will exclude unimportant light or dark surroundings in the scene that can mislead your exposure meter. In making close-up readings, be careful not to measure your shadow or the shadow from the meter or the camera.

Here are some examples of scenes that require selective meter readings to determine optimum exposure:

The most common situation that can mislead reflected-light meters is a scene that includes a large portion of the sky. The sky is brighter near the horizon than the other parts of the scene with average reflectance. Therefore, the meter may be overly influenced by the sky and will indicate too little exposure, causing underexposure of the subject which would be too dark. This effect is even greater on overcast days when the sky is whitish. Some manufacturers of reflected-light meters recommend that you tilt the meter downward at a slight angle to avoid undue influence from the sky. Most cameras with built-in exposure meters are designed to make the meter reading mainly from the center and bottom of the scene you're photographing to reduce the influence of the sky brightness. It's usually not necessary or practical to tilt cameras with built-in meters downward to avoid the sky. Consult your camera instruction manual for the correct use of your camera exposure meter.

RONALD DE MILT

PETE CULROSS

When there is a lot of sky in the background, make a close-up reading of your subject with an in-camera exposure meter or a separate handheld reflected-light meter.

110

NORM KERR

A light background, such as bright sand or snow, with average or dark subjects can fool a reflected-light meter. A reading made from the camera position will be too high and the subjects will be underexposed. For correct exposure, make a close-up meter reading of the subjects.

NEIL MONTANUS

Scenes with large light areas such as snow, light sand, or white concrete may mislead the exposure meter when the most important part of the scene is much darker than the surroundings. This will result in underexposure of the subject. In these situations, take a close-up meter reading of the principal subject for proper exposure.

When a large light area is the important part of the picture, such as a snow scene but not a close-up of a person, your reflected-light meter may be overly influenced by the bright snow, and the picture will be underexposed, with gray-looking snow. Here again, the exposure indicated by the meter would make the large light area a medium tone—too dark. The snow, of course, should look white in the photo. In a situation such as this, compare your meter reading with a Kodak exposure guide, such as the one on the film instructions. If your meter reading indicates much less than the recommended exposure for snow scenes in the exposure guide, you'll probably get better results by following the exposure guide. Or you can modify the reflected-light meter reading made from the camera position and use 1 stop more exposure than indicated by the meter. Conversely, when a large dark area is an important part of the picture, use 1 stop less exposure than an overall reflected-light meter reading indicates.

When the subject is much lighter than the surroundings, your exposure meter may indicate too much exposure, causing overexposure of the subject. An example of this is an outdoor scene with a bride in a white wedding dress standing in front of a dark foliage background with the camera at a medium distance. Because of the dark surroundings, your meter sees mostly the large dark area and therefore indicates an exposure that is too much for the lighter subject. As a result, the subject is overexposed. Once again, take a close-up meter reading of the face of the principal subject to determine the correct exposure.

In backlighted scenes the background is often sunlit and is therefore brighter than the subject. Also, light can shine directly into the light-sensitive meter cell. Both of these factors cause a high meter reading and underexposure results. The solution is to take a close-up meter reading while

JOHN VAETH   ROBERT KRETZER

When subjects are in the shade with a sunlit background, a reflected-light meter reading made from the camera position would respond too much to the bright background so that shaded subjects would be underexposed. Move in for a close-up meter reading.

shading the meter with your hand or some other object to block the sun (or lights) that may be directly illuminating the meter cell. Some cameras with built-in exposure meters have a backlight compensation button which increases exposure, usually 1½ to 2 stops, for use with backlighted subjects. See your camera manual.

You can make close-up meter readings with some built-in camera meters and then move back to take the picture. You can usually do this with a manually adjustable camera. Automatic cameras often have a means of letting you hold a close-up meter reading by partially pressing the shutter release or by pressing a memory-lock button while you move back to your original position to take the picture.

Another way you can make a close-up reading from the camera position is to use a single-lens reflex camera with through-the-lens metering equipped with a zoom lens. With the zoom lens adjusted to the telephoto setting, make the meter reading

of the important part of the subject. Then adjust the zoom control for the framing you want and take the picture.

An alternative method for obtaining correct exposure for backlighted subjects with a manually adjustable camera is to simply adjust exposure according to exposure guidelines. For close-ups of backlighted subjects illuminated by a large area of open sky, use a lens opening 2 stops larger than for frontlighted subjects; for backlighted subjects at a medium distance, use a lens opening 1 stop larger than normal; and for distant scenic views with no large shadow areas, use the same exposure as for frontlighting.

If you can't make close-up meter readings with your camera, you may be able to change the film-speed setting to a different number to compensate for unusual lighting or subject brightness. For photographing average or dark subjects in *very light* surroundings, divide the speed of your film by 2 and set the resulting *lower*

112

WALTER LEE

DON MAGGIO

A reflected-light meter reading made from the camera position would be too low because of the dark background, and the subject would be overexposed. A close-up meter reading will produce accurate exposure.

number on the film-speed dial of your camera for 1 stop more exposure. For example, if you were using KODACHROME 64 Film, ISO 64, in this type of situation, you would set 32 instead of 64 on the film-speed dial. For photographing average or light subjects in *very dark* surroundings, multiply the speed of your film by 2, and set the resulting *higher* number on your film-speed dial for 1 stop less exposure.

Instead of changing the setting on the film-speed dial to alter exposure for unusual scenes, many automatic cameras have an exposure compensation dial which lets you increase or decrease exposure by a fixed amount, such as ± 1, 1½, or 2 stops. Remember to reset your film-speed dial or exposure compensation dial to the normal setting when you've finished photographing the unusual scene.

Since operating procedures vary with different cameras, check your camera instruction manual for the recommended method to use with your built-in camera meter for making close-up meter readings or for altering the exposure.

Spot meters selectively measure the reflected light of small areas in a scene from the camera position. These meters measure only the small area toward which they are pointed. Therefore, they are not influenced by large light or dark surrounding areas. This type of meter is useful for telephoto pictures, which include only a small portion of the overall scene, and for scenes with uneven lighting or reflectance. However, since a spot meter reads one small area at a time, you must decide which areas in the scene are important to your picture. This is especially true when you're taking pictures with a normal or wide-angle camera lens, which usually includes many different areas of brightness in one picture. The important areas in the scene are the areas that you should measure with the spot meter. To determine correct exposure in this type of situation, take a meter reading of the lightest important area in the scene and the

BOB CLEMENS

NEIL MONTA

In these backlighted scenes, a reflected-light exposure meter would be influenced by the bright background, and the sun might shine into the light-sensitive cell of the meter. Both of these factors would result in underexposure. Make a close-up meter reading of the subjects.

darkest important area in the scene; then set your exposure halfway between the two. For example, if your exposure meter indicates that 1/250 second at $f/16$ is correct for the light area and 1/250 second at $f/4$ is correct for the dark area, then 1/250 second at $f/8$ is the average exposure which is the best compromise for the scene.

Because it is often necessary to make several exposure-meter readings, using a spot meter is more time-consuming and requires more knowledge of what to measure in the scene. Consequently, such meters are used primarily by experienced photographers.

Reflected-Light Readings of a Substitute Test Card

When you are photographing a subject indoors, the subject is frequently brighter than other parts of the scene, such as the background. A person lighted by photolamp illumination requires the same exposure to produce good flesh tones whether the person is in front of a dark background or a light one. But if you make reflected-light meter readings of such scenes from the camera position, the readings will be misleading because the meter will be influenced by a background which is much lighter or darker than the subject you're photographing.

To determine exposure for this type of scene, take a close-up reading with a conventional reflected-light meter, or use a spot meter from the camera position. If you make the meter reading of your subject's face, you must divide the film speed by 2 to compute your exposure. This is necessary because average Caucasian skin has twice as much reflectance as the average indoor scene, and exposure-meter calibration is based upon average scene reflectance.

Another way you can determine exposure accurately for these situations is to make reflected-light readings of a test card of known reflectance. Most indoor scenes have an average reflectance of about 18 percent. If you make a reflected-light reading of an 18-percent gray card held close to and in front of the principal subject, you should obtain accurate exposure for the scene. Photo dealers sell KODAK Gray Cards for this purpose. The gray cards come in a package of two, and are 8 × 10 inches in size. Each gray card has a gray side of 18-percent reflectance and a white side of approximately 90-percent reflectance. You can use the white side if necessary to get a higher meter reading in dim lighting. If you use the white side or any other matte white card of about 90-percent reflectance, divide the ISO speed of the film by 5 and set the answer on the film-speed dial of your exposure meter, using the

114

PETE CULROSS

HERB JONES

Since a spot meter measures a small area to determine exposure, it would come in handy for pictures such as these. You could make the meter reading of the important areas of the scenes from the camera position.

nearest film-speed number. Reset the film speed to the ISO speed of the film when you're through using the white-card meter reading-technique.

To make a meter reading of a gray or white card, place the card close in front of your subject and hold it straight up and down, facing halfway between the main light and your camera so there's no specular reflections on the card. Make the meter reading by holding your meter close to the card so that it reads only the card. Be sure that the meter doesn't read its own shadow. When you make the reading, turn on all the lights that will illuminate the subject. Shield your exposure meter from other lights that might shine directly into its light-sensitive cell.

You can also use the KODAK Gray Card for meter readings outdoors. This is particularly helpful when distance or a barrier of some sort makes it difficult to get an accurate reading of the light reflected from the subject or when unimportant light or dark areas can mislead your meter. It's desirable to place the card at or near the principal subject; but when it's impractical to do so, just make sure that the light on the gray card is the same as the light on the subject. When you make a meter reading from the gray card, your meter is not influenced by light or dark areas in the scene. Since exposure meters are calibrated for average reflectance, the meter reacts as though the subject has average reflectance.

When you use the card outdoors, exposure adjustments are necessary when the reflectance of the card differs from that of the scene. Complete instructions are included with the gray cards.

Indicent-Light Meters

An incident-light meter measures the light illuminating the scene. To make an incident-light reading, you position your meter in the same light that's illuminating the subject and point the meter toward the camera (unless the meter instruction book recommends a different technique). When possible, hold the meter at the subject position. To do this, you'll have to move close to your subject. This is the reason why cameras usually don't have incident-light meters. You can make an incident-light reading from the camera position if the light falling on the camera is the same as the light falling on the scene you are photographing. Point the meter in the same direction as you would if you were making the reading at the subject position, 180° from the subject.

Exposure determined by an incident-light meter assumes that the scene has average reflectance. Fortunately, most scenes have average reflectance, and as a result the exposure indicated by an incident-light meter is correct for most picture-taking situations.

Since an incident-light meter measures the illumination on the scene, scene reflectance does not influence the meter. This means that light or dark areas in the scene will not mislead the meter. If these areas are unimportant in your picture and the principal subject has average reflectance, your picture should be properly exposed when you use an incident-light meter. Or if you are photographing an evenly lighted scene which has a large brightness range where detail in the light and dark areas is of equal importance, an incident-light meter will indicate a compromise exposure that should be correct.

On the other hand, if either a very light area or a very dark area is the important part of the picture and you want to record detail in this area, you must modify the exposure indicated by your incident-light meter. If a light area is an important part of the picture, use a lens opening ½ to 1 stop smaller than your meter indicates. If a dark area is important, use a lens opening ½ to 1 stop larger than your meter indicates. Note that these exposure corrections are just the opposite of those for reflected-light meters.

116

When you can't get close enough to your subject to make an incident-light meter reading at the subject position, you can make the reading from the camera position if the light falling on the camera is the same as the light falling on the subject. Remember to aim the meter in the same direction as you would if you were at the subject position.

If a bright area, such as snow, is an important part of the picture, use a lens opening 1 stop smaller than your incident-light meter indicates.

When the scene has uneven lighting and you want the best overall exposure, make incident-light readings in the lightest and darkest areas of illumination that are important to your picture. Then use the exposure that is midway between the exposure settings indicated for these areas.

Many scenes, especially those outdoors in daylight, have average reflectance. For these scenes an incident-light meter and a reflected-light meter will work equally well and yield a high percentage of good exposures.

When lighting remains constant, as it does for most of the day in bright sunlight, you can use the same exposure for similarly lighted scenes with average reflectance. As a result, for average picture-taking conditions it is unnecessary to make a separate meter reading of each scene.

EXPOSURE BRACKETING

When you encounter scenes that are unusual or that are difficult to determine the correct exposure for and you're not sure of the proper camera settings, it's a good idea to bracket your exposures. Bracketing gives you more assurance of getting a picture with proper exposure. First determine the exposure as accurately as you can with your exposure meter or from an exposure guide, and then take a picture at this setting. Next take another picture at 1 stop less exposure and a third picture at 1 stop more exposure. If you want even more assurance of a properly exposed picture, take two *more* pictures—one at 2 stops under and one at 2 stops over the exposure recommended by your meter or the exposure guide.

Since color slide films have less exposure latitude than negative films, it's better to bracket the estimated exposure as described using $\frac{1}{2}$-stop increments to get the best exposure.

DON MAGGIO

Normal exposure—1/125 sec f/5.6, ISO 64, color slide film. Exposure bracketing gives you more confidence of getting a picture with proper exposure.

2 stops overexposed—1/125 sec f/2.8

1 stop overexposed—1/125 sec f/4

1 stop underexposed—1/125 sec f/8

2 stops underexposed—1/125 sec f/11

NEIL MONTANUS

Colors are often reproduced with more saturation when you use a polarizing screen. KODACHROME 64 Film (Daylight), 1/125 sec f/5.6

EXPOSURE WITH FILTERS

Since most filters absorb light, you must make an exposure compensation when you use them. With Kodak color films and the conversion filters recommended for various light sources, the compensation is included in the film speed given for each light source and filter combination. Use the speeds given on the instructions that come with the films or in the Film Data Sheets in this book. With Kodak black-and-white films, filter factors are given on some film instructions and the Data Sheets. Divide the ISO film speed by the filter factor to make the exposure compensation. Then set the corrected speed value on the film-speed dial of your camera or exposure meter.

Another way you can apply the filter factor for black-and-white film is to set your exposure meter for the speed of the film without a filter and then modify the camera settings indicated by the meter. For example, if the filter factor is 2 and the camera setting indicated by the meter reading made without a filter is 1/125 second at f/11, you can either double the exposure time to 1/60 second or open the lens 1 full stop to f/8. See the filter factor table below.

EQUIVALENT f-STOP CORRECTIONS FOR FILTER FACTORS

Filter Factor	f-Stops	Filter Factor	f-Stops	Filter Factor	f-Stops
1.2	+ $^1/_3$	3	+ 1$^2/_3$	8	+3
1.5	+ $^2/_3$	4	+2	10	+3$^1/_3$
2	+1	5	+2$^1/_3$	12	+3$^2/_3$
2.5	+ 1$^1/_3$	6	+2$^2/_3$	16	+4

The methods described so far are for determining exposure for filters for use with separate exposure meters or cameras that *do not* make the meter reading through a filter used over the lens. Many cameras with built-in exposure meters though, do measure the light through a filter placed over the camera lens. With most cameras of this type, you should set the built-in meter for the speed of the film *without a filter*. However, with some filters, built-in exposure meters that make the reading through the filter may require a correction in the film-speed setting to indicate the proper exposure. This is necessary since the meter and the film may not respond to colored light in the same way for exposure. Therefore, since camera instructions vary, check your instruction manual for details on how to set your camera.

If your camera manual doesn't adequately cover this situation, you can write for such information to the manufacturer or the American distributor for your camera. Or you can determine your own correction factor for filters by using the following procedure.

Select an average scene that's typical of the type of scenes and lighting you'll photograph using a particular filter. The lighting should remain constant and the subjects should not change position while you're making comparative exposure meter readings for this test.

Put your camera on a tripod. For *color film*, set the film-speed dial on your camera

HERB JONES

A polarizing screen with a filter factor of 2.5 was used to produce the dramatic sky in the picture on the top. To determine the correct exposure, divide the film speed by 2.5 or increase exposure by 1 1/3 stops. These exposure corrections are for use with meter readings made without the polarizing screen. Because of differences in camera exposure meter systems and the rotation position of the polarizing screen relative to the light from the scene, you should not rely on meter readings made through a polarizing screen.

With No. 21 orange filter

No filter   CAROLINE GRIMES

You can often use filters for creative picture-taking. Here the photographer put a No. 21 orange filter over the camera lens for the top picture taken at sunset in order to create a more colorful photo. Usually with this filter technique, making the meter reading through the filter gives good exposure. KODACHROME 64 Film (Daylight)

for the speed of the film *with the filter.* For *black-and-white film,* divide the speed of the film by the filter factor for the filter you're using and set the resulting number on the film-speed dial of your camera. Next make an exposure meter reading with your camera *without using the filter.* Note the shutter speed and *f*-number indicated by the meter reading. This tells you what the exposure should be *with* the filter.

Without moving the camera, put the filter over the lens and make an exposure meter reading of the same scene with the same lighting through the filter with your camera. Do not change the exposure settings; keep

the same shutter speed and *f*-number as before. Then adjust the film-speed dial on your camera to center the exposure meter needle or, depending on the exposure determination system in your camera, adjust the film-speed dial to obtain the same shutter speed and *f*-number combination. For example, with automatic cameras the exposure meter determines either the shutter speed or the lens opening or both.

Note the new ISO (ASA) setting on the film-speed dial. This shows you what the film speed should be for your camera when making meter readings through the filter.

DON MAGGIO

When you use high shutter speeds and medium or small lens openings with a camera that has a *leaf shutter*, you should use a smaller lens opening than normal. This exposure correction is more important for taking pictures on high-speed color slide film than it is for high-speed negative films because the negative films have more exposure latitude.

Compare this new ISO (ASA) setting with the film speed recommended for the film *without a filter*. This is the correction to use for the film, filter, and lighting conditions you used to make the test. You can make the same correction for other films for use with this filter.

For example, if the film has a speed of ISO 64 *without a filter* and you find from your meter-reading test that it should be ISO 50 when you make the meter reading through the filter with your camera exposure meter, then divide 50 by 64. The answer 0.8 is the multiplication-correction factor by which you should decrease (or increase for factors greater than 1) the speeds of other films for use with this filter when you make the meter reading through the filter.

Note that some black-and-white films have different basic filter factors for the same filter. For these exceptions, you'll need to make a separate exposure meter test to find the correction for each film that has a filter factor different from the film you used for your original test.

EXPOSURE FACTOR FOR SHUTTER EFFICIENCY

When you take pictures on high-speed film under certain conditions, there is an additional exposure factor you should consider. If you're using a camera with a leaf-type shutter under exposure conditions that require high shutter speeds and

medium or small lens openings, lens openings beginning about midway on the lens-opening scale of your camera, significant overexposure will result unless you make an exposure correction. This happens because shutter speeds are calibrated at the maximum lens opening of the camera, but shutter efficiency with a leaf-type shutter changes as the lens opening is decreased. At high shutter speeds and medium or small lens openings, the effective exposure times are longer than the shutter-speed settings indicated on your camera. At slow shutter speeds the difference between the effective exposure time and the indicated shutter-speed setting is relatively insignificant, and you can ignore it.

The exposure error may be equal to a half stop at 1/250 second and a full stop at 1/500 second. Because of the short exposure latitude of color slide films, the exposure error is more critical for high-speed color slide films than for high-speed color and black-and-white negative films. To correct for the exposure error, you should reduce the lens opening ½ stop at 1/250 second and 1 full stop at 1/500 second when exposure-meter readings indicate medium or small lens openings. *No such correction is necessary when you use a camera with a focal-plane shutter.*

These exposure corrections are given in the daylight exposure table on the Data Sheets for KODAK EKTACHROME 200 and 400 Films (Daylight) and on the instruction sheet supplied with the KODAK Special Processing Envelope, ESP-1, for doubling the speed of KODAK EKTACHROME Films.

USING EXPOSURE METERS IN COPYING

It's important that you adjust the lights so that the illumination over the copy area is even. To determine exposure for copying, you can either use an incident-light meter held in the plane of the original you are copying, pointed toward the camera, or use a reflected-light meter and take the reading from a gray card with 18-percent reflectance that you have substituted for the original. You can use the gray side of the KODAK Gray Card for this purpose. If you don't have the proper gray card, you can make a reflected-light reading from a matte white surface of 90-percent reflectance, such as the back of a sheet of double-weight white photographic paper as described on page 114. Remember to compensate for the high reflectance of the white surface by setting the meter calculator or film-speed dial at $^1/_5$ the normal film-speed number.

The film speeds for copying linework are intended for trial exposures. The exposure for linework is affected by the reflectance of the lines or dark areas of the original and the inherently short exposure latitude of high-contrast films. To obtain the best contrast between the background and the lines, you should use the maximum exposure that you can without causing filling-in or grayness of lines on the negative.

CORRECTION FOR LENS EXTENSION

In computing the exposure for copying or other close-up work for which you extend the camera lens by using extension tubes or bellows, make sure you allow for the effective increase in the indicated f-number unless your camera does this automatically. Otherwise, your pictures will be underexposed. For example, if you ignore this factor when determining exposure for taking a close-up picture of an object that will be the same size in your picture or a ratio of 1:1, your film will be underexposed by 2 f-stops. You should make an exposure compensation whenever the subject distance is less than 8 times the focal length of your lens. Close-up lenses require no exposure compensation unless you use a lens-extension device. The KODAK Pocket Photoguide (AR-21) provides a convenient calculator dial for determining the effective f-number quickly and easily.

You can also calculate the effective f-number by using the formula below. The lens-to-film distance is approximately equal to the focal length of your camera lens plus the distance the lens is extended beyond its position at infinity focus.

If your camera has a through-the-lens exposure meter that works with a bellows extension or extension tubes on the camera, the camera makes the exposure compensation automatically so you don't have to make the correction yourself. When you're using flash, you usually have to make the exposure compensation manually for lens extension. Some cameras, though, with through-the-lens metering for electronic flash also do this automatically. Check your camera, flash, and close-up equipment instruction manuals.

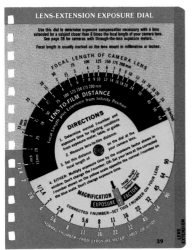

The KODAK Pocket Photoguide (AR-21) includes a handy Lens-Extension Exposure Dial for determining the effective f-number quickly and easily when you're using a lens-extension device.

$$\text{Effective } f\text{-number} = \frac{\text{Indicated } f\text{-number} \times \text{Lens-to-film distance}}{\text{Focal length}}$$

MODIFYING FILM-SPEED NUMBERS

Film speeds published by film manufacturers are an excellent basis for obtaining optimum exposure. To produce the quality you want in your pictures with your own equipment and procedures, though, it's sometimes necessary to modify recommended film-speed numbers. However, before you depart from the film speed recommended for a particular film, be sure that you are making careful exposure-meter readings using the technique recommended in your camera or meter instruction book. Then if your pictures are consistently unsatisfactory and indicate that you should change the film-speed setting on your meter, change it as follows: With normal development, if your films are consistently underexposed, increase exposure by using a lower film-speed number; if your films are consistently overexposed, reduce exposure by using a higher film-speed number. Divide the published film speed by 2 to produce 1 stop more exposure. Multiply by 2 to produce 1 stop less exposure.

FLASH EXPOSURE

The most important factor affecting flash exposure for a specific film and flash unit is the distance from the flash to your subject. Subjects close to the flash receive a lot of light, while subjects farther away receive less light. Many electronic flash units automatically adjust the light from the flash for proper exposure, and some cameras automatically adjust the lens opening for the proper flash exposure as you focus the lens. Other cameras have through-the-lens exposure meters that automatically adjust the light from electronic flash for proper exposure. With nonadjustable cameras, flash-to-subject distances of about 5 to 15 feet (1.5 to 4.5 metres) usually produce acceptable exposures. See your camera manual. With most adjustable cameras, however, flash guide numbers provide a convenient means for determining flash exposure manually.

The guide number you should use depends on the film you're using and on the output of your electronic flash unit. If you're using flashbulbs, the guide number

CHARLES A. CARNAGHI, K

Most electronic flash units determine the correct exposure automatically.

PETER G/

Flash-guide numbers provide a reliable method for determining exposure with nonautomatic electronic flash units, automatic electronic flash units set on manual, and flashbulbs.

124

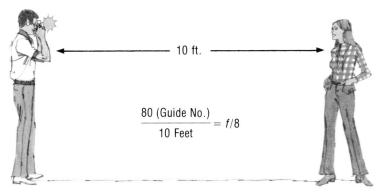

$$\frac{80\ (\text{Guide No.})}{10\ \text{Feet}} = f/8$$

The most important factor affecting flash exposure for a film and flash unit is the distance from the flash to your subject. To determine the f-number for average subjects, divide the proper guide number by the flash-to-subject distance in feet.

depends on the film, the type of flashbulb and reflector, the shutter speed, and the synchronization of your shutter. A flash exposure table in the Data Sheet for each film gives the recommended guide numbers for different light output values for electronic flash units. Guide numbers for flashbulbs are provided on flashbulb cartons.

Divide the proper guide number by the flash-to-subject distance in feet to find the f-number for average subjects. For example, if your guide number is 80 and the subject is 10 feet away from the flash, divide 80 by 10. The answer 8 means that you should

set your lens opening at f/8. If the answer is between two f-numbers marked on your camera lens, set the lens opening at the nearest f-number or halfway between the two, whichever is closer to the answer.

When using guide numbers, always use the distance units for which the guide numbers are calculated—feet or metres. You use guide numbers for metres in the same way as those for feet. Just divide the guide number for metres by the flash-to-subject distance in metres to obtain the f-number. In this book the guide numbers that are provided are for feet.

PETER GALES

Most flash units have convenient-to-use calculator dials to tell you the f-number setting for the speed of the film you're using and the flash-to-subject distance.

KEITH BOAS

This shot was taken with one electronic flash unit bounced from a reflecting umbrella which gives a soft, natural lighting effect. Since some light is lost when you bounce the flash off an umbrella, you must use about 1 stop more exposure than the exposure required for direct flash. TRI-X Pan Film, 1/60 sec f/11

Guide numbers are just *guides;* they are for average subjects in average-size rooms. They don't take into account subjects that are lighter or darker than average or small rooms with light-colored walls that reflect a lot of light. If you're photographing a light subject, use a lens opening ½ stop smaller than the guide number indicates; for a dark subject, use a lens opening ½ stop larger. In small rooms with light-colored walls, use 1 stop less exposure than the guide number indicates. For automatic electronic flash units, set the flash on manual if possible, and make the correction for small light-colored rooms manually.

If necessary, you can change the guide numbers to improve your results. If your pictures are consistently underexposed—if your negatives are too light or your slides are too dark—use a lower guide number. If your pictures are consistently overexposed—if your negatives are too

dark or your slides are too light—use a higher guide number.

When you're photographing subjects with a predominantly light or dark background using an automatic electronic flash unit, the light-sensitive photocell in the flash can be mislead by the background resulting in incorrect exposure for the subject. In these situations, operate the flash on manual and set the exposure manually.

The KODAK *Pocket Photoguide* (AR-21), described earlier, takes the arithmetic out of calculating flash exposure. It includes a convenient Flash Exposure Dial which indicates the correct *f*-number opposite each subject distance. The flash dial in the *Pocket Photoguide* provides a quick and easy method for determining the *f*-number setting for both electronic flash and flashbulbs.

Flash pictures of distant subjects, such as sports or other spectator events at distances of about 50 feet (15 metres) or farther away, are not very satisfactory. The foreground is usually shown as a large overexposed area which is distracting and spoils the picture. In addition, for subjects at great distances, the flash just won't carry that far. You can photograph these distant subjects much more effectively by the existing light.

You should *not* use flash to photograph the image on your television screen or projected images such as slides or movies. The bright light from the flash would overwhelm the image you want to photograph, and all you would get is a blank area on the film. Here again, photograph these subjects by the existing light. For techniques on photographing television and computer screen images, you may want to obtain the book on existing-light photography mentioned on page 60.

GARY WHELPLEY

Storage and Care of KODAK Films

TRI-X Pan Film

Photographic films are perishable products and are damaged by high temperatures, high relative humidities, and harmful gases. Some photographic characteristics—speed, color balance, and contrast of color films and speed, contrast, and fog level of black-and-white films—change gradually after manufacture. Adverse storage conditions accelerate these changes. Color films are more seriously affected than black-and-white films because adverse conditions usually affect the three or more emulsion layers of a color film to different degrees.

Moisture may also cause various physical defects such as mottle and abrasions.

For best results, handle and store unprocessed films properly both before and after exposure, with adequate protection against heat, moisture, and harmful gases. Unprocessed films must be protected from x-rays and radioactive substances. When the climate is moderate, storage precautions are few and simple. Greater care is necessary under hot and humid conditions. Processed films also require proper storage and care for long-term keeping.

128

PANATOMIC-X Film

JERRY McCUNE, KINSA

STORAGE IN THE ORIGINAL PACKAGE

Kodak supplies 135, 110, 126, disc, roll, and 144 instant color films in water-vapor-tight packaging. The 135 films are packaged in snap-cover plastic cans; the other films in heat-sealed foil pouches. The vapor-tight packaging provides necessary protection from humidity in areas such as tropical regions or any other locality where high relative humidities (RH) prevail. You may encounter such conditions in a number of areas, especially during the warm summer months.

Protection from Humidity. Kodak films supplied in vapor-tight packaging require no additional protection against high humidities until you open the package. *So don't open the vapor-tight packaging until you are ready to use the film.* Otherwise the protection originally provided is no longer effective.

You can determine the relative humidity with a humidity indicator such as the type sold for home use.

Protection from Heat. *Vapor-tight packaging is not heatproof.* Regardless of the type of packaging, don't leave your films near heat registers, steam pipes, or other sources of heat. In warm weather, do not leave film in areas on the top floors of uninsulated buildings or in hot places in a car, especially when it's parked in the sun on a warm or hot day.

As we mentioned earlier, Kodak color negative films and Kodak color slide films are both available in films designed for general use and in films designed for professional use. The requirements for storing and handling color films for critical photography by professional photographers are more rigid than those for films for general use.

When Kodak color films for general use are made, the changes in speed, color

KODACOLOR Film

balance, and contrast that will occur from natural aging are anticipated. The film is manufactured to have optimum quality when it is most likely to be used by the photographer. Kodak color films for general use are designed for storage at normal room temperature before use. The film should be protected from heat.

Kodak professional color films are designed for optimum performance to make the best pictures close to the time of manufacture. To retain the original characteristics for critical photography for professional purposes where small color deviations would be important, professional color films should be stored under refrigeration, 55°F (13°C) or lower, before exposure. Cold storage is recommended for these films because it helps maintain their excellent color balance and contrast until the film is needed for photography. No allowance is made for changes that may occur under nonprofessional or general use without following the refrigerated storage recommendations for the film.

Refrigerated storage for professional color films, though, is not as critical as you may believe. Storage of these films at normal room temperatures for short periods of time will not cause any noticeable change in the film. For example, two weeks at room temperature would not cause any significant shift in color balance or contrast. Professional color film does not have to be rushed from cold storage to camera, and then on to processing within a few hours. It is enough to exercise reasonable care and judgment. Typically, a roll of professional color film will be exposed within a week of being removed from refrigerated storage and processed within the next week.

Most Kodak films for professional use and for general use are equally as stable for photographic quality when they are used under identical conditions.

For normal temperature conditions, 75°F (24°C) or below, Kodak color films for general use and most Kodak black-and-white films do not require refrigeration. Storage instructions for each kind of Kodak film are printed on the film carton and on the instruction sheet packaged with some of the films. The storage recommendations for Kodak films for general use provided on the

film carton are to protect the film from heat. Those for Kodak professional black-and-white films recommend storing the film in a cool, dry place. The storage instructions for Kodak professional color films specify storage at 55°F (13°C) or lower. KODAK INSTAGRAPHIC Color Print Film, for professional use, specifies storage at 45°F (7°C) before use. A few special-purpose films require storage temperatures of 0 to −10°F (−18 to −23°C). Storage recommendations for Kodak films that require refrigerated storage are also given on the Data Sheets in this book.

During summer heat, with temperatures over 75°F (24°C) for extended periods of time, we recommend refrigerated storage for keeping all Kodak films cool, provided they are in vapor-tight packages or in sealed cans or jars. To avoid condensation of moisture on cold film surfaces, remove unopened film packages from cold storage and allow 1½ hours for them to reach approximate room temperature before you open the package.

Keep KODAK TRIMPRINT™ Instant Color Film and KODAK Instant Color Film (and KODAK INSTAGRAPHIC Color Print Film) in the original vapor-tight packages when you store them in a refrigerator or freezer. Upon removal from the refrigerator, wait at least 24 hours before using the film pack to allow the film and processing chemistry to reach equilibrium with room temperature. If you store the film at temperatures lower than 35°F (2°C), allow at least 48 hours to reach room temperature. Prolonged storage at temperatures above 75°F (24°C) will result in color changes. (Refrigerated storage is required for INSTAGRAPHIC Color Print Film.)

When the ambient temperature has returned to normal, 75°F (24°C) or below, remove Kodak color films for general use from refrigerated storage so they can age normally as anticipated in manufacture.

If after testing some rolls of film, you want to maintain the film at that specific color balance for an extended period, you can store other rolls of the same emulsion in a refrigerator or freezer. The emulsion number is printed on the film carton.

You can store unexposed black-and-white films under normal temperature conditions, temperatures that don't exceed

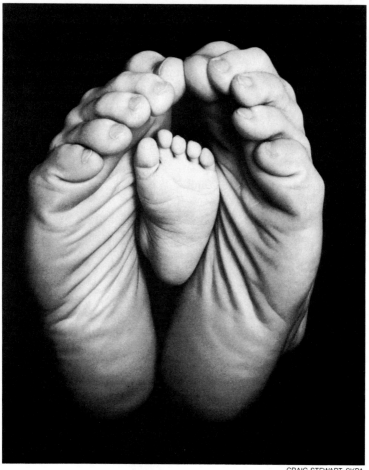

TRɪ-X Pan Film, electronic flash, 1/60 sec f/16

75°F (24°C). For storage over long periods of time, it's desirable, when possible, to maintain the following storage temperatures for black-and-white films:

For storage periods up to	2 months	6 months	12 months
Keep black-and-white films below	75°F 24°C	60°F 16°C	50°F 10°C

When you're traveling in a car, don't leave your film in a closed car parked in the sun on a warm or hot, sunny day. The temperature can quickly reach 140°F (60°C) or more. If this is unavoidable, keep your film in an insulated container, such as an ice chest like those used for camping or an insulated picnic bag.

Avoid keeping your film in the glove compartment, on the rear window shelf, over hot spots on the car floor, or in areas in direct sunlight inside the car.

The coolest area for protecting your film from heat in a car in the sun is in the passenger compartment with the air conditioner on or the windows open, especially when the car is moving. The best location is on the car floor in the shade away from hot areas over the exhaust system or transmission. With a light-color car parked in the sun on a warm or hot day with the engine off and windows closed, the car trunk is usually somewhat cooler and is a better storage area for the insulated container than the hot passenger compartment. With a dark-color car the

132

passenger compartment, though hot, is usually slightly cooler than the trunk. However, if there is a build-up of heat from the engine and exhaust system in a parked car after traveling at highway speeds, it may be better to put your insulated film container in the trunk which, although hot, may be slightly cooler than the passenger compartment. It's good practice to limit subjecting your film to heat in a car during warm or hot weather to as short a time as possible.

If ice or cold packs are available, you can use them to help keep your film cool. If you use ice, keep the film packages dry. Also, see "Protection of Films After You Open the Package," page 136.

Expiration Date. *Use the film promptly.* You should expose and process each roll of Kodak film before the expiration date printed on the package. Films kept beyond this date may be unsatisfactory due to changes in speed, contrast, fog, stain, color balance, and color reproduction. The last three effects, of course, apply only to color films. The magnitude of changes in a film is largely dependent on the conditions of storage. Proper storage conditions decrease the rate of changes inherent in films but won't eliminate changes entirely.

Extension of film life through refrigeration is not recommended. While such techniques may be somewhat successful with Kodak black-and-white films, the risks of detrimental effects will be higher with color films. These precautions are especially important for high-speed color films, such as KODACOLOR VR 1000 Film. You should not attempt to extend the life of these films beyond their normal expiration dates by storing the films in the refrigerator or freezer. High speed film used after its expiration date may show excessive graininess due to the effects of cosmic and gamma radiation that's naturally present in the environment all around us. Neither refrigeration nor freezing will retard this effect. Similarly, storage in lead containers, such as lead-foil bags will do little to retard ambient radiation effects. You can avoid the objectionable results of terrestrial radiation by simply exposing and processing the film before the expiration date.

EKTACHROME 200 Film (Daylight)   GARY WHELPLEY

NEIL MONTANUS
KODACHROME 25 Film (Daylight), 1/250 sec f/5.6

Protection from X-rays. X-ray equipment can fog your unprocessed film when the radiation level is high or the film receives several low-level doses. The effect of exposure to x-rays is cumulative. Film which has been processed, however, is not affected.

For the protection of travelers, many airports, airlines, and law-enforcement agencies around the world are using electronic devices to check passengers and x-ray equipment to check their luggage for

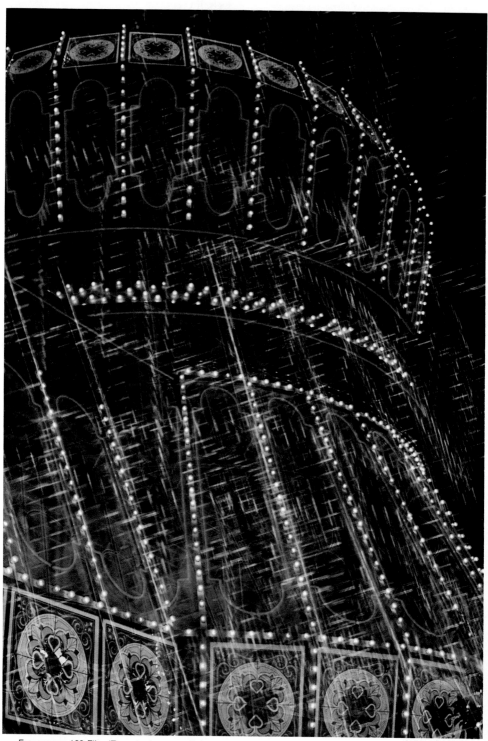

EKTACHROME 160 Film (Tungsten), exposed through diffraction grating, 1/30 sec f/4

concealed bombs and weapons. If you travel by commercial airline, your luggage may be subjected to x-ray examination each time you prepare to board the aircraft. All carry-on luggage is x-rayed unless you can obtain a visual inspection instead. Checked luggage may also be x-rayed.

While some x-ray exposure can usually be tolerated, excessive amounts may result in objectionable fog and extraneous shadow images on film contained in the luggage. X-rays are particularly damaging to KODACOLOR VR 1000 Film which is a very high-speed film and is highly sensitive to x-rays. It is usually possible for passengers to avoid this danger to their unprocessed film by hand-carrying their supply, including loaded cameras, and requesting a *visual* rather than an x-ray inspection of it. Carrying your film in a clear plastic bag will speed up and simplify this visual inspection. The walk-through and handheld electronic devices used at many airports to check passengers separately from their luggage, are not x-ray equipment and have no effect on film.

In the United States, at the airport boarding gates for domestic airline flights, federal regulations require that x-ray inspection be conducted only with low-output devices. These subject luggage to less than 1 milliroentgen of x-ray exposure per inspection which should not perceptibly fog most camera-type films. But if you are carrying KODACOLOR VR 1000 Film, you should request a visual inspection. This film should not be subjected to x-ray inspection. However, since the effects of x-rays on film are cumulative, it is possible for films to be significantly fogged by repeated exposures of less than 1 milliroentgen each but totaling 5 milliroentgens or higher. So for travel within the United States, requests for visual inspections should be unnecessary— unless more than five inspections are encountered with the same film or when you are carrying very high-speed film.

Visual inspection of film is particularly important when traveling abroad, including traveling by airline from international air terminals in the United States. A wide variety of luggage-inspection systems may be encountered both for checked and carry-on luggage. Some of these systems are known to operate at relatively high x-ray

levels. If you are unable to obtain a visual inspection, you should ask pertinent questions of airline authorities to determine in doubtful situations whether your film can be damaged.

In general, it is a good idea to avoid repeated exposure of your film to x-rays. If you plan to use KODAK Processing Mailers, you can send your exposed film to a Kodak Processing Lab instead of carrying it with you and risking exposure to x-rays.

If you're in doubt about the safety of the equipment in use, or if your luggage will be examined more than five times, or when you're traveling to a country outside the United States, you can minimize the possibility of damage to your film in the following ways.

• Carry your film in a clear plastic bag in hand luggage, arrive early, and ask airport authorities for a visual inspection at each checkpoint, stressing the fact that the sensitive photo material you're carrying might be ruined by x-rays. Not all inspectors will cooperate; however, those who do will help reduce the possibility of film damage.

• Each time you pack your bag, arrange the contents so that the film is not always oriented in the same way. You can achieve a similar effect by orienting your bag differently each time it passes through x-ray inspection.

• Carry KODAK Processing Mailers or other photofinishing mailers on your trip, and mail each roll of film in for processing as soon as it has been exposed. As an added bonus, your processed film may already be waiting for you when you return home.

• If your trip will simply be from one city to another in the United States and back again, there's probably little need for concern unless you're carrying very high-speed film. But the 12 countries-in-10-days, whirlwind-tour sort of trip may present a problem to your film.

Sometimes mailed packages are also x-rayed or fluoroscoped, so if you include unprocessed film in a package, label the package "Undeveloped Photographic Film. Please Do Not X-Ray." Film mailed in processing mailers provided by processors—and clearly marked as film— usually is not subject to x-ray or fluoroscope inspection.

BAHIA

NEIL MONTANUS

EKTACHROME 200 Film (Daylight)

PROTECTION OF FILMS AFTER YOU OPEN THE PACKAGE

When the vapor-tight film package is opened, the film is no longer protected from the damaging effects of high humidity and harmful gases. *So expose and process your films promptly after you open the package.* When films for general use are manufactured, an average delay after exposure before the film can be processed is planned for. You get the best results, however, when you have your exposed film processed promptly. Process professional films soon after exposure. If you can't have professional film processed promptly, you should keep it refrigerated until you can have it processed.

High relative humidity and high temperature often cause undesirable changes in the latent image—the undeveloped image on exposed film. Therefore, under these conditions, it's particularly important that you have your exposed films processed as soon as

possible. Do not deposit film in an outdoor metal mailbox where high temperature from the sun may occur, especially when pickup is delayed.

Under adverse conditions of heat or humidity, don't keep films in your camera any longer than necessary. Protect your films by keeping them in a carrying case, and shield the case from direct sunlight; otherwise, the temperature inside the case may become extremely high even in a temperate region. Similarly, don't leave your films in a closed car parked in the sun on a warm or hot, sunny day. Follow the same recommendations for films kept in cars given on page 132 under "Protection from Heat," except that you *should not refrigerate the container* the film is kept in because there is no humidity protection for the film after you open the vapor-tight packaging.

Putting 135 films back into their plastic film cans will protect them from being subjected to additional humidity or harmful gases.

Don't store opened packages of film in damp basements, iceboxes, refrigerators, or other places where the relative humidity is high. A moderate temperature and moderate relative humidity, such as 60°F (16°C) and 40 percent RH, are better than a low temperature with high relative humidity, such as 40°F (4°C) and 80 percent RH. The ideal relative humidity for storage of such film packages is between 40 and 50 percent, preferably near 40 percent.

When you can't avoid humid storage locations, or when you must store your films in a refrigerator to keep them cool, place opened packages of film in a can or jar which you can seal tightly to provide moisture protection. For 135-size films, you can put them back in the plastic film cans they came in. Instead of these containers you can put the film in KODAK Storage Envelopes for Processed Film described on page 141 even though the film has not been processed. Or you can use three wraps of aluminum foil each tightly sealed with tape to protect the film from moisture. See page 142.

If the prevailing relative humidity is above 60 percent, dry your films with a suitable desiccating agent, such as activated silica gel, before storing them in cans, jars, KODAK

NICHOLAS C. SCOTT, KINSA

EASTMAN KODAK COMPANY

This is one type of static markings on film caused by static discharges. Friction generated while winding the film too rapidly in the camera is the main cause of static charges. As a rule, static is most troublesome when the relative humidity is low.

Storage Envelopes or aluminum foil in humid or cold locations. You can buy silica gel from chemical-supply firms. Packages of silica gel convenient for photography are produced by such companies as W. R. Grace & Co., Davison Chemical Division, P.O. Box 2117, Baltimore, Maryland 21203. You can contact them for the name of a local distributor.

Keep opened packages of film away from chemical fumes, such as industrial gases, motor exhausts, mothballs and similar moth repellents, formaldehydes, paints, solvents, cleaners, mildew or fungus preventives, chipboard, glues, foam-in-place insulation, insecticides, sulfides, and fabric treatments, for example, permanent press and stain inhibitors. Do not store films or cameras in drawers of furniture made from chipboard

or that may be contaminated with photographically harmful fumes from mothballs, mildew inhibitors, wood preservers, paints, varnishes, and wood glues. Since clothes closets often contain moth repellent chemicals or mildew and fungus preventives, check carefully to be sure you don't store films and cameras in compartments containing these chemicals.

Static. Advancing and rewinding roll film too rapidly or other careless handling can produce discharges of static electricity which cause marks to show up on the processed film. Static discharges occur most often when the relative humidity is low, such as indoors during winter months. Marks produced by static can appear as lightning streaks, small dots, or fogging. High-speed films are more susceptible to the effects of static than are medium- or low-speed films. When the humidity is low, you can minimize static discharges by slowly advancing the film for each picture, slowly rewinding 135 film in your camera after the last exposure, and handling the film carefully. After film has been processed, static discharges won't make marks on the film.

STORAGE AND CARE OF PROCESSED FILMS AND PRINTS

Some photographs are used for only brief periods to satisfy immediate needs while other photographs are used or stored for extended periods of time. How long a picture will be kept depends on many personal factors so that only the person who owns the picture can determine when a picture is no longer of any value. This section gives some suggestions for storage and care of negatives, slides, and photographic prints.

Storage conditions for processed black-and-white films and prints are less demanding than those for color photographs. You can store black-and-white negatives (or black-and-white slides), which are on safety base, and black-and-white prints at normal temperatures—about 70°F (21°C) or cooler. All Kodak films are now made with a safety base and have been for many years. Store black-and-white negatives and prints where it's dry, between

137

30- and 50-percent relative humidity. Avoid a relative humidity below 30 percent because excessive brittleness may result. High relative humidities above 60 percent are also harmful because of the possibility of mold or fungus growth. It's best to have temperature and humidity remain at constant values rather than varying up and down daily. If the temperature is moderately higher temporarily, this should cause no harm providing the relative humidity remains less than 40 percent. Temperatures exceeding 75°F (24°C) together with relative humidity exceeding 60 percent are the most damaging, causing accelerated growth of mold or fungus, deterioration of the image, fading of color images, and sticking together or glazing of film surfaces.

Since the silver image may be attacked by oxidizing gases in polluted atmosphere, protect your negatives and prints from fumes of certain sulfur compounds, such as hydrogen sulfide and coal gas and from fumes of oxides of nitrogen, peroxides, formaldehyde, ozone, and other harmful gases. Fumes from areas freshly painted with oil-base paints can cause serious discoloration of black-and-white images. Do not return black-and-white prints and negatives to a freshly painted area (oil-based paint) for at least 4 weeks after painting. No adverse effects have been found with latex paints.

For long-term keeping of processed black-and-white and color films and photographic papers, follow the most current processing recommendations very closely. Incorrect processing procedures, such as faulty agitation, excessive times in certain solutions, insufficient fixing, and inadequate or excessive washing, can result in defects after long-term storage that were not apparent shortly after processing. For example, insufficient time in some solutions or inadequate rinsing and washing can leave unwanted chemical residues in the film or paper which later cause harmful effects to the pictures.

In addition, KODAK Hypo Eliminator HE-1 *should never* be used on films that you want to store under long-term storage conditions. You should not use KODAK Hypo Eliminator for treating prints in place of an adequate wash cycle, but only to

CAROLINE GRIMES

EKTACHROME 200 Film (Daylight), 210 mm telephoto lens, 1/800 sec f/8

remove the last traces of fixer from photographic papers, if its presence would create a problem for a toning process. When you use HE-1 Hypo Eliminator for prints, you should protect the image from external attack by conversion of the image to a less reactive form. You can do this by treating the prints, for example, with one of the recommended Kodak toners at the concentration stated for optimum use and storage in an inert environment. The Kodak book, *Conservation of Photographs*, (F-40), referred to on page 142, provides comprehensive information on processing and storage for preservation of photographic materials.

Generally you can provide additional protection to black-and-white prints and extend their life by toning the image. Prints that have been toned by one of the processes that convert metallic silver to silver sulfide or silver selenide are generally more stable than untoned prints. For information on toning prints, see your photo dealer for purchasing a copy of the Kodak booklet, *The ABCs of Toning*, (G-23).

Commercial laboratories are aware of the important part that processing plays in the image stability of negatives, slides, and prints. If you do your own processing, carefully follow the manufacturer's instructions.

When black-and-white negatives and prints are processed properly and are stored under optimum conditions, they will last a very long time. For additional protection, you can put your negatives (on safety base) and prints in KODAK Storage Envelopes for Processed Film. Although these envelopes are recommended for cold storage of processed Kodak color films, you can use them for long-term storage of black-and-white photographs as well. Do not intermix black-and-white materials with color, however, in the same envelope. The storage envelopes and recommendations for their use are described on page 141.

The long-term storage and care requirements for color negatives, color slides, and color prints are somewhat different than those for black-and-white materials. The images in color photographs are formed by dyes while the images in most black-and-white photographs are formed by metallic silver. In time, all dyes may change. The dyes used in Kodak color films and color photographic papers provide the best possible stability while meeting other essential requirements.

The primary factors affecting the stability of color photographs are heat, humidity, light, and cleanliness of the storage conditions. Store processed color films and color prints (see page 141) where it's dark, dry, cool, and free of contamination. You can store processed color films and color prints for extended periods of time in normal room conditions, such as in many areas on the main floors of buildings but never damp basements or in hot attics. For color slides, color negatives, and color prints a relative humidity between 30 and 50 percent and a temperature about 70°F (21°C) or below are satisfactory. Cooler temperatures are even better for storing color photographs. Again it's best to have temperature and humidity remain constant than change up and down daily. Avoid a relative humidity below 30 percent because excessive brittleness may result. High relative humidities above 60 percent are also harmful because of the increased possibility of fungus growth or color changes. Keep the storage container that contains your photographs away from sources of heat, like radiators, warm-air registers, walls that may contain hot-air ducts or chimneys, and windows where sunlight can strike the container.

Dye images can deteriorate particularly when they are exposed to bright light or to normal light levels for a long period of time. Therefore, dark storage is best for color photographic materials. Dark storage for color negatives and color slides is an easy condition to achieve since these images are exposed to light for only brief periods when they are used, and are then returned to storage. You can store color negatives and color slides in the dark by using metal containers, such as file boxes or drawers. Metal is preferred over wood or plastic because the last two kinds of materials may contain preservatives or volatile substances harmful to stored negatives or slides.

You can print color negatives many times without causing perceptible fading due to light. Use a heat-absorbing glass in the enlarger between the lamp and the negative unless your enlarger already includes a heat-rejection device. Return the negatives to dark storage after use. Properly processed and stored, you can expect Kodak color negative films to give acceptable results for extended periods of time.

Color slide films are intended for projection. The use and storage of color slides is similar to that for color negatives— slides are usually projected on a screen with a bright light for several seconds and then returned to storage.

Kodak color slide films are remarkably stable. As previously discussed in other sections of this book, there are many photographic factors in choosing a color slide film to use. But if longevity is the deciding factor, and if you store your slides in the dark, perhaps the best choice is KODACHROME Film. A second choice, certainly, for extended dark storage is KODAK EKTACHROME Film. EKTACHROME Films withstand the effects of light better than KODACHROME Films.

KODAK EKTACHROME Film

If you project your slides frequently or project them for long periods of time, it's wise to have duplicate slides made on KODAK EKTACHROME Slide Duplicating Film 5071. Then you can project the duplicates and preserve your original slides.

Color prints are viewed in many ways—in albums, on walls, in wallets and on desks. In most cases you can have replacement prints made from the negatives or slides if the original prints fade or are damaged. If you don't have the negative or slide or if it's an instant print, care of the print becomes very important.

Storage recommendations for color prints are the same as for color negatives and color slides. Some prints, though, are exposed to light for a much longer period of time. Whenever possible display these prints in subdued light, such as household lighting, as far from the light source as possible, and away from direct sunlight and long exposure to fluorescent lamps. Avoid temperatures above 70°F (21°C), humidities above 50 percent RH, and damaging chemicals and fumes. If you can't

avoid less-than-ideal conditions, keep in mind that prints will change faster as a result. A color photographic print that is on continuous display, even under the best conditions, is likely to change in time because light, heat, humidity, and contaminants in the air are affecting the print for long periods. If you're going to display a traditional print, store the negative or slide it was made from properly so that you can have new prints made if the original prints begins to fade.

A convenient way to store your prints for easy viewing and good long-term storage is to put them in photo albums. Make sure that all materials used to make the photo album are recommended for archival, or long-term, storage. See the reference for standards that specify storage materials on page 142. Of course, it's important to keep the album in rooms free of contaminants, out of direct sunlight, and where the temperature and humidity are within the recommendations specified earlier.

If your color prints were made with KODAK TRIMPRINT Instant Color Film or KODAK Instant Color Film with the TRIMPRINT Feature and have been separated from their backing materials, you can display these TRIMPRINT Pictures right along with traditional prints in photo albums. The album pages should not be colored, and no adhesives should be used to mount the prints. If you want to put unseparated KODAK Instant Prints in a photo album when each picture unit has been left intact, use albums recommended for unseparated instant pictures. Instant print albums, such as KODAK GALLERY Instant Photo Albums, let air circulate to the pictures to help them dry internally.

Freshly processed color prints made with KODAK TRIMPRINT Instant Color Film and KODAK Instant Color Film contain moisture from the processing chemicals. If you leave your instant prints intact—unseparated, keep them at moderate temperatures for the first 2 or 3 weeks in a manner which will provide sufficient air circulation to allow the moisture to leave the prints.

Unseparated KODAK Instant Prints stored in unbound stacks on top of a table or in a drawer or file cabinet should normally receive adequate air circulation. Do not bind stacks of unseparated processed prints

KODAK EKTACHROME Film

together with rubber bands or place them in a closed container like a box or a plastic bag that will not provide sufficient air circulation to allow the prints to dry. After this initial time period, you can store your instant prints in the same manner as traditional photographic prints.

If you have separated your TRIMPRINT Pictures from their backing materials, you can store them in the same manner as traditional prints after the back is dry, which is usually within a few minutes after you have separated them.

To minimize changes in the color dyes of your instant prints, keep them in a cool, dry place, and protect them from long exposure to bright light, high temperatures, and high humidity. For extended storage periods, follow the same temperature, humidity, and other storage conditions recommended for traditional color photographic prints.

Best Conditions for Extended Storage of Color Photographs

Storage of color photographs under normal room conditions is a practical recommendation relatively easy to achieve. You can keep color pictures under these conditions for extended periods of time; but to keep changes in color photographs due to fading at a minimum, store them in the dark under refrigeration at a temperature of 0°F (− 18°C) and a relative humidity of between 30 and 35 percent.

Since refrigerators and freezers usually have high relative humidity, you should put your color negatives, color slides, or color prints into KODAK Storage Envelopes for Processed Film before refrigerating them. These envelopes, sold by photo dealers, provide moistureproof packaging for your photographs. The envelopes are available in 4 × 5-inch and 8 × 10-inch sizes. Before putting your negatives, slides, or prints into the envelopes, condition the photographs for an hour, or, if the prints are on resin-coated paper,* for 2 days, in a room or cabinet at 70°F (21°C) or lower and 25- to 30-percent RH. The room or cabinet should be free of dust and fumes. Then insert the negatives, slides, or prints into the envelopes under these temperature and humidity conditions. Segregate the different classes of films or prints and put them in individual storage envelopes, such as color negatives in one envelope, color

*You can determine if your prints were made on resin-coated paper by the smooth, plastic-like surface on the back of the prints.

slides in another envelope, and instant color prints in a third envelope. Before storing color prints from KODAK TRIMPRINT Instant Color Film and KODAK Instant Color Film in KODAK Storage Envelopes, allow 6 weeks for unseparated prints to dry completely internally after processing. It's better to separate TRIMPRINT Pictures from their backing materials within one week from the time the pictures were taken, for extended cold storage in KODAK Storage Envelopes. Then condition the separated prints at 70°F (21°C) or lower and 25 to 30 percent RH before placing in storage envelopes.

Seal the envelopes according to the instructions that come with the envelopes. If your color prints are larger than 8 × 10 inches, you can protect them from moisture by using three wraps of aluminum foil and sealing the folds and seams with moisture-proof tape.

If you store several negatives, slides, or prints in the same envelope, separate them with sheets of paper. Be sure that the paper is of archival quality free of harmful chemicals. See the standards reference for storage materials below.

With refrigerated storage there is the possibility of a power failure, so you may want to have an alarm signal installed by an electrician for your refrigerator or freezer in order to alert you if a power outage occurs. The humidity rises rapidly to high levels in refrigerators or freezers when the power fails. This could damage photographs stored under refrigeration if they are not protected from high humidity.

Power failures with a refrigerator should not cause a humidity problem when color photographs are sealed in KODAK Storage Envelopes. The humidity inside the envelopes is established at the time of sealing and remains stable as long as the seal is not broken. A power failure with a freezer is more serious because of the possibility of puddles of water forming from melting ice and frost on the freezer compartment walls. In this situation remove the storage envelopes from the freezer until power is restored. When the storage envelopes are in the freezer for cold storage, it's a good idea to place them in an elevated position to avoid any moisture that could form on the bottom of the freezer.

Such elaborate care that has been discussed in this section is needed only for color photographs that you want to store for a very long time.

An alternative for long-term storage of color photographs is to have three color-separation negatives of the color image made on black-and-white film. Since these separation negatives have silver images, you can expect the negatives to last as long as other properly processed black-and-white negatives stored under the best conditions. You can have color images made from the separation negatives any time in the future. Custom processing laboratories do this type of work. The process, though, is expensive and requires skilled photographic procedures.

For a more thorough discussion of long-term keeping of photographs, see your photo dealer for the Kodak publications, *Storage and Care of KODAK Films and Papers—(Before and After Processing)*, (E-30), and *Conservation of Photographs*, (F-40). Or you can obtain single copies of E-30 from the address given on page 65.

Protection from Physical Damage.
Keep slides and negatives as clean and dustfree as possible. A good rule is never to touch the film with your fingers, except by the edges. The best way to protect negatives is to store them in envelopes with side seams. The paper or plastic and adhesive should meet the requirements of *American National Standard for Photography (Processing)—Processed Films, Plates, and Papers—Filing Enclosures and Containers for Storage*, PH1.53—1984. Other ANSI publications that you might find helpful are *American National Standard for Photography (Film)—Storage of Processed Safety Film*, PH1.43—1983 and *American National Standard for Photography (Films and Slides)—Black and White Photographic Paper Prints—Practice for Storage*, PH1.48—1982. You can purchase American National Standards from the American National Standards Institute, Inc., 1430 Broadway, New York, New York 10018. Stores that sell photo products usually offer a variety of containers for storing slides.

Don't store color negatives or slides near moth-preventive chemicals, which tend to crystalize on the films and damage the

adhesive used in slide mounts. Exposure to nitrogen oxides, hydrogen sulfide, or sulfur dioxide gas may cause slow fading of color dyes. The solvents and chemicals used in insecticides and fungicide sprays may be harmful to processed films and slide mounts. Keep films away from chemical dust; alkaline dust particles and hypo particles on the emulsion may cause dye fading after a prolonged storage period. Protect your film from insects, because some species will eat the gelatin emulsion and possibly the film base, too.

Care in Projection of Slides

You can use slides that are properly cared for for many years. However, the light and heat that result from prolonged projection with high-wattage lamps will shorten the life and may even distort the slides. Avoid projection times longer than 1 minute. Never remove the heat-absorbing glass or use a lamp of higher wattage than recommended for the projector. Do not obstruct the air intake or outlet for cooling the projector.

Binding slides in glass will protect them from physical damage such as dirt and scratches. When you use glass-mounted slides in high-wattage projectors, moisture may condense on the inside of the glass. You can usually eliminate the moisture by storing slides with activated silica gel.

HOW TO TREAT FILMS DAMAGED BY WATER

Water from floods, firefighting, sprinkler systems, overflowing sinks, burst pipes, backed-up sewers, and leaky roofs can cause serious damage to stored negatives and slides. There are also other situations where moisture can make film unusable, such as poor humidity control in areas where your processed film is stored. Water damage may also take the following forms:

• Films sticking together because of water absorption. Separating the films may pull the emulsion from either or both film surfaces.

• Transfer of paper fibers or coatings on storage sleeves caused by the film sticking to the storage sleeves.

• Ferrotyping of film surfaces to plastic sleeves; i.e.; shiny surface areas on the film.

• Embedded material from dirt or foreign matter in water.

• Differential drying due to the film drying untreated.

• Biological growths.

Treatment

It's important to treat the films immediately or as soon as practical. You can keep the damage to a minimum when you act quickly to salvage the films. The first thing to remember is to keep the water-soaked negatives and slides and their enclosures, such as slide mounts, envelopes, and sleeves, wet. Never let water damaged photographic materials dry out before treatment. If you can't rewash the immersed films within a few days, freeze the films by placing them in a freezer compartment to retard further deterioration.

Immerse the films completely in plastic containers of cold water, 70° F (21° C) or below, containing the following chemicals per litre of water:

Solution A

Quadrafos*	0.6 gram per litre
Sodium Acid Sulfate (NaHSO$_4$)	7.0 grams per litre
Sodium Tetraborate-Borax (Na$_2$B$_4$O$_7$/10H$_2$O)	15.0 grams per litre
Sodium Sulfate (Na$_2$SO$_4$)	195.0 grams per litre
Formalin (37.5 percent solution)	20.0 mL

*Quadrafos is a registered trademark of Monsanto for sodium hexametaphosphate.

143

EKTACHROME 100 Film (Daylight)   BOB CLEMENS

If these chemicals are not readily available, you can instead use solution B containing 15 mL of 37-percent formaldehyde (formalin) solution (by weight) per litre of water at 65°F (18°C) or below. If necessary, use ice to keep the temperature of the soaking solution down. The cold water and the formaldehyde will help prevent swelling and softening of the gelation emulsion which are the major causes of damage, and the growth of bacteria.

The first solution, Solution A, is better because it hardens the emulsion to help minimize damage. When handling chemicals, be sure to observe and follow the precautionary information printed on the chemical containers.

As soon as possible, while soaking the films in either Solution A or Solution B, carefully separate the negatives and slides from their sleeves, enclosures, or each other. Use extreme care because the wet emulsion is very susceptible to physical damage. To remove any traces of mud, silt, paper, or other foreign particles, wash the films for approximately 30 minutes in the soaking solution. Where necessary, you can clean the films by gently swabbing the film surfaces with a tuft of cotton or a soft foam rubber brush *under the surface of the solution* to remove any traces of mud, paper, grit, or other material. Again use extreme care to minimize damage. Avoid any sudden temperature changes in the solution or wash water. For water-damaged films with little or no foreign particles, wash for 10 to 15 minutes in the soaking solution.

After treatment in Solution A, wash the films in running water for 10 minutes at 70°F (21°C) or below; or after treatment in Solution B, wash in running water for 10 to 15 minutes at 65°F (18°C) or below. *Never* use warm water for washing because it may cause frilling or even melting of already soft gelatin emulsion. *Note:* Never use water above 67°F (19°C) for washing when using Solution B because treatment in this solution is more temperature sensitive. Following the washing procedure, treat the films as follows:

• For Kodak black-and-white films and color slides made on KODACHROME Film, rinse for 1 minute in a diluted solution of KODAK PHOTO-FLO Solution, 65°F (18°C).

• For color slides made on KODAK EKTACHROME Film, rinse for 10 to 15 seconds in a working solution of KODAK Stabilizer, Process E-6, 65°F (18°C).

• For color negatives made on Kodak color negative films, rinse for 1 minute in a working solution of KODAK Stabilizer, Process C-41, 65°F (18°C).

• Dry in a dust-free area.

For exposed water-soaked film that has not been processed, keep it wet and process it as soon as possible.

These recommendations do not apply to KODAK TRIMPRINT Instant Color Film and KODAK Instant Color Film. For these films, rinse water-soaked separated TRIMPRINT Pictures or unseparated picture units in fresh water at 65°F (18°C) or below. Allow unseparated picture units to air dry for several weeks. Let separated TRIMPRINT Pictures air dry for 24 hours.

Prevention

Some methods of preventing water damage are obvious, of course. Wherever possible store film:

• Above the water level anticipated from flooding that could occur in your area.

• In areas free of water pipes and/or plumbing.

• In an area with proper humidity to prevent the films from absorbing moisture from the air which increases the possibility of damage.

• In waterproof or water-resistant containers, such as sealing valuable films in KODAK Storage Envelopes as previously recommended.

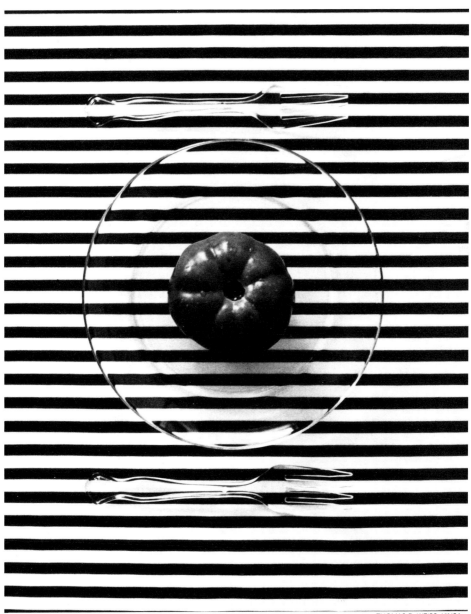

PLUS-X Pan Film

Condensed Information

KODAK COLOR FILMS FOR STILL CAMERAS

KODAK Film	Type of Pictures	For Use with	ISO Film Speed and Filter			Film Code Numbers and Sizes Available	Processed by	Process
			Daylight	Photolamps 3400 K	Tungsten 3200 K			
KODACOLOR VR100 (CP)	Color Prints	Daylight, Electronic Flash, or Blue Flash	100	32 No. 80B	25 No. 80A	5094—135-12, 135-24, 135-36, 6094—size 120	Kodak, other labs, or users	C-41
KODACOLOR VR200 (CL)	Color Prints	Daylight, Electronic Flash, Blue Flash, or Existing Light	200	64 No. 80B	50 No. 80A	5093—sizes 135-12, 135-24, 135-36 7093—size 110-12 7098—size 110-24 8098—sizes 126-12, 126-24 6093—sizes 620, 127	Kodak, other labs, or users	C-41
KODACOLOR VR400 (CM)	Color Prints		400	125 No. 80B	100 No. 80A	5079—sizes 135-12, 135-24, 135-36, 110-12 7079—size 110-24 6079—size 120	Kodak, other labs, or users	C-41
KODACOLOR VR1000 (CF)	Color Prints		1000	320 No. 80B	250 No. 80A	5090—sizes 135-12, 135-24, 135-36	Kodak, other labs, or users	C-41
KODACOLOR VR Disc (CVR)	Color Prints		200	64 No. 80B	50 No. 80A	4175—Disc-15	Kodak and other labs	C-41A
TRIMPRINT™ Instant Color (HS)	Instant Color Prints	Daylight, Electronic Flash, or Blue Flash	320	100 No. 80B	80 No. 80A	Size 144-10	Users	Instant
Instant Color (PR)	Instant Color Prints		160	50 No. 80B	40 No. 80A	Size 144-10	Users	Instant
KODACHROME 25* (Daylight) (KM)	Color Slides	Daylight, Electronic Flash, or Blue Flash	25	8 No. 80B	6 No. 80A	5073—sizes 135-24, 135-36	Kodak and other labs	Commercial Laboratory K-14
KODACHROME 64* (Daylight) (KR)	Color Slides		64	20 No. 80B	16 No. 80A	5032—sizes 135-24, 135-36, 110-20, 126-20	Kodak and other labs	Commercial Laboratory K-14
KODACHROME 40 5070 (Type A) (KPA)	Color Slides	Photolamps 3400K	25 No. 85	40	32 No. 82A	5070—size 135-36	Kodak and other labs	Commercial Laboratory K-14

for KODAK Color Films

Film	Color Slides	Light Source	EI	Filter No. 80B	Filter No. 80A	Film Code / Size	Processed by	Process
EKTACHROME 64 (Daylight) (ER)†	Color Slides	Daylight, Electronic Flash, or Blue Flash	64	20 / No. 80B	16 / No. 80A	5031—sizes 110-20, 126-20	Kodak, other labs, or users	E-6
EKTACHROME 100 (Daylight) (EN)†	Color Slides	Daylight, Electronic Flash, or Blue Flash	100	32 / No. 80B	25 / No. 80A	5039—sizes 135-24, 135-36	Kodak, other labs, or users	E-6
EKTACHROME 200 (Daylight) (ED)†	Color Slides		200 / 400‡	64 / No. 80B / 125‡ No. 80B	50 / No. 80A / 100‡ No. 80A	5076—sizes 135-24, 135-36	Kodak, other labs, or users	E-6
EKTACHROME 400 (Daylight) (EL)	Color Slides	Daylight, Electronic Flash, Blue Flash, or Existing Daylight	400 / 800‡	125 No. 80B / 250‡ No. 80B	100 No. 80A / 200‡ No. 80A	5074—sizes 135-24, 135-36 / 6074—size 120	Kodak, other labs, or users	E-6
EKTACHROME P800/1600 Professional (Daylight) (EES)	Color Slides		EI 800‡ / EI 1600§	EI 250‡ No. 80B / EI 500§ No. 80B	EI 200‡ No. 80A / EI 400§ No. 80A	5020—size 135-36	Kodak, other labs, or users	E-6P
EKTACHROME 160 (Tungsten) (ET)†	Color Slides	Tungsten Lamps 3200 K or Existing Tungsten Light	100 No. 85B / 200‡ No. 85B	125 No. 81A / 250‡ No. 81A	160 / 320‡	5077—sizes 135-24, 135-36	Kodak, other labs, or users	E-6
EKTACHROME Slide Duplicating 5071	Color Slides	Tungsten Lamps 3200 K or Daylight**	12**	—	12**	5071—size 135-36	Kodak, other labs, or users	E-6
EKTACHROME SE Duplicating SO-366	Color Slides	Electronic Flash or Daylight**	16**	—	—	SO-366—size 135-36	Kodak, other labs, or users	E-6

Note: See page D1 for an explanation of the code letters after each film name.

*Professional versions of these films are available.

†Size 135 magazines and 120 rolls are available in the professional versions of these films. See pages 47 and 48.

‡With KODAK EKTACHROME P800/1600, 400, 200, and 160 Films, 135 and 120 sizes, and ESP-1 Processing (Push 1). See page 66.

§With Push 2 Processing to EI 1600.

**See Data Sheet pages D24 and D25 for exposure and filter information.

Condensed Information for KODAK Black-and-White Films

KODAK BLACK-AND-WHITE FILMS FOR STILL CAMERAS

KODAK Film	Film Speed	Definition				Film Code Numbers and Sizes Available	Processed by
		Graininess	Resolving Power Lines per mm	Sharpness	Degree of Enlargement Potential*		
VERICHROME Pan (VP)	ISO 125	Extremely Fine	High 100	Very High	High	7042—size 110-12 8041—size 126-12 6041—size 120	Kodak, other labs, or users
PLUS-X Pan (PX)†	ISO 125	Extremely Fine	High 125	Very High	High	5062—sizes 135-24, 135-36	Kodak, other labs, or users
PANATOMIC-X (FX)†‡	ISO 32	Extremely Fine	Very High 200	Very High	Very High	5060—sizes 135-24, 135-36	Kodak, other labs, or users
TRI-X Pan (TX)	ISO 400	Fine	High 100	Very High	Moderate	5063—sizes 135-24, 135-36 6043—size 120	Kodak, other labs, or users
ROYAL-X Pan (RX)	ISO 1250	Medium	High 100	High	Moderately Low	6046—size 120	Other labs or users
Recording 2475 (RE)	EI 1000	Coarse	Medium 63	Very High	Low	2475—size 135-36	Other labs or users
High Speed Infrared 2481 (HIE)	EI 125§ No. 25 Filter	Fine	Medium 80	Medium	Moderately Low	2481—size 135-36	Other labs or users
Technical Pan 2415, 6415 (TP)	EI 25**	Micro Fine	Extremely High 320	Extremely High	Extremely High	2415—size 135-36 6415—size 120	Other labs or users

*For good-quality negatives.

†Professional versions of these films are available in 120 size.

‡With special reversal processing, PANATOMIC-X Film in 135 size will produce black-and-white positive slides. See page D 35 for film speeds.

§Speed for tungsten light.

**Developed in KODAK TECHNIDOL Liquid Developer for pictorial results.

Film Data Sheets

KODAK Films for General Use

The following Data Sheets provide detailed information to help you obtain the best possible results with each film. Since recommendations may change, whenever these Data Sheets do not agree with the instructions included with the film, follow the film instructions. The instructions in the film package are updated more frequently.

The film code letter designation and the film code number for each film are given on the Data Sheets. The code letter designation is printed on the film carton, on 135 magazines, 110 and 126 cartridges, rolls, discs, and packs to help identify the kind of film. For example, KODACHROME 64 Film (Daylight) is identified by the letters "KR." This film in 135 size with 24 exposures, is identified as KR135-24.

The film code number is printed on the actual film itself for most sizes so that you can identify the film after it's processed, if necessary. The film code number for KODACHROME 64 Film (Daylight) is 5032, for example.

KODAK COLOR FILMS

KODAK BLACK-AND-WHITE FILMS

For Color Prints

A color negative film designed for use in disc cameras with characteristics similar to those of KODACOLOR VR 200 Film but with even finer grain. KODACOLOR VR Disc Film is excellent for general photography with daylight and flash. It reproduces colors superbly together with high-quality definition and a fast speed of ISO 200. The film's generous speed coupled with the exposure capabilities of many disc cameras provide considerable versatility by utilizing high shutter speeds to stop some action and minimize the results of camera motion, and large lens openings to extend the flash distance range and to photograph some scene detail in marginal lighting beyond the maximum flash distance. Disc film is for use with daylight, electronic flash, or blue flashbulbs. The film has wide exposure latitude which helps contribute to its versatility. The combination of KODACOLOR VR Disc Film and disc cameras produce excellent color pictures over a wider range of conditions than was previously possible with simple cameras.

Film Code Letter Designation: CVR.

Film Code Number and Size Available: 4175—size disc-15 exposures.

Storage and Handling: Protect unprocessed film from heat. Have your film processed promptly after exposure. Protect negatives from extended exposure to strong light and store in a cool, dry, and dark place.

NOTE: Since most disc cameras are automatic and require no exposure settings, the following data and text is for informational purposes.

EXPOSURE

Speeds and Filter Recommendations:

Type of Light	Film Speed	Filter
DAYLIGHT	**ISO 200**	**None**
PHOTOLAMPS 3400 K	ISO 64	No. 80B*
TUNGSTEN 3200 K	ISO 50	No. 80A*

*For critical use.

Daylight Exposure Table: For average subjects.

Shutter Speed 1/250 Second						
Bright or Hazy Sun Distinct Shadows		**Weak Hazy Sun Soft Shadows**	**Cloudy Bright No Shadows**	**Heavy Overcast**	**Open Shade†**
On Light Sand or Snow	**Average Subjects**				
f/16	f/11*	f/8	f/5.6	f/4	f/4

Exposure table adjusted for increased underexposure latitude.
*For frontlighted subjects. For backlighted close-up subjects use f/5.6 at 1/250 second.
†Subject shaded from the sun but lighted by a large area of sky.

Electronic Flash Guide Numbers: You can use this table as a starting point in determining the correct guide number for electronic flash units rated in beam candlepower seconds (BCPS). Divide the proper guide number by the flash-to-subject distance in feet to determine the f-number for average subjects. Or you can divide the proper guide number by the f-number to determine the flash-to-subject distance in feet for average subjects.

Output of Unit—BCPS	350	500	700	1000	1400	2000	2800	4000	5600	8000
Guide Numbers*	60	70	85	100	120	140	170	200	240	280

*If your prints are consistently too blue, use a No. 81B filter and increase your exposure by 1/3 stop.

Reciprocity Characteristics: The following table gives the exposure compensation for different exposure times.

Exposure Time in Seconds						
1/10,000	1/1000	1/100	1/10	1	10	100
None No Filter	None No Filter	None No Filter	None No Filter	+ 1/2 stop No Filter	NR*	NR*

*Not recommended for critical use.

PROCESSING

You can have your film developed and printed by Kodak or another processing lab by returning the film to your photo dealer, or by mailing it directly with the appropriate prepaid processing mailer.

Your dealer can also order enlargements from your negatives.

The film is not recommended for processing in home darkrooms.

DEFINITION

Graininess	Resolving Power	Sharpness	Degree of Enlargement Potential*
Micro Fine	High 100 lines per mm	Very High	Very High

*For good-quality negatives.

For Color Prints

This is the sharpest color negative film ever produced by Kodak. Its sharpness plus extremely fine grain give you more clarity for capturing fine detail. The film has adequate speed for many situations—ISO 100, and produces superb color. These qualities make it an excellent film for general photography when you want maximum image quality for making large prints with a high degree of magnification. You can take pictures with this film by daylight or electronic flash. KODACOLOR VR 100 Film is noted for its wide exposure latitude, which minimizes the effects of exposure errors. This film is designed for producing color prints, but color slides and black-and-white prints can also be made from the negatives.

Film Code Letter Designation: CP.

Film Code Numbers and Sizes Available: 5094—sizes 135-12 exposures, 135-24 exposures, 135-36 exposures; 6094—size 120.

Storage and Handling: Protect unprocessed film from heat. Have your film processed promptly after exposure. Protect negatives from extended exposure to strong light and store in a cool, dry, and dark place.

EXPOSURE

Speeds and Filter Recommendations:

Type of Light	Film Speed	Filter
DAYLIGHT	ISO 100	None
PHOTOLAMPS 3400 K	ISO 32	No. 80B
TUNGSTEN 3200 K	ISO 25	No. 80A

NOTE: If your camera has a built-in exposure meter that makes the reading through a filter used over the lens, see your camera manual for instructions on exposure with filters. Also, see page 119.

Daylight Exposure Table: For average subjects.

Shutter Speed 1/125 Second						
Bright or Hazy Sun Distinct Shadows		**Weak Hazy Sun Soft Shadows**	**Cloudy Bright No Shadows**	**Heavy Overcast**	**Open Shade†**
On Light Sand or Snow	**Average Subjects**				
f/16	f/11*	f/8	f/5.6	f/4	f/4

Exposure table adjusted for increased underexposure latitude.
*For frontlighted subjects. For backlighted close-up subjects use f/5.6 at 1/125 second.
†Subject shaded from the sun but lighted by a large area of sky.

Electronic Flash Guide Numbers: Use this table as a starting point in determining the correct guide number for electronic flash units rated in beam candlepower seconds (BCPS).

Divide the proper guide number by the flash-to-subject distance in feet to determine the f-number for average subjects.

Output of Unit—BCPS	350	500	700	1000	1400	2000	2800	4000	5600	8000
Guide Numbers*	40	50	60	70	85	100	120	140	170	200

*If your prints are consistently too blue, use a No. 81B filter and increase your exposure by 1/3 stop.

Reciprocity Characteristics: The following table gives the exposure and filter compensation for different exposure times. The exposure increase includes the adjustment required when a filter is indicated.

Exposure Time in Seconds						
1/10,000	1/1000	1/100	1/10	1	10	100
None No Filter	None No Filter	None No Filter	None No Filter	+1 stop CC10R	+2 stops CC10R + CC10Y	NR*

*Not recommended for critical use.

PROCESSING

You can have your film developed and printed by Kodak or another processing lab by returning the film to your photo dealer, or by mailing it directly with the appropriate prepaid processing mailer. Your dealer can also order enlargements or color slides from your negatives.

You can develop KODACOLOR VR 100 Film in your own darkroom and print the negatives on KODAK EKTACOLOR Paper or EKTAFLEX Materials.

Process the film in the KODAK HOBBY-PACTM Color Negative Kit for Processing KODACOLOR and KODAK VERICOLOR Films or in KODAK FLEXICOLOR Chemicals, Process C-41, or equivalent, available from photo dealers. If you want black-and-white prints from your color negatives, you can use KODAK PANALURE Papers. Instructions are included with the papers and with the processing chemicals.

DEFINITION	Graininess	Resolving Power	Sharpness	Degree of Enlargement Potential*
	Extremely Fine	High 100 lines per mm	Very High	High

*For good-quality negatives.

For Color Prints

An ideal general-purpose color negative film that offers vibrant color, excellent sharpness, and extremely fine grain combined with ample speed of ISO 200. These qualities make this Kodak's most versatile film for color prints. The film's speed is fast enough for stopping some moderate action, for using high shutter speeds for sharp pictures with telephoto lenses, and for increasing depth of field while using high shutter speeds. The 200 speed will also let you photograph some dimly lighted subjects and extend the distance range for flash pictures. KODACOLOR VR 200 Film is intended for use with daylight, electronic flash, or blue flashbulbs. It has wide exposure latitude to help minimize moderate exposure errors. VR 200 film's definition characteristics are excellent for enlargements. The film is primarily for color prints but you can also have color slides or black-and-white prints made from the negatives.

Film Code Letter Designation: CL.

Film Code Numbers and Sizes Available: 5093—sizes 135-12 exposures, 135-24 exposures, 135-36 exposures; 7093—size 110-12 exposures; 7098—size 110-24 exposures; 8098—sizes 126-12 exposures, 126-24 exposures; 6093—sizes 620, 127.

Storage and Handling: Protect unprocessed film from heat. Have your film processed promptly after exposure. Protect negatives from extended exposure to strong light and store in a cool, dry, and dark place.

EXPOSURE

Speeds and Filter Recommendations:

Type of Light	Film Speed	Filter
DAYLIGHT	ISO 200	None
PHOTOLAMPS 3400 K	ISO 64	No. 80B*
TUNGSTEN 3200 K	ISO 50	No. 80A*

NOTE: If your camera has a built-in exposure meter that makes the reading through a filter used over the lens, see your camera manual for instructions on exposure with filters. Also, see page 119. *For critical use.

Daylight Exposure Table: For average subjects.

Shutter Speed 1/250 Second					
Bright or Hazy Sun Distinct Shadows		Weak Hazy Sun Soft Shadows	Cloudy Bright No Shadows	Heavy Overcast	Open Shade†
On Light Sand or Snow	Average Subjects				
f/16	f/11*	f/8	f/5.6	f/4	f/4

Exposure table adjusted for increased underexposure latitude.
*For frontlighted subjects. For backlighted close-up subjects use f/5.6 at 1/250 second.

†Subject shaded from the sun but lighted by a large area of sky.

Electronic Flash Guide Numbers: Use this table as a starting point in determining the correct guide number for electronic flash units rated in beam candlepower seconds (BCPS). Divide the proper guide number by the flash-to-subject distance in feet to determine the f-number for average subjects.

Output of Unit—BCPS	350	500	700	1000	1400	2000	2800	4000	5600	8000
Guide Numbers*	60	70	85	100	120	140	170	200	240	280

*If your prints are consistently too blue, use a No. 81B filter and increase your exposure by 1/3 stop.

D 4

Existing-Light Exposure Table: Use an exposure meter or a camera with built-in meter if you have one. For cameras without working exposure meters or for scenes that are difficult to meter, try the settings suggested in the table. These exposures are *guides*; for more assurance, bracket your exposures 1 stop on each side of the suggested exposure.

Picture Subject	Shutter Speed	Lens Opening
Interiors with Bright Fluorescent Light*	1/30	f/4
Indoor, Outdoor Christmas Lighting at Night	1†	f/5.6
Brightly Lighted Downtown Street Scenes at Night	1/30	f/2.8
Brightly Lighted Theatre Districts—Las Vegas or Times Square	1/30	f/4
Neon Signs, Other Lighted Signs	1/60	f/4
Store Windows at Night	1/30	f/4
Floodlighted Buildings, Fountains, Monuments	1/2†	f/4
Distant View of City Skyline at Night	1†	f/2
Skylines—10 minutes after sunset	1/60	f/4

*Use exposure times longer than 1/60 second.

Picture Subject	Shutter Speed	Lens Opening
Fairs, Amusement Parks	1/30	f/2
Aerial Fireworks Displays— Keep camera shutter open on BULB for several bursts	BULB†	f/11
Night Football, Soccer, Baseball, Racetracks	1/60	f/2.8
Basketball, Hockey, Bowling	1/60	f/2
Boxing, Wrestling	1/125	f/2
Stage Shows— Average lighting Bright lighting	1/30 1/60	f/2.8 f/4
Circuses—Floodlighted acts	1/30	f/2.8
Ice Shows—Floodlighted acts	1/60	f/2.8
Ice Shows, Circuses— Spotlighted acts (carbon arc)	1/125	f/2.8
Swimming Pool—Indoors, tungsten lights above water	1/30	f/2

†Use a tripod or other firm camera support for exposure times longer than 1/30 second.

Reciprocity Characteristics: The following table gives the exposure and filter compensation for different exposure times. The exposure increase includes the adjustment required when a filter is indicated.

Exposure Time in Seconds						
1/10,000	1/1000	1/100	1/10	1	10	100
None No Filter	None No Filter	None No Filter	None No Filter	+ 1 stop CC10R	+ 2 stops CC10R + CC10Y	NR*

*Not recommended for critical use.

PROCESSING

You can have your film developed and printed by Kodak or another processing lab by returning the film to your photo dealer, or by mailing it directly with the appropriate prepaid processing mailer. Your dealer can also order enlargements or color slides from your negatives.

You can develop KODACOLOR VR 200 Film in your own darkroom and print the negatives on KODAK EKTACOLOR Paper or EKTAFLEX Materials.

Process the film in the KODAK HOBBY-PAC™ Color Negative Kit for Processing KODACOLOR and KODAK VERICOLOR Films or in KODAK FLEXICOLOR Chemicals, Process C-41, or equivalent, available from photo dealers. If you want black-and-white prints from your color negatives, you can use KODAK PANALURE Papers. Instructions are included with the papers and with the processing chemicals.

DEFINITION			
Graininess	Resolving Power	Sharpness	Degree of Enlargement Potential*
Extremely Fine	High 100 lines per mm	High	High

*For good-quality negatives.

For Color Prints

This color negative film features high speed, ISO 400, plus extremely fine grain together with rich, saturated colors, and realistic reproduction of flesh tones. The film is a good choice for photographing dimly lighted subjects, such as those in existing light; fast action; subjects that require good depth of field and high shutter speeds; and for using telephoto lenses and high shutter speeds; and for extending the flash distance range. KODACOLOR VR 400 Film is the film to use when you need high speed and want enlargements. The film is color-balanced for daylight, electronic flash, or blue flash. It also has special sensitizing charateristics that give you pleasing pictures exposed with other light sources, such as household light bulbs and fluorescent lamps, without using filters on your camera. VR 400 Film has considerable versatility with wide exposure latitude. You can use it to photograph subjects ranging from bright sunlight to dim light, depending on your camera.

Film Code Letter Designation: CM.

Film Code Numbers and Sizes Available: 5079—sizes 135-12 exposures, 135-24 exposures, 135-36 exposures, 110-12 exposures; 7079—size 110-24 exposures; 6079—size 120.

Storage and Handling: Protect unprocessed film from heat. Load and unload camera in subdued light. Have your film processed promptly after exposure. Protect negatives from extended exposure to strong light and store in a cool, dry, and dark place.

EXPOSURE

Speeds and Filter Recommendations:

Type of Light	Film Speed	Filter
DAYLIGHT	**ISO 400**	**None**
PHOTOLAMPS 3400 K	ISO 125	No. 80B*
TUNGSTEN 3200 K	ISO 100	No. 80A*

NOTE: If your camera has a built-in exposure meter that makes the reading through a filter used over the lens, see your camera manual for instructions on exposure with filters. Also, see page 119. *For critical use.

Daylight Exposure Table: For average subjects.

Shutter Speed 1/500 Second					
Bright or Hazy Sun Distinct Shadows		Weak Hazy Sun Soft Shadows	Cloudy Bright No Shadows	Heavy Overcast	Open Shade†
On Light Sand or Snow	Average Subjects				
f/16	f/11*	f/8	f/5.6	f/4	f/4

Exposure table adjusted for increased underexposure latitude. *For frontlighted subjects. For backlighted close-up subjects use f/5.6 at 1/500 second. †Subject shaded from the sun but lighted by a large area of sky.

Electronic Flash Guide Numbers:
Use this table as a starting point in determining the correct guide number for electronic flash units rated in beam candlepower seconds (BCPS). Divide the proper guide number by the flash-to-subject distance in feet to determine the f-number for average subjects.

Output of Unit—BCPS	350	500	700	1000	1400	2000	2800	4000	5600	8000
Guide Numbers*	85	100	120	140	170	200	240	280	340	400

*If your prints are consistently too blue, use a No. 81B filter and increase your exposure by 1/3 stop.

D 6

Existing-Light Exposure Table: Use an exposure meter or a camera with built-in meter if you have one. For cameras without working exposure meters or for scenes that are difficult to meter, try the settings suggested in the table. These exposures are *guides*; for more assurance, bracket your exposures 1 stop on each side of the suggested exposure.

Picture Subject	Shutter Speed	Lens Opening
Home Interiors at Night— Areas with average light Areas with bright light	1/30 1/30	f/2 f/2.8
Candlelighted Close-Ups	1/15*	f/2
Interiors with Bright Fluorescent Light†	1/60	f/4
Indoor, Outdoor Christmas Lighting at Night	1/15*	f/2
Brightly Lighted Downtown Street Scenes at Night	1/60	f/2.8
Brightly Lighted Theatre Districts—Las Vegas or Times Square	1/60	f/4
Neon Signs, Other Lighted Signs	1/125	f/4
Store Windows at Night	1/60	f/4
Floodlighted Buildings, Fountains, Monuments	1/15*	f/2
Distant View of City Skyline at Night	1*	f/2.8
Skylines—10 minutes after sunset	1/60	f/5.6

*Use a tripod or other firm camera support for exposure times longer than 1/30 second.

Picture Subject	Shutter Speed	Lens Opening
Fairs, Amusement Parks	1/30	f/2.8
Aerial Fireworks Displays— Keep camera shutter open on BULB for several bursts	BULB*	f/16
Night Football, Soccer, Baseball, Racetracks	1/125	f/2.8
Basketball, Hockey, Bowling	1/125	f/2
Boxing, Wrestling	1/250	f/2
Stage Shows— Average lighting Bright lighting	1/60 1/125	f/2.8 f/4
Circuses—Floodlighted acts	1/60	f/2.8
Ice Shows—Floodlighted acts	1/125	f/2.8
Ice Shows, Circuses— Spotlighted acts (carbon arc)	1/250	f/2.8
School—Stage and auditorium	1/30	f/2
Swimming Pool—Indoors, tungsten lights above water	1/60	f/2
Church Interiors— Tungsten lights	1/30	f/2

†Use exposure times longer than 1/60 second.

Reciprocity Characteristics: The following table gives the exposure compensation for different exposure times.

Exposure Time in Seconds						
1/10,000	1/1000	1/100	1/10	1	10	100
None No Filter	None No Filter	None No Filter	None No Filter	+ 1/2 stop No Filter	+ 1 stop No Filter	+ 2 stops No Filter

PROCESSING

You can have your film developed and printed by Kodak or another processing lab by returning the film to your photo dealer, or by mailing it directly with the appropriate prepaid processing mailer. Your dealer can also order enlargements or color slides from your negatives.

You can develop KODACOLOR VR 400 Film in your own darkroom and print the negatives on KODAK EKTACOLOR Paper or EKTAFLEX Materials.

Process the film in the KODAK HOBBY-PAC™ Color Negative Kit for Processing KODACOLOR and KODAK VERICOLOR Films or in KODAK FLEXICOLOR Chemicals, Process C-41, or equivalent, available from photo dealers. If you want black-and-white prints from your color negatives, you can use KODAK PANALURE Papers. Instructions are included with the papers and with the processing chemicals.

DEFINITION

Graininess	Resolving Power	Sharpness	Degree of Enlargement Potential*
Extremely Fine	Medium 80 lines per mm	Medium	Moderate

*For good-quality negatives.

For Color Prints

Kodak's fastest color negative film with a very high speed of ISO 1000, lets you photograph subjects under a wide range of conditions from average to the extremes. KODACOLOR VR 1000 Film is remarkable—when the light is faint you can still capture beautiful color and detail without using flash, depending on your camera. This is the film to use under adverse lighting conditions or for fast action. Use it for existing-light photography outdoors at night, or indoors where flash is inappropriate, or wherever you want to capture the natural lighting that may be dim. It's good for telephoto pictures under marginal lighting, for increasing depth of field by using a smaller lens opening, and for increasing flash-to-subject distances when you want to use flash. VR 1000 film is color balanced for exposure by daylight or electronic flash. But it also features special sensitization that gives pleasing results under a variety of different lighting situations without using filters over your camera lens, for example, tungsten light bulbs in homes and fluorescent lamps in public buildings.

Film Code Letter Designation: CF.

Film Code Number and Size Available:
5090—size 135-12 exposures, 135-24 exposures, 135-36 exposures.

Storage and Handling: Protect unprocessed film from heat and x-rays. Take special precautions to load and unload camera in subdued light because of the film's very high speed. Have your film processed promptly after exposure. Protect negatives from extended exposure to strong light and store in a cool, dry, and dark place.

EXPOSURE

Speeds and Filter Recommendations:

Type of Light	Film Speed	Filter
DAYLIGHT	ISO 1000	None
PHOTOLAMPS 3400 K	ISO 320	No. 80B*
TUNGSTEN 3200 K	ISO 250	No. 80A*

NOTE: If your camera has a built-in exposure meter that makes the reading through a filter used over the lens, see your camera manual for instructions on exposure with filters. Also, see page 119. *For critical use.

Daylight Exposure Table*: For average subjects.

Shutter Speed 1/1000 Second					
Bright or Hazy Sun Distinct Shadows		**Weak Hazy Sun Soft Shadows**	**Cloudy Bright No Shadows**	**Heavy Overcast**	**Open Shade‡**
On Light Sand or Snow	Average Subjects				
f/22	f/16†	f/11	f/8	f/5.6	f/5.6

*If your camera is unable to accommodate the minimum exposure settings in the table, use the highest shutter speed and smallest lens opening available. Film exposure latitude will compensate for up to 3 stops of overexposure.

†For frontlighted subjects. For backlighted close-up subjects use f/8 at 1/1000 second.
‡Subject shaded from the sun but lighted by a large area of sky.

Electronic Flash Guide Numbers: Use this table as a starting point in determining the correct guide number for electronic flash units rated in beam candlepower seconds (BCPS). Divide the proper guide number by the flash-to-subject distance in feet to determine the f-number for average subjects.

Output of Unit—BCPS	350	500	700	1000	1400	2000	2800	4000	5600	8000
Guide Numbers*	130	160	190	220	260	320	380	450	530	630

*If your prints are consistently too blue, use a No. 81B filter and increase your exposure by 1/3 stop.

Existing-Light Exposure Table: Use an exposure meter or a camera with built-in meter if you have one. For cameras without working exposure meters or for scenes that are difficult to meter, try the settings suggested in the table. These exposures are *guides*; for more assurance, bracket your exposures 1 stop on each side of the suggested exposure.

Picture Subject	Shutter Speed	Lens Opening
Home Interiors at Night—		
Areas with average light	1/30	f/2.8
Areas with bright light	1/30	f/4
Candlelighted Close-Ups	1/30	f/2
Interiors with Bright Fluorescent Light*	1/60	f/5.6
Indoor, Outdoor Christmas Lighting at Night	1/30	f/2
Brightly Lighted Downtown Street Scenes at Night	1/60	f/4
Brightly Lighted Theatre Districts—Las Vegas or Times Square	1/125	f/4
Neon Signs, Other Lighted Signs	1/125	f/5.6
Store Windows at Night	1/60	f/5.6
Floodlighted Buildings, Fountains, Monuments	1/30	f/2
Distant View of City Skyline at Night	1†	f/4
Skylines—10 minutes after sunset	1/125	f/5.6

*Use exposure times longer than 1/60 second.
†Use a tripod or other firm camera support for exposure times longer than 1/30 second.

Picture Subject	Shutter Speed	Lens Opening
Fairs, Amusement Parks	1/60	f/2.8
Aerial Fireworks Displays— Keep camera shutter open on BULB for several bursts	BULB†	f/22‡
Night Football, Soccer, Baseball, Racetracks	1/250	f/2.8
Basketball, Hockey, Bowling	1/125	f/2.8
Boxing, Wrestling	1/250	f/2.8
Stage Shows—		
Average lighting	1/125	f/2.8
Bright lighting	1/250	f/4
Circuses—Floodlighted acts	1/125	f/2.8
Ice Shows—Floodlighted acts	1/250	f/2.8
Ice Shows, Circuses— Spotlighted acts (carbon arc)	1/250	f/4
School—Stage and auditorium	1/30	f/2.8
Swimming Pool—Indoors, tungsten lights above water	1/60	f/2.8
Church Interiors— Tungsten lights	1/30	f/2.8

‡If f/22 is not available on your camera, you can use f/16.

Reciprocity Characteristics: The following table gives the exposure and filter compensation for different exposure times. The exposure increase includes the adjustment required when a filter is indicated.

Exposure Time in Seconds						
1/10,000	1/1000	1/100	1/10	1	10	100
None No Filter	None No Filter	None No Filter	None No Filter	+ 1 stop CC10G	+ 2 stops CC20G	+ 3 stops CC30G + CC10B

PROCESSING

You can have your film developed and printed by Kodak or another processing lab by returning the film to your photo dealer, or by mailing it directly with the appropriate prepaid processing mailer. Your dealer can also order enlargements or color slides from your negatives.

You can develop KODACOLOR VR 1000 Film in your own darkroom and print the negatives on KODAK EKTACOLOR Paper or EKTAFLEX Materials.

Process the film in the KODAK HOBBY-PAC™ Color Negative Kit for Processing KODACOLOR and KODAK VERICOLOR Films or in KODAK FLEXICOLOR Chemicals, Process C-41, or equivalent, available from photo dealers. If you want black-and-white prints from your color negatives, you can use KODAK PANALURE Papers. Instructions are included with the papers and with the processing chemicals.

DEFINITION

Graininess	Resolving Power	Sharpness	Degree of Enlargement Potential*
Very Fine	Medium 80 lines per mm	Medium	Moderately Low

*For good-quality negatives.

For Color Prints

KODAK TRIMPRINT Instant Color Film (HS) and KODAK Instant Color Film (PR) are designed for use in instant cameras and instant film backs that accept KODAK Instant Film. These films produce color prints directly from the camera which develop in a matter of minutes. You don't have to time development. The films provide attractive color reproduction and excellent grain and sharpness. The two films are color balanced for daylight, electronic flash, and blue flash. Both films have the exclusive TRIMPRINT Feature that gives you the option of separating the prints from their backing materials. TRIMPRINT Pictures have a KODAK SATINLUXE™ Finish. This surface, which is hard and dry from the moment the prints are ejected, lets you handle prints without fingerprinting and with a minimum of scratching. The professional film is called KODAK INSTAGRAPHIC™ Color Print Film.

Film Code Letters: HS—KODAK TRIMPRINT Instant Color Film. PR—KODAK Instant Color Film.

Size Available: 144-10 exposures.

Picture Size: The overall size of a separated print is 3 1/2 x 4 inches (8.9 x 10.2 cm). The actual image size within the borders is 2 5/8 x 3 9/16 inches (6.8 x 9.1 cm). The overall size of an unseparated print, including the white borders, is 3 13/16 x 4 inches (9.7 x 10.2 cm).

Storage and Handling: Protect unprocessed film from heat. Prolonged storage at temperatures above 75°F (24°C) will result in color changes.

Camera Loading: Before loading your camera, check to see that the rollers are clean. If the rollers need cleaning, follow the instructions in your camera manual. Hold the film pack by the edges only. Remove the protective wrapping by grasping the flap and pulling it in the direction of the arrows printed on the wrapping. Don't squeeze the pack or apply pressure to the film cover, since this could allow light to fog your pictures and/or ruin them by starting the instant process prematurely.

EXPOSURE

Speeds and Filter Recommendations for Adjustable Cameras:

Type of Light	ISO Film Speed*		Filter
	KODAK TRIMPRINT Instant Color Film (HS)	KODAK Instant Color Film (PR)	
DAYLIGHT	320	160	None
PHOTOLAMPS 3400 K	100	50	No. 80B
TUNGSTEN 3200 K	80	40	No. 80A

*Film speeds in the table are for temperatures between 60°F (16°C) and 100°F (38°C). At temperatures below 60°F (16°C) film speed increases and above 100° F (38°C) film speed decreases.

Lighten/Darken Control for Automatic Cameras: Under most conditions, you will want to take pictures with the Lighten/Darken control on your camera in the center position. However, the lightness or darkness of your prints can be affected by such factors as temperature and type and brightness of subject. The Lighten/Darken control helps you to compensate for these effects. After taking a picture, if you want to take a lighter or darker picture of the same subject in the same location without changing the lighting or your position, adjust the Lighten/Darken control *before* taking the next picture. To take a lighter picture, move the control toward Lighten; for a darker picture, move the control toward Darken.

Flash for Automatic Cameras: Use electronic flash or blue flash within the flash distance range recommended for your camera. See your camera and electronic flash instruction manuals for detailed information on taking flash pictures.

Electronic Flash Guide Numbers for Adjustable Cameras: Use this table as a starting point in determining the correct guide number for electronic flash units rated in beam candlepower seconds (BCPS). Divide the proper guide number by the flash-to-subject distance in feet to determine the *f*-number for average subjects.

Output of Unit—BCPS	350	500	700	1000	1400	2000	2800	4000	5600	8000
Guide Numbers—KODAK TRIMPRINT Instant Color Film (HS)	75	90	110	130	150	180	210	250	300	360
Guide Numbers—KODAK Instant Color Film (PR)	55	65	75	90	110	130	150	180	210	250

Reciprocity Characteristics for Adjustable Cameras: The following table gives the exposure compensation for different exposure times.

Exposure Time in Seconds					
1/250	1/100	1/20	1/2	1	10
− 1/3 stop No Filter	None No Filter	+ 1/3 stop No Filter	+ 2/3 stop No Filter	+ 1 stop No Filter	+ 2 stops No Filter

DEVELOPMENT

Pictures begin to develop as they are ejected from the camera. It's important to handle prints carefully during the first 10 minutes after exposure. If you plan to separate your prints from the backing materials, wait at least one hour. Hold the prints by their borders, and don't bend, flex, or attempt to fold them. Never leave prints in direct sunlight or on hot surfaces during development.

An image will begin to appear in about 35 seconds under normal room temperature conditions, 72°F (22°C). Do not attempt to make a judgment of print appearance until development is sufficiently advanced. You can judge expression and composition in about 90 seconds and exposure usually after 2 or 3 minutes under normal temperature conditions. Development is essentially complete after about 6 minutes at this temperature. Development will be slower at cooler temperatures and faster at warmer temperatures. Prints will appear lighter when judged in direct sunlight than they will under normal room lighting.

Temperature Effects on Prints: The recommended temperature range during development of prints is 60 to 100°F (16 to 38°C). At temperatures below 60°F (16°C), place your prints in a warm place—an inside pocket, for example—as soon as they are ejected from the camera, and leave them there during development. Otherwise, your prints may appear too light. It may be desirable at the upper end of the temperature range—approaching 100°F (38°C)—to set the Lighten/Darken control toward Lighten to keep prints from becoming too dark.

SEPARATION OF *TRIMPRINT* PICTURES

For thinner, more compact prints, you can separate your prints from the backing materials at the slit after one hour. For acceptable print separation, the temperature should be no lower than 68°F (20°C). If you choose to separate your prints, you'll get best results if you do so within a week from the time you took the pictures. Occasionally a residue may appear on the back of the separated print. Use a piece of transparent tape to lift off the residue. Print separation is optional—leave the picture unit intact if you prefer.

To prevent damage to your separated prints, keep moisture away from the back side. Don't place a print in contact with the waste portion or against the back of another freshly separated print.

STORAGE AND CARE OF FILM AND PRINTS

Avoid storing your camera and film in a hot place such as the glove compartment or rear-window shelf of a car in the sun because this may result in poor picture quality and a permanently damaged camera. If you inadvertently leave your camera and film in a hot place, allow them to cool for at least one hour before taking any pictures. Also, allow them to return to normal temperature if they have been left in a cold place.

Don't mount prints with glue or paste. You can display separated TRIMPRINT Pictures in the same manner as traditional prints in regular albums; cut them to fit frames, wallets, lockets, or photo cubes; mail them; or store them compactly.

Store your prints in a cool, dry place. Color dyes may change over a period of time. Print colors will remain unchanged longer if you protect your pictures from long exposure to bright light.

You can use a soft-tip pen or marker with permanent, waterproof ink to write on the white borders of the prints. You may want to write the date, location, or special event on the print border, for example. Select a pen with ink that's fast-drying, and adheres to nonporous surfaces without smearing. If you want to write on the back of separated TRIMPRINT Pictures, *use only a soft lead pencil to write on the back of dry prints.* Otherwise damage to the image can occur through the back from abrasion or scratching.

CAUTION: Picture units in the film pack contain a caustic fluid. Upon ejection from the camera, the fluid in the picture unit begins to neutralize, and in approximately 10 minutes any chance of harm is minimal. Should any fluid escape from the picture unit, avoid contact with eyes, mouth, and skin. Also avoid fluid contact with fabrics, carpeting, and furniture to prevent stain.

In case of contact with eyes, immediately flush with plenty of water and get medical attention. In case of any other contact, wash thoroughly at once.

The empty film pack has sharp internal edges. Discard out of the reach of children.

ADDITIONAL PRINTS AND SLIDES

You can have additional color prints and color enlargements made from your orginal instant color prints. The original prints can be separated or unseparated for copying. You can also have color slides made from your color prints.

For Color Slides

A favorite for color slides because of its excellent color quality, extremely high sharpness, and extremely fine grain. This film is great for bright lighting conditions where you want the best possible image quality. The film produces rich color saturation and superb flesh tones while retaining good detail in both highlights and shadow areas. Its speed is adequate for many picture-taking situations, and it has good exposure latitude which yields acceptable results even with moderate overexposure or underexposure.

This film is designed for use in daylight or with electronic flash. It's also sold in a professional version—KODACHROME 25 Professional Film (Daylight). See page 47.

Film Code Letter Designation: KM.

Film Code Number and Size Available: 5073—sizes 135-24 exposures, 135-36 exposures.

Storage and Handling: Protect unprocessed film from heat. Have your film processed promptly after exposure. Store your slides in a cool, dry place.

EXPOSURE

Speeds and Filter Recommendations:

Type of Light	Film Speed	Filter
DAYLIGHT	ISO 25	None
PHOTOLAMPS 3400 K	ISO 8	No. 80B
TUNGSTEN 3200 K	ISO 6	No. 80A

NOTE: If your camera has a built-in exposure meter that makes the reading through a filter used over the lens, see your camera manual for instructions on exposure with filters. Also, see page 119.

Daylight Exposure Table: For average subjects.

Shutter Speed 1/125 Second					Shutter Speed 1/60 Second	
Bright or Hazy Sun Distinct Shadows		Weak Hazy Sun Soft Shadows	Cloudy Bright No Shadows	Heavy Overcast	Open Shade†	
On Light Sand or Snow	Average Subjects					
f/11	f/8*	f/5.6	f/4	f/4	f/4	

*For frontlighted subjects. For backlighted close-up subjects use f/4 at 1/125 second.

†Subject shaded from the sun but lighted by a large area of sky.

Electronic Flash Guide Numbers: Use this table as a starting point in determining the correct guide number for electronic flash units rated in beam candlepower seconds (BCPS).

Divide the proper guide number by the flash-to-subject distance in feet to determine the f-number for average subjects.

Output of Unit—BCPS	350	500	700	1000	1400	2000	2800	4000	5600	8000
Guide Numbers*	20	24	30	35	40	50	60	70	85	100

*If your prints are consistently too blue, use a No. 81B filter and increase your exposure by 1/3 stop.

Reciprocity Characteristics: The following table gives the exposure compensation for different exposure times.

Exposure Time in Seconds						
1/10,000	1/1000	1/100	1/10	1	10	100
None No Filter	None No Filter	None No Filter	None No Filter	+ 1/2 stop No Filter	NR*	NR*

*Not recommended for critical use.

PROCESSING

You can have your film processed by Kodak or another processing lab by returning the film to your photo dealer, or by mailing it directly with the appropriate prepaid processing mailer. Your dealer can also order duplicate slides, color prints, or enlargements from your slides.

You can't process KODACHROME Films successfully in your own darkroom because the process is highly complex and requires commercial photofinishing equipment.

DEFINITION	Graininess	Resolving Power	Sharpness
	Extremely Fine	High 100 lines per mm	Extremely High

For Color Slides

A medium-speed, color slide film for general picture-taking. KODACHROME 64 Film exhibits remarkable sharpness and freedom from graininess—its definition characteristics are outstanding. Color rendition is excellent—colors are clean, crisp, and saturated with beautiful flesh tones. The ISO 64 speed makes the film a good choice, compared with KODACHROME 25 Film (Daylight), for making color slides when lighting conditions are less than ideal. Under sunlight conditions, you can use high shutter speeds or small lens openings. The film is for use with daylight, electronic flash, or blue flashbulbs. A professional version, KODACHROME 64 Professional Film (Daylight), is also available.

Film Code Letter Designation: KR.

Film Code Number and Sizes Available: 5032—sizes 135-24 exposures, 135-36 exposures; 110-20 exposures; 126-20 exposures.

Storage and Handling: Protect unprocessed film from heat. Have your film processed promptly after exposure. Store your slides in a cool, dry place.

EXPOSURE

Speeds and Filter Recommendations:

Type of Light	Film Speed	Filter
DAYLIGHT	ISO 64	None
PHOTOLAMPS 3400 K	ISO 20	No. 80B
TUNGSTEN 3200 K	ISO 16	No. 80A

NOTE: If your camera has a built-in exposure meter that makes the reading through a filter used over the lens, see your camera manual for instructions on exposure with filters. Also, see page 119.

Daylight Exposure Table: For average subjects.

Shutter Speed 1/125 Second						
Bright or Hazy Sun Distinct Shadows		Weak Hazy Sun Soft Shadows	Cloudy Bright No Shadows	Heavy Overcast	Open Shade†
On Light Sand or Snow	Average Subjects				
f/16	f/11*	f/8	f/5.6	f/4	f/4

*For frontlighted subjects. For backlighted close-up subjects use f/5.6 at 1/125 second.

†Subject shaded from the sun but lighted by a large area of sky.

Electronic Flash Guide Numbers: Use this table as a starting point in determining the correct guide number for electronic flash units rated in beam candlepower seconds (BCPS). Divide the proper guide number by the flash-to-subject distance in feet to determine the f-number for average subjects.

Output of Unit—BCPS	350	500	700	1000	1400	2000	2800	4000	5600	8000
Guide Numbers*	32	40	45	55	65	80	95	110	130	160

*If your prints are consistently too blue, use a No. 81B filter and increase your exposure by 1/3 stop.

Reciprocity Characteristics: The following table gives the exposure and filter compensation for different exposure times. The exposure increase includes the adjustment required when a filter is indicated.

Exposure Time in Seconds						
1/10,000	1/1000	1/100	1/10	1	10	100
None No Filter	None No Filter	None No Filter	None No Filter	+ 1 stop CC10R	NR*	NR*

*Not recommended for critical use.

PROCESSING

You can have your film processed by Kodak or another processing lab by returning the film to your photo dealer, or by mailing it directly with the appropriate prepaid processing mailer. Your dealer can also order duplicate slides, color prints, or enlargements from your slides.

You can't process KODACHROME Films successfully in your own darkroom because the process is highly complex and requires commercial photofinishing equipment.

	Graininess	Resolving Power	Sharpness
DEFINITION	Extremely Fine	High 100 lines per mm	Extremely High

For Color Slides

KODACHROME 40 Film is for use with 3400 K photolamps. It has extemely fine grain, extremely high sharpness, and superior color quality. It has exceptional definition for which KODACHROME Films are noted. Its speed is sufficient for photolamp illumination. KODACHROME 40 Film is excellent for informal portraits, close-ups, title slides, and for copying color originals. You can also take pictures in daylight or by electronic flash with this film by using a No. 85 filter over your camera lens.

Film Code Letter Designation: KPA.

Film Code Number and Size Available: 5070—size 135-36 exposures.

Storage and Handling: Protect unprocessed film from heat. Have your film processed promptly after exposure. Store your slides in a cool, dry place.

EXPOSURE

Speeds and Filter Recommendations:

Type of Light	Film Speed	Filter
PHOTOLAMPS 3400 K	**ISO 40**	**None**
TUNGSTEN 3200 K	ISO 32	No. 82A
DAYLIGHT	ISO 25	No. 85

NOTE: If your camera has a built-in exposure meter that makes the reading through a filter used over the lens, see your camera manual for instructions on exposure with filters. Also, see page 119.

Photolamps—3400 K: The following table is based on the use of two 500-watt reflector-type photolamps 3400 K, such as General Electric DXC and Sylvania DXC reflector floodlamps. Use one lamp as a fill-in light close to the camera at lens level; the other as the main light on the opposite side of the camera, 2 to 4 feet (0.6 to 1.2 metres) higher, and at a 45-degree angle from the camera-subject axis. Position both lights the same distance from the subject.

EXPOSURE TABLE FOR 500-WATT REFLECTOR-TYPE PHOTOLAMPS 3400 K			
Set Shutter Speed at 1/60 Second			
Lamp-to-Subject Distance	4½ ft (1.4 m)	6 ft (1.8m)	9 ft (2.7m)
Lens Opening	f/4	f/2.8	f/2

NOTE: Use these camera settings as guides only. The lamp-to-subject distances give a lighting ratio of 2:1. For a 3:1 ratio, place the fill-in light at a distance from the subject 1.4 times the distance for the main light and use a lens opening 1/2 stop larger. This table is based on the use of new lamps. After the lamps have burned for 1 hour, use a lens opening 1/2 stop larger; after 2 hours, use a lens opening 1 stop larger.

Daylight Exposure Table: For average subjects. *Use a No.85 filter.*

Shutter Speed 1/125 Second				Shutter Speed 1/60 Second	
Bright or Hazy Sun Distinct Shadows		Weak Hazy Sun Soft Shadows	Cloudy Bright No Shadows	Heavy Overcast	Open Shade†
On Light Sand or Snow	Average Subjects				
f/11	f/8*	f/5.6	f/4	f/4	f/4

*For frontlighted subjects. For backlighted close-up subjects use f/4 at 1/125 second.
†Subject shaded from the sun but lighted by a large area of sky.

Electronic Flash Guide Numbers: *Use a No. 85 filter.* This table is intended as a starting point in determining the correct guide number for electronic flash units rated in beam candlepower seconds (BCPS). Divide the proper guide number by the flash-to-subject distance in feet to determine the f-number for average subjects.

Output of Unit—BCPS	350	500	700	1000	1400	2000	2800	4000	5600	8000
Guide Numbers	20	24	30	35	40	50	60	70	85	100

Reciprocity Characteristics: The following table gives the exposure compensation for different exposure times.

Exposure Time in Seconds							
1/10,000	1/1000	1/100	1/10	1	5	10	100
None No Filter	None No Filter	None No Filter	None No Filter	+ 1/2 stop No Filter	+ 1 stop No Filter	NR*	NR*

*Not recommended for critical use.

PROCESSING

You can have your film processed by Kodak or another processing lab by returning the film to your photo dealer, or by mailing it directly with the appropriate prepaid processing mailer. Your dealer can also order duplicate slides, color prints, or enlargements from your slides.

You can't process KODACHROME Films successfully in your own darkroom because the process is highly complex and requires commercial photofinishing equipment.

DEFINITION

Graininess	Resolving Power	Sharpness
Extremely Fine	High 100 lines per mm	Extremely High

For Color Slides

An excellent film for general picture-taking when you want color slides. EKTACHROME 64 Film produces vivid colors, clean highlights, and neutral shadows with good detail. It has very high sharpness and low graininess which gives very good image quality. The medium speed of the film helps you to take high-quality pictures in the shade or on overcast days. It's balanced for daylight; for flash pictures, use electronic flash or blue flashbulbs. A feature of this film, as with all KODAK EKTACHROME Films, is that you can process it in your own darkroom if you want to. The film is also supplied as a professional film; it's called EKTACHROME 64 Professional Film (Daylight). See page 47.

Film Code Letter Designation: ER.

Film Code Number and Sizes Available: 5031—sizes 110-20 exposures; 126-20 exposures.

Storage and Handling: Protect unprocessed film from heat. Have your film processed promptly after exposure. Store your slides in a cool, dry place.

EXPOSURE

Speeds and Filter Recommendations:

Type of Light	Film Speed	Filter
DAYLIGHT	**ISO 64**	**None**
PHOTOLAMPS 3400 K	ISO 20	No. 80B
TUNGSTEN 3200 K	ISO 16	No. 80A

NOTE: If your camera has a built-in exposure meter that makes the reading through a filter used over the lens, see your camera manual for instructions on exposure with filters. Also, see page 119.

Daylight Exposure Table: For average subjects.

Shutter Speed 1/125 Second						
Bright or Hazy Sun Distinct Shadows		Weak Hazy Sun Soft Shadows	Cloudy Bright No Shadows	Heavy Overcast	Open Shade†
On Light Sand or Snow	Average Subjects				
f/16	f/11*	f/8	f/5.6	f/4	f/4

*For frontlighted subjects. For backlighted close-up subjects use f/5.6 at 1/125 second.

†Subject shaded from the sun but lighted by a large area of sky.

Electronic Flash Guide Numbers: Use this table as a starting point in determining the correct guide number for electronic flash units rated in beam candlepower seconds (BCPS).

Divide the proper guide number by the flash-to-subject distance in feet to determine the f-number for average subjects.

Output of Unit—BCPS	350	500	700	1000	1400	2000	2800	4000	5600	8000
Guide Numbers*	32	40	45	55	65	80	95	110	130	160

*If your prints are consistently too blue, use a No. 81B filter and increase your exposure by 1/3 stop.

Reciprocity Characteristics: The following table gives the exposure compensation for different exposure times.

Exposure Time in Seconds						
1/10,000	1/1000	1/100	1/10	1	10	100
None No Filter	None No Filter	None No Filter	None No Filter	+ 1/2 stop No Filter	+ 1 stop No Filter	NR*

*Not recommended for critical use.

PROCESSING

You can have your film processed by Kodak or another processing lab by returning the film to your photo dealer, or by mailing it directly with the appropriate prepaid processing mailer. Your dealer can also order duplicate slides, color prints, or enlargements from your slides.

To process the film yourself, use the.KODAK HOBBY-PAC™ Color Slide Kit or KODAK EKTACHROME Film Processing Kit, Process E-6, or equivalent, sold by photo dealers.

DEFINITION	Graininess	Resolving Power	Sharpness
	Very Fine	High 125 lines per mm	Very High

KODAK EKTACHROME 100 Film (Daylight)

For Color Slides

When you want color slides, this is an excellent film to use for general, all around photography. This film features outstanding color reproduction—excellent highlight detail, superb flesh tones, and accurately recorded neutrals, such as those in open shade conditions. EKTACHROME 100 Film's generous speed of ISO 100 enhances the film's exposure capabilities while producing admirable definition quality—very fine grain and very high sharpness. The film is color balanced for daylight or electronic flash.

The professional version of this film is named KODAK EKTACHROME 100 Professional Film (Daylight). See page 48.

Film Code Letter Designation: EN.

Film Code Number and Size Available: 5039—size 135-24 exposures, 135-36 exposures.

Storage and Handling: Protect unprocessed film from heat. Have your film processed promptly after exposure. Store your slides in a cool, dry place.

EXPOSURE

Speeds and Filter Recommendations:

Type of Light	Film Speed	Filter
DAYLIGHT	**ISO 100**	**None**
PHOTOLAMPS 3400 K	ISO 32	No. 80B
TUNGSTEN 3200 K	ISO 25	No. 80A

NOTE: If your camera has a built-in exposure meter that makes the reading through a filter used over the lens, see your camera manual for instructions on exposure with filters. Also, see page 119.

Daylight Exposure Table: For average subjects.

Shutter Speed 1/250 Second		Shutter Speed 1/125 Second				
Bright or Hazy Sun Distinct Shadows		**Weak Hazy Sun Soft Shadows**	**Cloudy Bright No Shadows**	**Heavy Overcast**	**Open Shade†**
On Light Sand or Snow	**Average Subjects**				
f/16	f/16*	f/11	f/8	f/5.6	f/5.6

*For frontlighted subjects. For backlighted close-up subjects use f/8 at 1/125 second.

†Subject shaded from the sun but lighted by a large area of sky.

Electronic Flash Guide Numbers: Use this table as a starting point in determining the correct guide number for electronic flash units rated in beam candlepower seconds (BCPS).

Divide the proper guide number by the flash-to-subject distance in feet to determine the f-number for average subjects.

Output of Unit—BCPS	350	500	700	1000	1400	2000	2800	4000	5600	8000
Guide Numbers*	40	50	60	70	85	100	120	140	170	200

*If your prints are consistently too blue, use a No. 81B filter and increase your exposure by 1/3 stop.

Reciprocity Characteristics: The following table gives the exposure compensation for different exposure times.

Exposure Time in Seconds						
1/10,000	1/1000	1/100	1/10	1	10	100
None No Filter	None No Filter	None No Filter	None No Filter	NR*	NR*	NR*

*Not recommended for critical use.

PROCESSING

You can have your film processed by Kodak or another processing lab by returning the film to your photo dealer, or by mailing it directly with the appropriate prepaid processing mailer. Your dealer can also order duplicate slides, color prints, or enlargements from your slides.

To process the film yourself, use the KODAK HOBBY-PAC™ Color Slide Kit or KODAK EKTACHROME Film Processing Kit, Process E-6, or equivalent, sold by photo dealers.

DEFINITION	Graininess	Resolving Power	Sharpness
	Very Fine	High 100 lines per mm	Very High

For Color Slides

A fast, versatile color slide film for photographing fast action, subjects that require good depth of field and high shutter speeds, some dimly lighted subjects, and for extending the distance range for flash pictures. EKTACHROME 200 Film combines extra speed with excellent definition characteristics—very fine grain and high sharpness. The film gives pleasing color quality with good separation between similar colors. It is designed for use with daylight or electronic flash. This is a great film to use when exposure requirements are demanding but not severe enough to require a high-speed film, such as for photographing subjects in daylight outdoors when conditions are less than optimum and you want to stop action or use a telephoto lens. Another use for EKTACHROME 200 Film is for existing-light subjects, such as performers illuminated by carbon-arc spotlights or indoor scenes illuminated by existing daylight. A beneficial feature is that with special processing, you can expose the film at speeds higher than its normal speed. The professional version of this film is called KODAK EKTACHROME 200 Professional Film (Daylight). See page 48.

Film Code Letter Designation: ED.

Film Code Number and Size Available: 5076—size 135-24 exposures, 135-36 exposures.

Storage and Handling: Protect unprocessed film from heat. Have your film processed promptly after exposure. Store your slides in a cool, dry place.

EXPOSURE

Speeds and Filter Recommendations:

Type of Light	Film Speed	Filter
DAYLIGHT	ISO 200	None
PHOTOLAMPS 3400 K	ISO 64	No. 80B
TUNGSTEN 3200 K	ISO 50	No. 80A

NOTE: If your camera has a built-in exposure meter that makes the reading through a filter used over the lens, see your camera manual for instructions on exposure with filters. Also, see page 119.

Daylight Exposure Table—ISO 200: For average subjects. Exposure recommendations are for cameras with focal-plane shutters. For leaf-type shutters, see explanation below table.

Shutter Speed 1/500 Second*		Shutter Speed 1/250 Second*				
Bright or Hazy Sun Distinct Shadows		Weak Hazy Sun Soft Shadows	Cloudy Bright No Shadows	Heavy Overcast	Open Shade‡
On Light Sand or Snow	Average Subjects				
f/16	f/16†	f/11	f/8	f/5.6	f/5.6

*When using a camera with a leaf-type shutter under lighting conditions that require high shutter speeds and medium or small lens openings (lens openings beginning about midway on your camera lens-opening scale), reduce exposure as follows: At 1/250 second, use a lens opening 1/2 stop smaller than indicated; at 1/500 second, use a lens opening 1 stop smaller than indicated.

†For frontlighted subjects. For backlighted close-up subjects use f/8 at 1/250 second.

‡Subject shaded from the sun but lighted by a large area of sky.

Electronic Flash Guide Numbers—ISO 200: Use this table as a starting point in determining the correct guide number for electronic flash units rated in beam candlepower seconds (BCPS). Divide the proper guide number by the flash-to-subject distance in feet to determine the f-number for average subjects.

Output of Unit—BCPS	350	500	700	1000	1400	2000	2800	4000	5600	8000
Guide Numbers*	60	70	85	100	120	140	170	200	240	280

*If your slides are consistently too blue, use a No. 81B filter and increase your exposure by 1/3 stop.

D 18

Existing-Light Exposure Table—ISO 200: Use an exposure meter or a camera with built-in meter if you have one. For cameras without working exposure meters or for scenes that are difficult to meter, try the settings suggested in the table. These exposures are *guides*; for more assurance, bracket your exposures 1 stop on each side of the suggested exposure.

Picture Subject	Shutter Speed	Lens Opening
Skylines—10 minutes after sunset	1/60	f/4
Interiors with Bright Fluorescent Light*	1/30	f/4
Ice Shows, Circuses— Spotlighted acts (carbon arc)	1/125	f/2.8
Brightly Lighted Downtown Street Scenes at Night	1/30	f/2.8
Brightly Lighted Nightclub or Theatre Districts at Night— Las Vegas or Times Square Store Window Displays at Night	1/30	f/4

*May require correction filters for optimum results. See page 58. Use exposure times longer than 1/60 second.

Picture Subject	Shutter Speed	Lens Opening
Neon and Other Lighted Signs at Night	1/60	f/4
Floodlighted Buildings, Fountains, Monuments	1/2†	f/4
Christmas Lighting, Trees— Indoors and outdoors at night	1†	f/5.6
Fairs, Amusement Parks at Night	1/30	f/2
Night Football, Soccer, Baseball, Racetracks	1/60	f/2.8

†Use a camera support for exposure times longer than 1/30 second.

▢ Tungsten light produces yellow-red color rendition.

Reciprocity Characteristics: The following table gives the exposure compensation for different exposure times.

Exposure Time in Seconds						
1/10,000	1/1000	1/100	1/10	1	10	100
None No Filter	None No Filter	None No Filter	None No Filter	+ 1/2 stop No Filter	NR*	NR*

*Not recommended for critical use.

PROCESSING

You can have your film processed by Kodak or another processing lab by returning the film to your photo dealer, or by mailing it directly with the appropriate prepaid processing mailer. Your dealer can also order duplicate slides, color prints, or enlargements from your slides.

Special Processing for Increased Film Speed: You can increase the effective speed of this film 2 times to ISO 400 when you order special processing by Kodak. Use the KODAK Special Processing Envelope, ESP-1, sold by photo dealers. The cost of the ESP-1 Envelope is in addition to the regular charge for processing

KODAK EKTACHROME Film. Follow the instructions and exposure recommendations included with the envelope. Other labs may process this film to various film speeds. This special processing service is not available from Kodak in most countries outside the United States.

You Can Process the Film Yourself: Use the KODAK HOBBY-PAC™ Color Slide Kit or KODAK EKTACHROME Film Processing Kit, Process E-6, or equivalent, sold by photo dealers. By changing the first development time, you can change the speed of the film to any of a variety of film speeds. See page 67.

DEFINITION

Graininess	Resolving Power	Sharpness
Very Fine	High 125 lines per mm	High

For Color Slides

A high-speed color slide film for photographing dimly lighted subjects, such as those in existing light; fast action; and subjects that require both good depth of field and high shutter speeds. It lets you take flash pictures at greater distances than other Kodak color slide films with less speed. The film is color-balanced for daylight or electronic flash. You can also use this film for photographing performers illuminated by carbon-arc spotlights, and the film is excellent for indoor scenes illuminated by existing daylight.

EKTACHROME 400 Film has fine grain in addition to its high speed of ISO 400. A versatile feature of this film is the fine results you can obtain with special processing to achieve a film speed of ISO 800. The film can also be processed to various other speeds.

Film Code Letter Designation: EL.

Film Code Numbers and Sizes Available: 5074—size 135-24 exposures, 135-36 exposures; 6074—size 120.

Storage and Handling: Protect unprocessed film from heat. Load and unload camera in subdued light. Have your film processed promptly after exposure. Store your slides in a cool, dry place.

EXPOSURE

Speeds and Filter Recommendations:

Type of Light	Film Speed	Filter
DAYLIGHT	**ISO 400**	**None**
PHOTOLAMPS 3400 K	ISO 125	No. 80B
TUNGSTEN 3200 K	ISO 100	No. 80A

NOTE: If your camera has a built-in exposure meter that makes the reading through a filter used over the lens, see your camera manual for instructions on exposure with filters. Also, see page 119.

Daylight Exposure Table—ISO 400: For average subjects. Exposure recommendations are for cameras with focal-plane shutters. For leaf-type shutters, see explanation below table.

Shutter Speed 1/1000 Second		Shutter Speed 1/500 Second*				
Bright or Hazy Sun Distinct Shadows		Weak Hazy Sun Soft Shadows	Cloudy Bright No Shadows	Heavy Overcast	Open Shade‡
On Light Sand or Snow	Average Subjects				
f/16	f/16†	f/11	f/8	f/5.6	f/5.6

*When using a camera with a leaf-type shutter under lighting conditions that require high shutter speeds and medium or small lens openings (lens openings beginning about midway on your camera lens-opening scale), reduce exposure as follows: At 1/500 second, use a lens opening 1 stop smaller than indicated. If you set your shutter at 1/250 second, use a lens opening 1/2 stop smaller than the intended exposure.

†For frontlighted subjects. For backlighted close-up subjects use f/8 at 1/500 second.
‡Subject shaded from the sun but lighted by a large area of sky.

Electronic Flash Guide Numbers—ISO 400:

Use this table as a starting point in determining the correct guide number for electronic flash units rated in beam candlepower seconds (BCPS). Divide the proper guide number by the flash-to-subject distance in feet to determine the f-number for average subjects.

Output of Unit—BCPS	350	500	700	1000	1400	2000	2800	4000	5600	8000
Guide Numbers*	85	100	120	140	170	200	240	280	340	400

*If your slides are consistently too blue, use a No. 81B filter and increase your exposure by 1/3 stop.

Existing-Light Exposure Table—ISO 400:

Use an exposure meter or a camera with built-in meter if you have one. For cameras without working exposure meters or for scenes that are difficult to meter, try the settings suggested in the table. These exposures are *guides*; for more assurance, bracket your exposures 1 stop on each side of the suggested exposure.

Picture Subject	Shutter Speed	Lens Opening
Skylines—10 minutes after sunset	1/60	f/5.6
Distant View of City Skyline at Night	1*	f/2.8
Interiors with Bright Fluorescent Light†	1/60	f/4
Ice Shows, Circuses— Spotlighted acts (carbon arc)	1/250	f/2.8
Brightly Lighted Downtown Street Scenes at Night	1/60	f/2.8
Brightly Lighted Nightclub or Theatre Districts at Night— Las Vegas or Times Square Store Window Displays at Night	1/60	f/4

*Use a camera support for exposure times longer than 1/30 second.

Picture Subject	Shutter Speed	Lens Opening
Neon and Other Lighted Signs at Night	1/125	f/4
Floodlighted Buildings, Fountains, Monuments	1/15*	f/2
Christmas Lighting, Trees— Indoors and outdoors at night	1/15*	f/2
Fairs, Amusement Parks at Night	1/30	f/2.8
Night Football, Soccer, Baseball, Racetracks	1/125	f/2.8
Stage Shows— Average lighting Bright lighting	1/60 1/125	f/2.8 f/4

†May require correction filters for optimum results. See page 58. Use exposure times longer than 1/60 second.

⬜ Tungsten light produces yellow-red color rendition.

Reciprocity Characteristics: The following table gives the exposure compensation for different exposure times. The exposure increase includes the adjustment for the filter indicated.

Exposure Time in Seconds						
1/10,000	1/1000	1/100	1/10	1	10	100
None No Filter	None No Filter	None No Filter	None No Filter	+ ½ stop No Filter	+ 1½ stops CC10C	+ 2½ stops CC10C

PROCESSING

You can have your film processed by Kodak or another processing lab by returning the film to your photo dealer, or by mailing it directly with the appropriate prepaid processing mailer. Your dealer can also order duplicate slides, color prints, or enlargements from your slides.

Special Processing for Increased Film Speed: You can increase the effective speed of this film 2 times to ISO 800 when you order special processing by Kodak. Use the KODAK Special Processing Envelope, ESP-1, sold by photo dealers. The cost of the ESP-1 Envelope is in addition to the regular charge for KODAK EKTACHROME Film processing. Follow the instructions and exposure recommendations included with the envelope. Other labs may process this film to various film speeds. This special processing service is not available from Kodak in most countries outside the United States.

You Can Process the Film Yourself: Use the KODAK HOBBY-PAC™ Color Slide Kit or KODAK EKTACHROME Film Processing Kit, Process E-6, or equivalent, sold by photo dealers. By changing the first development time, you can change the speed of the film to any of a variety of film speeds up to ISO 1600. See page 67.

DEFINITION

Graininess	Resolving Power	Sharpness
Fine	Medium 80 lines per mm	High

For Color Slides

This film is an excellent choice whenever you require maximum speed in a color slide film. The film's extraordinary high speed is extremely useful for low-light level existing-light photography, for action or sports photography in poor light, for photographing with telephoto lenses which require high shutter speeds, or for increasing depth of field with small lens openings under adverse lighting conditions. In addition P800/1600 film extends the distance range for taking flash pictures farther than any other Kodak color slide film.

EKTACHROME P800/1600 Film is specifically designed for push processing to attain its very high speeds. It produces the best picture quality at EI 800 or EI 1600; however, you can obtain acceptable results with some loss of quality at EI 3200 or EI 400, depending on your needs, with appropriate adjustments in development time when the film is processed. Exposing the film at EI 400 requires the use of a KODAK Color Compensating Filter CC10Y to avoid a bluish color balance.

EKTACHROME P800/1600 Film's color reproduction is very good; it distinguishes well between similar colors. P800/1600 film is color balanced for daylight or electronic flash, and is designed for optimum color balance for quality pictorial results at EI 800 or EI 1600. Color rendition is also very good in slides of scenes illuminated by carbon-arc spotlights. The film has high sharpness and adequate graininess characteristics.

Film Code Letter Designation: EES.

Film Code Number and Size Available: 5020—size 135-36 exposures.

Storage and Handling: Keep unexposed film in a refrigerator at 55°F (13°C) or lower in the original sealed package. Allow film to warm up to room temperature before opening package to avoid moisture condensation on film surfaces. Load and unload camera in subdued light. Have your film processed promptly after exposure. Store your slides in a cool, dry place.

EXPOSURE

Speeds and Filter Recommendations:

Type of Light	Film Speed		Filter
	Push 1	Push 2	
DAYLIGHT	EI 800	EI 1600	None
PHOTOLAMPS 3400 K	EI 250	EI 500	No. 80B
TUNGSTEN 3200 K	EI 200	EI 400	No. 80A

NOTE: If your camera has a built-in exposure meter that makes the reading through a filter used over the lens, see your camera manual for instructions on exposure with filters. Also, see page 119.

Daylight Exposure Table: For average subjects. Exposure recommendations are for cameras with focal-plane shutters. For leaf-type shutters, see explanation below table.

Exposure Index	Shutter Speed 1/1000 Second						
	Bright or Hazy Sun Distinct Shadows		Weak Hazy Sun Soft Shadows	Cloudy Bright No Shadows	Heavy Overcast	Open Shade†
	On Light Sand or Snow	Average Subjects				
EI 800	f/22‡	f/16*	f/11	f/8	f/5.6	f/5.6
EI 1600	f/32‡	f/22*‡	f/16	f/11	f/8	f/8

*For frontlighted subjects. For backlighted close-up subjects use f/8 for EI 800 and f/11 for EI 1600 at 1/1000 second.
†Subject shaded from the sun but lighted by a large area of sky.
‡The smaller lens openings recommended in the table may not be available on various lenses. If not, use a higher shutter speed, or an appropriate neutral density filter, or expose and process the film to a slower speed.

Appropriate neutral density filters sold by photo dealers are: ND 0.3 filter—use 1 stop larger lens opening; ND 0.6 filter—use 2 stops larger lens opening; ND 0.9 filter—use 3 stops larger lens opening.
Note: Most cameras with leaf shutters will overexpose many of the conditions in the daylight exposure table because of shutter efficiency at small lens openings, a minimum shutter speed of 1/500 second, and a minimum lens opening of f/16.

Electronic Flash Guide Numbers: Use this table as a starting point in determining the correct guide number for electronic flash units rated in beam candlepower seconds (BCPS). Divide the proper guide number by the flash-to-subject distance in feet to determine the f-number for average subjects.

Output of Unit—BCPS	350	500	700	1000	1400	2000	2800	4000	5600	8000
Guide Numbers* EI 800	120	140	170	200	240	280	330	400	470	560
Guide Numbers* EI 1600	170	200	240	280	340	400	480	560	670	800

*If your slides are consistently too blue, use a No. 81B filter and increase your exposure by 1/3 stop.

Existing-Light Exposure Table: Use an exposure meter or a camera with built-in meter if you have one. For cameras without working exposure meters or for scenes that are difficult to meter, try the settings suggested in the table. These exposures are *guides*; for more assurance, bracket your exposures 1 stop on each side of the suggested exposure.

Picture Subject	Shutter Speed and Lens Opening	
	EI 800	EI 1600
Skylines—10 minutes after sunset	1/125 f/5.6	1/125 f/8
Distant View of City Skyline at Night	1* f/4	1* f/5.6
Interiors with Bright Fluorescent Light†	1/60 f/5.6	1/60 f/8
Ice Shows, Circuses— Spotlighted acts (carbon arc)	1/250 f/4	1/250 f/5.6
Brightly Lighted Downtown Street Scenes at Night	1/60 f/4	1/125 f/4
Brightly Lighted Nightclub or Theatre Districts at Night— Las Vegas or Times Square Store Window Displays at Night	1/125 f/4	1/125 f/5.6

*Use a camera support for exposure times longer than 1/30 second.

▭ Tungsten light produces yellow-red color rendition.

Picture Subject	Shutter Speed and Lens Opening	
	EI 800	EI 1600
Neon and Other Lighted Signs at Night	1/125 f/5.6	1/125 f/8
Floodlighted Buildings, Fountains, Monuments	1/30 f/2	1/30 f/2.8
Christmas Lighting, Trees— Indoors and outdoors at night	1/30 f/2	1/30 f/2.8
Fairs, Amusement Parks at Night	1/60 f/2.8	1/60 f/4
Night Football, Soccer, Baseball, Racetracks	1/250 f/2.8	1/250 f/4
Stage Shows— Average lighting	1/125 f/2.8	1/125 f/4
Bright lighting	1/250 f/4	1/250 f/5.6

†May require correction filters for optimum results. See page 58. Use exposure times longer than 1/60 second.

Reciprocity Characteristics: The following table gives the exposure compensation for different exposure times.

Exposure Time in Seconds						
1/10,000	1/1000	1/100	1/10	1	10	100
None No Filter	None No Filter	None No Filter	None No Filter	NR*	NR*	NR*

*Not recommended for critical use.

PROCESSING

This film requires special processing, called push processing, to obtain its high speeds. The film magazine has a writable surface so that you can circle the speed you used to expose the film in order to obtain correct processing. The speeds printed on the magazine are: 400 E-6; 800 P1; 1600 P2; 3200 P3.

You can have your film processed by Kodak or another processing lab by returning the film to your photo dealer. When you expose the film at EI 800, which requires Push 1 processing, you can choose to mail it directly to a Kodak lab in a KODAK Processing Mailer for prepaid processing together with a KODAK Special Processing Envelope, ESP-1. If you expose the film at EI 1600, which requires Push 2 processing, see your photo dealer for push processing by Kodak to this speed. Kodak does not process EKTACHROME P800/1600 Film to EI 3200, which requires Push 3 processing. See your photo dealer for push processing to EI 3200 by other processing labs. If you want your film processed to EI 400, have the film processed normally without push processing by Kodak or another lab.

Your dealer can also order duplicate slides, color prints, or enlargements from your slides.

You Can Process the Film Yourself: Use the KODAK HOBBY-PAC™ Color Slide Kit or KODAK EKTACHROME Film Processing Kit, Process E-6, or equivalent, sold by photo dealers. By changing the first development time, you can change the speed of the film to any of a variety of film speeds up to EI 3200. See page 67. The process is referred to as Process E-6P when the film is push processed in the regular processing chemicals, such as those recommended here.

	Film Speed	Graininess	Resolving Power	Sharpness
DEFINITION	EI 800	Medium	Medium 80 lines per mm	High
	EI 1600	Moderately Course	Medium 63 lines per mm	High

For Color Slides

A fast color slide film for photographing subjects lighted by tungsten light. EKTACHROME 160 Film (Tungsten) features excellent color reproduction, very fine grain, and high sharpness together with extra film speed. It's designed for use with 3200 K tungsten lamps, but it's excellent for existing tungsten light, such as the light from household lamps and other general-purpose tungsten lamps. Outdoors at night you can use this film for pictures of illuminated buildings, fountains, statues, signs, street scenes, and similar subjects. You can take pictures in daylight or with electronic flash when you use a No. 85B filter over your camera lens. A versatile feature is that with special processing, you can expose the film at speeds higher than its normal speed. KODAK EKTACHROME 160 Professional Film (Tungsten) is also available. See page 48.

Film Code Letter Designation: ET.

Film Code Number and Size Available: 5077—size 135-24 exposures, 135-36 exposures.

Storage and Handling: Protect unprocessed film from heat. Have your film processed promptly after exposure. Store your slides in a cool, dry place.

EXPOSURE

Speeds and Filter Recommendations:

Type of Light	Film Speed	Filter
TUNGSTEN 3200 K	ISO 160	None
PHOTOLAMPS 3400 K	ISO 125	No. 81A
DAYLIGHT	ISO 100	No. 85B

NOTE: If your camera has a built-in exposure meter that makes the reCading through a filter used over the lens, see your camera manual for instructions on exposure with filters. Also, see page 119.

Tungsten Lamps 3200 K—ISO 160: The following table is based on the use of two reflector-type photolamps 3200 K. Use one lamp as a fill-in light close to the camera at lens level; the other as the main light on the opposite side of the camera, 2 to 4 feet (0.6 to 1.2 metres) higher, and at a 45-degree angle from the camera-subject axis.

EXPOSURE TABLE FOR TUNGSTEN LAMPS 3200 K						
Lamp-to-Subject Distance in Feet (Metres) • Set Shutter Speed at 1/60 Second						
Lamp	Lens Opening	f/8	f/5.6	f/4	f/2.8	
General Electric EAL 500 watts (reflector type)	Main Light	4 (1.2 m)	5½ (1.7 m)	8 (2.4 m)	11 (3.4 m)	
	Fill-in Light	5½ (1.7 m)	8 (2.4 m)	11 (3.4 m)	15½ (4.7 m)	
Sylvania DXH Type R-32, 375 watts (reflector type)	Main Light	5 (1.5 m)	7 (2.1 m)	10 (3 m)	13½ (4.1 m)	
	Fill-in Light	7 (2.1 m)	10 (3 m)	13½ (4.1 m)	20 (6 m)	

NOTE: Use these camera settings as guides only. The lamp-to-subject distances give a lighting ratio of about 3:1. For a 2:1 ratio, place the fill-in light at the same distance from the subject as the main light and use a lens opening 1/2 stop smaller. This table is based on the use of new lamps. After the lamps have burned for 1 hour, use a lens opening 1/2 stop larger; after 2 hours, use a lens opening 1 stop larger.

Daylight Exposure Table—ISO 100: For average subjects. *Use a No.85B filter.*

Shutter Speed 1/250 Second		Shutter Speed 1/125 Second				
Bright or Hazy Sun Distinct Shadows		Weak Hazy Sun Soft Shadows	Cloudy Bright No Shadows	Heavy Overcast	Open Shade†	
On Light Sand or Snow	Average Subjects					
f/16	f/16*	f/11	f/8	f/5.6	f/5.6	

*For frontlighted subjects. For backlighted close-up subjects use f/8 at 1/125 second. †Subject shaded from the sun but lighted by a large area of sky.

Electronic Flash Guide Numbers: *Use a No. 85B filter.* This table is intended as a starting point in determining the correct guide number for electronic flash units rated in beam candlepower seconds (BCPS). Divide the proper guide number by the flash-to-subject distance in feet to determine the f-number for average subjects.

Output of Unit—BCPS	350	500	700	1000	1400	2000	2800	4000	5600	8000
Guide Numbers	40	50	60	70	85	100	120	140	170	200

D 24

Existing-Light Exposure Table—ISO 160:
Use an exposure meter or a camera with built-in meter if you have one. For cameras without working exposure meters or for scenes that are difficult to meter, try the settings suggested in the table. These exposures are *guides*; for more assurance, bracket your exposures 1 stop on each side of the suggested exposure.

Picture Subject	Shutter Speed	Lens Opening
Home Interiors at Night—		
Areas with average light	1/15*	f/2
Areas with bright light	1/30	f/2
Candlelighted Close-Ups	1/8*	f/2
Indoor, Outdoor Christmas Lighting at Night	1*	f/5.6
Brightly Lighted Downtown Street Scenes at Night	1/30	f/2.8
Brightly Lighted Theatre Districts—Las Vegas or Times Square	1/30	f/4
Neon Signs, Other Lighted Signs	1/60	f/4
Store Windows at Night	1/30	f/4
Floodlighted Buildings, Fountains, Monuments	1/2*	f/4
Distant View of City Skyline at Night	1*	f/2
Fairs, Amusement Parks	1/30	f/2

*Use a camera support for exposure times longer than 1/30 second.

Picture Subject	Shutter Speed	Lens Opening
Aerial Fireworks Displays— Keep camera shutter open on BULB for several bursts	BULB*	f/11
Night Football, Soccer, Baseball, Racetracks†	1/60	f/2.8
Basketball, Hockey, Bowling	1/60	f/2
Boxing, Wrestling	1/125	f/2
Stage Shows—		
Average lighting	1/30	f/2.8
Bright lighting	1/60	f/4
Circuses—Floodlighted acts	1/30	f/2.8
Ice Shows—Floodlighted acts	1/60	f/2.8
School—Stage and auditorium	1/15*	f/2
Swimming Pool—Indoors, tungsten lights above water	1/30	f/2
Church Interiors— Tungsten lights	1/15*	f/2

†When lighting at these events is provided by mercury-vapor lamps, you'll get better results by using Daylight film.

Reciprocity Characteristics: The following table gives the exposure and filter compensation for different exposure times. The exposure increase includes the adjustment for the filter indicated.

Exposure Time in Seconds						
1/10,000	1/1000	1/100	1/10	1	10	100
None CC025G	None CC05C	None No Filter	None No Filter	+ 1/2 stop CC025M	NR*	NR*

*Not recommended for critical use.

PROCESSING

You can have your film processed by Kodak or another processing lab by returning the film to your photo dealer, or by mailing it directly with the appropriate prepaid processing mailer. Your dealer can also order duplicate slides, color prints, or enlargements from your slides.

Special Processing for Increased Film Speed: You can increase the effective speed of this film 2 times to ISO 320 when you order special processing by Kodak. Use the KODAK Special Processing Envelope, ESP-1, sold by photo dealers. The cost of the ESP-1 Envelope is in addition to the regular charge for processing

KODAK EKTACHROME Film. Follow the instructions and exposure recommendations included with the envelope. Other labs may process this film to various film speeds. This special processing service is not available from Kodak in most countries outside the United States.

You Can Process the Film Yourself: Use the KODAK HOBBY-PAC™ Color Slide Kit or KODAK EKTACHROME Film Processing Kit, Process E-6, or equivalent, sold by photo dealers. By changing the first development time, you can change the speed of the film to any of a variety of film speeds. See page 67.

DEFINITION

Graininess	Resolving Power	Sharpness
Very Fine	High 125 lines per mm	High

For Color Slides

These films are for making duplicate color slides from original slides made on color slide films, such as KODACHROME or KODAK EKTACHROME Films. EKTACHROME Slide Duplicating Film 5071 is designed for slow exposure times with tungsten illumination 3200 K. EKTACHROME SE Duplicating Film SO-366 is intended for short exposure times with electronic flash. Both of the films can also be used with sunlight. These films produce excellent color slide duplicates. It's often difficult to distinguish between the duplicate and the original when appropriate filters are used during exposure. Since a duplicate slide, however, is a photograph of another photograph, there may be a slight reduction in photographic quality when critical quality standards are applied.

Film Code Number and Size Available:
5071—135-36 exposures; SO-366—135-36 exposures. Catalog Number for SO-366 Film: CAT NO. 159 0223.

Storage and Handling: Keep unexposed film in a refrigerator at 55°F (13°C) or lower in the original sealed package. Allow film to warm up to room temperature before opening package to avoid moisture condensation on film surfaces. Have your film processed promptly after exposure. Store your slides in a cool, dry place.

EXPOSURE

You can make duplicate slides by using a single-lens reflex camera with a through-the-lens exposure meter and a slide-duplicating attachment or slide-duplicating equipment. You can also use a contact printer. Using a diffused light source and a lens to transmit the image of the original onto the duplicating film offers the least difficulty with dust and scratches.

The 5071 film is primarily for use at exposure times of approximately 1 second with 3200 K tungsten illumination, such as tungsten photo enlarger lamps or tungsten halogen lamps. The SO-366 film is primarily for use at a short exposure time of 1/1000 second with electronic flash. In addition you can use both films with sunlight at exposure times of 1 second with the 5071 film and of 1/10 second with the SO-366 film. Exposure with fluorescent lamps is not recommended.

Camera Exposure: For exposure meters marked for ISO or ASA speeds or Exposure Indexes. Use these speed ranges as starting points for determining proper exposure. The speed for a specific film emulsion is provided with the film.

Type of Light	Film Speed Range for Trial Exposures	Film
TUNGSTEN 3200 K	EI 3−32	5071*
ELECTRONIC FLASH	EI 3−32	SO-366
DAYLIGHT†	EI 3−32	5071*, SO-366†

*For an exposure time of 1 second. If the ISO/ASA speed dial on your camera or meter does not have these low-speed numbers on it, you can set the dial for a higher speed, such as 25, for example, and increase the exposure indicated on your exposure meter by 2 stops when the exposure index provided with the film is EI 6; or +1 stop for EI 12; or +3 stops for EI 3.
†Set a piece of white paper on the ground in sunlight and point your camera with a slide-copying attachment at the paper. Make the meter reading of the original slide in the attachment, not of the white paper directly.
‡For an exposure time of 1/10 second.
  These film speed ranges are for use with exposure meter readings made through the filters given on the film carton and in the table at the top of page D 27. Make exposure tests to determine the best exposure index to use with your equipment and duplicating technique. You can do this by making an exposure series starting with a meter reading of EI 32, and increasing exposure using 1/3 stop increments to EI 3. The exposure index scale for this range is: EI 32, 25, 20, 16, 12, 10, 8, 6, 5, 4, and 3. With SO-366 film and electronic flash, make exposure tests by varying the lens opening in 1/2-stop increments, or by varying the flash-to-slide distance to determine the best lens opening and distance to use.
  To avoid small changes in color balance once you have determined a satisfactory exposure time and filter pack, keep the exposure time constant and vary the lens opening to change exposure. This is necessary for original slides that are darker or lighter than normal.

Filter Recommendations: Use these filter packs as starting points for camera exposures.

KODAK Film Original to be Duplicated	Use the Filter Pack Data Given on the Film Carton Plus the Filter Data Listed in the Table			
	Light Source			
	5071 Film		SO-366 Film	
	Tungsten 3200 K§	Sunlight§	Electronic Flash**	Sunlight††
EKTACHROME 64*, 100* 160*, 200*, 400 50 Professional, P800/1600 Professional EKTACHROME Slide Duplicating 5071, SE Duplicating SO-366, KODACHROME II†, KODACHROME-X†	+ No. 2B	+ No. 85B + No. 2B	+ No. 2B	+10R + 10Y + No. 2B
EKTACHROME-X† High Speed EKTACHROME† EKTACHROME Infrared	−15C + No. 2B	−15C + No. 85B + No. 2B	−15C + No 2B	−25C + 10Y + No. 2B
KODACHROME 25‡, 40, 64‡	+10C + No. 2B	+10C + No. 85B + No. 2B	+10C + No. 2B	+10Y + No. 2B

*Also EKTACHROME Professional Films, Process E-6.
†Discontinued Kodak films.
‡Also KODACHROME Professional Films.
§For 1-second exposure.
**If you use an automatic electronic flash unit, set it on manual.
††For 1/10-second exposure.
Note: Except for the No. 2B and No. 85B filters, the filters in the table are KODAK Color Compensating Filters, CC, or KODAK Color Printing Filters, CP, sold by photo dealers. CC filters are for use in the image-forming light, such as between the camera lens and the original slide, and CP filters are for use only in nonimage-forming light, such as between the light source and the original slide. You can also use CC filters in nonimage-forming light instead of CP filters. With dichroic filters some adjustment in filtration may be required.

It's best to place the filters between the slide and light source. Since the filter data are starting points, take test pictures with the filters listed and with filters of all six colors that vary at least plus and minus CC10 from the starting point filters. Bracket your exposures.

Adjusting the Filter Pack: To evaluate color balance, project the duplicate slides in a darkened room or compare them with the original slides on an illuminator. If corrections are necessary, determine what color is in excess. You can do this by viewing the duplicates through various CC or CP filters. When judging the color, look at the middletones instead of the highlights or shadows. To adjust the filter pack, you can either remove a filter of the color of the overall hue that's in excess or add a filter that's complementary to the overall hue.

Overall color balance of original	Subtract these filters or—	Add these filters
Yellow	Yellow	Magenta + Cyan, (or Blue)
Magenta	Magenta	Yellow + Cyan, (or Green)
Cyan	Cyan	Yellow + Magenta, (or Red)
Blue	Magenta + Cyan, (or Blue)	Yellow
Green	Yellow + Cyan, (or Green)	Magenta
Red	Yellow + Magenta, (or Red)	Cyan

Keep the number of filters in the filter pack to a minimum by removing filters from the pack whenever possible. For example, if a slide is too red, remove yellow and magenta (or red) filters rather than add a cyan filter. If all three subtractive colors—cyan, magenta, and yellow— are in the filter pack, they form neutral density which increases exposure time without making any correction in color rendition. You should eliminate neutral density by removing the color that has the lowest value and reducing the other two colors by the same amount. For example, if the pack contains 40C + 40M + 20Y, remove 20 filtration from all three filters.

Filter Pack	40 C	+ 40M	+ 20Y	
Subtract	20 C	+ 20M	+ 20Y	Removes 0.20 neutral density.
Minimum Filter Pack	20 C	+ 20M		

You can reduce the 20C + 20M filters further to a 20B filter which is the equivalent. When you change the filter pack, you'll have to adjust the camera exposure settings due to the difference in light absorption of the filters and the number of filter surfaces. If a primary color—red, green, or blue—is in the filter pack with other filters and you want to determine if neutral density would be present when you change the filter pack, convert the primary color to its equivalents in the subtractive colors for the calculation. For example, 40G = 40C + 40Y.

Adjustment for Emulsion Number Changes: Each quantity of film has an emulsion number which is printed on the film carton. When you change to a new film emulsion number, an appreciable change in both exposure and filter pack may be necessary. To help you determine the best filter pack to use with a new roll of film with a different emulsion number, filter data is printed on the film carton. The filter data is expressed in cyan and yellow filtration.

If you haven't used the film before, refer to the filter data in the table at the top of page D 27 and on the film carton for a starting filter pack.

When you change to a new emulsion number, subtract the data on the old film carton from the data on the new film carton. Remember that in subtracting, a minus value is equivalent to adding. To subtract, change the signs of the data subtrahend from plus to minus or from minus to plus, and then add. Apply the difference to the filter pack you were using. For example:

Exposure data on new film carton.	+ 15C + 05Y
Exposure data on old film carton.	+ 05C + 15Y Subtract
Change in filter pack.	+ 10C − 10Y

The difference in filter data from the old emulsion to the new one applies regardless of the filter pack you were using for the old emulsion. Assume with the old emulsion that you used a filter pack of CC30C plus CC50Y. Change the filter pack by adding CC10C (or by subtracting CC10R) and subtracting CC10Y (or adding CC10B). For example:

Used for old emulsion.	+ CC30C + CC50Y
Change for new emulsion.	Add + CC10C − CC10Y
Use for new emulsion.	+ CC40C + CC40Y

If there is not enough cyan or yellow filtration in the pack to remove, add the complementary filter. Since you may have to alter exposure when you use a new emulsion, you can either change the lens opening or you can change the exposure time for a small change in exposure of ± 1 stop or less. An additional adjustment in filtration or exposure may be necessary when you change exposure time. For a large change in exposure, change just the aperture.

DEFINITION*		
Graininess	**Resolving Power**	**Sharpness**
Extremely Fine	High 125 lines per mm	Very High

*These classifications apply to EKTACHROME Slide and EKTACHROME SE Duplicating Films only. The definition quality of duplicate slides will be a function of the original slides being duplicated and the quality of the duplicating equipment.

PROCESSING

You can have your film processed by Kodak or another processing lab by returning the film to your photo dealer, or by mailing it directly with the appropriate prepaid processing mailer. Your dealer can also order duplicate slides, color prints, or enlargements from your slides.

You Can Process the Film Yourself: Use the KODAK HOBBY-PAC™ Color Slide Kit or KODAK EKTACHROME Film Processing Kit, Process E-6, or equivalent, sold by photo dealers.

Selecting a KODAK Developer for Black-and-White Film— Key Properties

KODAK Developer

D-76 Long a favorite of pictorialists, it is well known for superior performance. This developer produces full emulsion speed and maximum shadow detail with normal contrast, and produces fine grain with a wide selection of black-and-white films. It produces a long density scale, and its excellent development latitude permits push processing with relatively low fog. If you want to use one developer for all types of roll film, we highly recommend KODAK Developer D-76. For greater sharpness, but with a slight sacrifice in graininess, you can dilute the developer 1:1. You can use KODAK Replenisher D-76R, sold by photo dealers, to extend the useful life of the developer. Instructions are included with the developer and the replenisher.

HC-110 A highly active general purpose developer for rapid processing of most black-and-white films. HC-110 Developer produces full film speed, maximum shadow detail, and long tonal range. It gives low fog level with push processing. This developer yields sharp images and fine grain with a large variety of black-and-white films. Both developer and replenisher are conveniently supplied in highly concentrated liquid form in plastic bottles which makes them easy to mix and use. Dilution A gives short development times; Dilution B is for longer development times which yield better development uniformity.

HOBBY-PAC™ Black-and-White Film Developer Provides photographic results similar to those produced by KODAK HC-110 Developer (Dilution B). KODAK HOBBY-PAC Black-and-White Film Developer is part of the KODAK HOBBY-PAC Black-and-White Film Processing Kit which contains developer, stop bath, and fix in liquid concentrate form in easy-to-use snip-and-pour foil packets. The developer is also available separately.

DK-50 A popular general-purpose developer which works well with or without dilution. Moderately fast acting, it produces crisp, clean negatives with good highlight detail and medium grain. You can use KODAK Replenisher DK-50R to extend the capacity of the developer.

MICRODOL-X An excellent fine-grain developer which is designed to produce low graininess and high sharpness with minimum speed loss. This developer is particularly suited for developing small negatives intended for making big enlargements. It is clean-working and has a long life. You can obtain even greater image sharpness by using MICRODOL-X Developer diluted 1:3, but with a slight increase in graininess. You can purchase this developer in either powder or liquid form. A powder replenisher is also available to extend the developer's capacity.

TECHNIDOL Liquid Produced specifically for KODAK Technical Pan Film 2415 and 6415 for pictorial photography. The developer provides pictorial contrast with an inherently high-contrast film while retaining useful film speed. It enhances edge effects and apparent sharpness. TECHNIDOL Liquid Developer produces micro-fine grain, extremely high resolving power—320 lines per mm resolution, and extremely high sharpness with Technical Pan Film. The developer/film combination features 25X and greater enlargements with little apparent grain. The developer is easy to mix in its convenient liquid form, and is recommended for both 135 and 120 size Technical Pan Film.

TECHNIDOL LC This developer has characteristics similar to KODAK TECHNIDOL Liquid Developer and is used for the same pictorial purposes with KODAK Technical Pan Film 2415. TECHNIDOL LC Developer is recommended for the 135 size film only. The developer and film provide extremely fine grain, extremely high resolving power—320 lines per mm resolution, and extremely high sharpness. TECHNIDOL LC Developer is supplied in powder form. It is intended for mixing just prior to use, used once, and then discarded.

D-19 A high-capacity, rapid-working developer yielding brilliant, high-contrast negatives. It is especially suited to copying and technical applications where higher-than-normal contrast is required.

DEKTOL Primarily a paper developer, DEKTOL Developer is also used for some high-contrast applications with specific films, such as KODAK Technical Pan Film. The developer is supplied in powder form.

For Black-and-White Prints

A medium-speed panchromatic film with extremely fine grain and very high sharpness. Its rich gradation and wide exposure latitude make it ideally suited to most picture-taking situations. It is an excellent choice among black-and-white films for general use in cartridge and 120-size cameras—from simple cameras to the most advanced models.

Film Code Letter Designation: VP.

Film Code Numbers and Sizes Available: 7042—size 110-12 exposures; 8041—size 126-12 exposures; 6041—size 120.

Storage and Handling: Protect unprocessed film from heat. Have your film processed promptly after exposure.

EXPOSURE

Daylight Exposure Table: For average subjects.

Speed: ISO 125

Shutter Speed 1/250 Second				Shutter Speed 1/125 Second		
Bright or Hazy Sun Distinct Shadows		Weak Hazy Sun Soft Shadows	Cloudy Bright No Shadows	Heavy Overcast	Open Shade†
On Light Sand or Snow	Average Subjects				
f/16	f/11*	f/8	f/8	f/5.6	f/5.6

*For frontlighted subjects. For backlighted close-up subjects use f/8 at 1/125 second.　　　†Subject shaded from the sun but lighted by a large area of sky.

Filter Factors: Increase the normal exposure by the filter factor in the table. However, if your camera has a built-in exposure meter that makes the reading through a filter used over the lens, see your camera manual for instructions on exposure with filters. Also, see page 119.

Filter	No. 6	No. 8	No. 15	No. 11	No. 25	No. 58	No. 47	Polarizing Screen
Daylight	1.5	2*	2.5	4	8	6	6	2.5
Tungsten	1.5	1.5	1.5	4*	5	6	12	2.5

*For correct gray-tone rendering of colored objects.

Electronic Flash Guide Numbers: Use this table as a starting point in determining the correct guide number for electronic flash units rated in beam candlepower seconds (BCPS).

Divide the proper guide number by the flash-to-subject distance in feet to determine the f-number for average subjects.

Output of Unit—BCPS	350	500	700	1000	1400	2000	2800	4000	5600	8000
Guide Numbers	45	55	65	80	95	110	130	160	190	220

Reciprocity Characteristics: The following table gives the exposure and development compensation for different exposure times.

Exposure Time in Seconds	Either		Change Developing Time by
	Increase Lens Opening by	Or Use Corrected Exposure Time in Seconds	
1/100,000	+1 stop	Use lens opening correction	+20 percent
1/10,000	+½ stop	Use lens opening correction	+15 percent
1/1000	None	No change	+10 percent
1/100	None	No change	None
1/10	None	No change	None
1	+1 stop	2	−10 percent
10	+2 stops	50	−20 percent
100	+3 stops	1200	−30 percent

Note: Make exposure corrections for long or short exposure times as indicated in the table. Make the development correction only if you want the whole roll of film processed for the corrected development time. If correcting the development is not practical because of significantly different exposure times used for different pictures on the roll, develop the film for the normal development time. Usually you can make the contrast correction for reciprocity effect by using higher- or lower-contrast photographic paper as necessary when you make the prints.

Processing Services: You can have your film developed and printed by Kodak or another processing lab by returning the film to your photo dealer. Your dealer can also order enlargements from your negatives from other labs.

Processing the Film Yourself: You can develop your film in your own darkroom by following the steps below.

Safelight: *Total darkness required.* However, when development is half completed, you can use a safelight at 4 feet (1.2 metres) for a *few* seconds. Equip the safelight with a KODAK 3 Safelight Filter (dark green), or equivalent, and a 15-watt bulb.

Developing Times are for small roll-film tanks with agitation for 5 seconds at 30-second intervals throughout development. See page 100 for method of agitation. The most widely used times and temperature are in heavy type. If your negatives are consistently too low in contrast, increase development time; if too high in contrast, decrease development time.

KODAK Packaged Developers	Developing Times in Minutes*				
	65°F (18°C)	68°F (20°C)	70°F (21°C)	72°F (22°C)	75°F (24°C)
D-76	8	**7**	5½	5	4½
D-76 (1:1)†	11	**9**	8	7	6
MICRODOL-X	10	**9**	8	7	6
MICRODOL-X (1:3)†	15	14	13	12	**11**
HC-110 (Dilution B)	6	**5**	4½	4	2
HOBBY-PAC™ Black-and-White Film Developer	6	**5**	4½	4	2

*Unsatisfactory uniformity may result with development times shorter than 5 minutes.

†For greater sharpness.

Rinse in KODAK Indicator Stop Bath, KODAK HOBBY-PAC™ Black-and-White Film and Paper Stop Bath, or KODAK Stop Bath SB-5, at 65 to 75°F (18 to 24°C), for 30 seconds with agitation. You can use a running-water rinse if an acid stop bath is not available.

Fix in KODAK Fixer, KODAK HOBBY-PAC™ Black-and-White Film and Paper Fixer, or KODAK Fixing Bath F-5 for 5 to 10 minutes, or KODAK Rapid Fixer or KODAFIX Solution for 2 to 4 minutes, at 65 to 75°F (18 to 24°C) with agitation.

Wash the film for 20 to 30 minutes in running water at 65 to 75°F (18 to 24°C). To minimize drying marks, treat the film in KODAK PHOTO-FLO Solution after washing, or wipe the surfaces carefully with a KODAK Photo Chamois or a soft viscose sponge.

Note: Keep temperatures of rinse, fix, and wash close to developer temperature.

Dry in a dust-free place.

Also, see pages 96–99.

DEFINITION

Graininess	Resolving Power	Sharpness	Degree of Enlargement Potential*
Extremely Fine	High 100 lines per mm	Very High	High

*For good-quality negatives.

For Black-and-White Prints

A general-purpose panchromatic film for 35 mm cameras that offers the optimum combination of medium speed, extremely fine grain, and excellent picture sharpness even at high degrees of enlargement. PLUS-X Pan Film's performance is superb, it produces high-quality photographs where you require fine detail, wide tonal range, and adequate speed for average or bright lighting conditions. It's ideally suited to most picture-taking situations. KODAK PLUS-X Pan Professional Film is supplied in 120 and 220 sizes. See page 83.

Film Code Letter Designation: PX.

Film Code Number and Size Available: 5062—size 135-24 exposures, 135-36 exposures.

Storage and Handling: Protect unprocessed film from heat. Have your film processed promptly after exposure.

EXPOSURE

Daylight Exposure Table: For average subjects.

Speed: ISO 125

Shutter Speed 1/250 Second			Shutter Speed 1/125 Second		
Bright or Hazy Sun Distinct Shadows		**Weak Hazy Sun Soft Shadows**	**Cloudy Bright No Shadows**	**Heavy Overcast**	**Open Shade†**
On Light Sand or Snow	**Average Subjects**				
f/16	f/11*	f/8	f/8	f/5.6	f/5.6

*For frontlighted subjects. For backlighted close-up subjects use f/8 at 1/125 second.

†Subject shaded from the sun but lighted by a large area of sky.

Filter Factors: Increase the normal exposure by the filter factor in the table. However, if your camera has a built-in exposure meter that makes the reading through a filter used over the lens, see your camera manual for instructions on exposure with filters. Also, see page 119.

Filter	No. 6	No. 8	No. 15	No. 11	No. 25	No. 58	No. 47	Polarizing Screen
Daylight	1.5	2*	2.5	4	6	8	6	2.5
Tungsten	1.2	1.5	1.5	4*	4	8	12	2.5

*For correct gray-tone rendering of colored objects.

Electronic Flash Guide Numbers: Use this table as a starting point in determining the correct guide number for electronic flash units rated in beam candlepower seconds (BCPS). Divide the proper guide number by the flash-to-subject distance in feet to determine the f-number for average subjects.

Output of Unit—BCPS	350	500	700	1000	1400	2000	2800	4000	5600	8000
Guide Numbers	45	55	65	80	95	110	130	160	190	220

Reciprocity Characteristics: The following table gives the exposure and development compensation for different exposure times.

Exposure Time in Seconds	Either		Change Developing Time by
	Increase Lens Opening by	**Or Use Corrected Exposure Time in Seconds**	
1/100,000	+1 stop	Use lens opening correction	+20 percent
1/10,000	+½ stop	Use lens opening correction	+15 percent
1/1000	None	No change	+10 percent
1/100	None	No change	None
1/10	None	No change	None
1	+1 stop	2	−10 percent
10	+2 stops	50	−20 percent
100	+3 stops	1200	−30 percent

Note: Make exposure corrections for long or short exposure times as indicated in the table. Make the development correction only if you want the whole roll of film processed for the corrected development time. If correcting the development is not practical because of significantly different exposure times used for different pictures on the roll, develop the film for the normal development time. Usually you can make the contrast correction for reciprocity effect by using higher- or lower-contrast photographic paper as necessary when you make the prints.

Processing Services: You can have your film developed and printed by Kodak or another processing lab by returning the film to your photo dealer. Your dealer can also order enlargements from your negatives from other labs.

Processing the Film Yourself: You can develop your film in your own darkroom by following the steps below.

Safelight: *Total darkness required.* However, when development is half completed, you can use a safelight at 4 feet (1.2 metres) for a *few* seconds. Equip the safelight with a KODAK 3 Safelight Filter (dark green), or equivalent, and a 15-watt bulb.

Developing Times are for small roll-film tanks with agitation for 5 seconds at 30-second intervals throughout development. See page 100 for method of agitation. The most widely used times and temperature are in heavy type. If your negatives are consistently too low in contrast, increase development time; if too high in contrast, decrease development time.

KODAK Packaged Developers	Developing Times in Minutes*				
	65°F (18°C)	68°F (20°C)	70°F (21°C)	72°F (22°C)	75°F (24°C)
D-76	6½	**5½**	5	4½	3¾
D-76 (1:1)†	8	**7**	6½	6	5
MICRODOL-X	8	**7**	6½	6	5½
MICRODOL-X (1:3)†	—	—	11	10	**9½**
HC-110 (Dilution B)	6	**5**	4½	4	3½
HOBBY-PAC™ Black-and-White Film Developer	6	**5**	4½	4	3½

*Unsatisfactory uniformity may result with development times shorter than 5 minutes.   †For greater sharpness.

Rinse in KODAK Indicator Stop Bath, KODAK HOBBY-PAC™ Black-and-White Film and Paper Stop Bath, or KODAK Stop Bath SB-5, at 65 to 75°F (18 to 24°C), for 30 seconds with agitation. You can use a running-water rinse if an acid stop bath is not available.

Fix in KODAK Fixer, KODAK HOBBY-PAC™ Black-and-White Film and Paper Fixer, or KODAK Fixing Bath F-5 for 5 to 10 minutes, or KODAK Rapid Fixer or KODAFIX Solution for 2 to 4 minutes, at 65 to 75°F (18 to 24°C) with agitation.

Wash the film for 20 to 30 minutes in running water at 65 to 75°F (18 to 24°C). To minimize drying marks, treat the film in KODAK PHOTO-FLO Solution after washing, or wipe the surfaces carefully with a KODAK Photo Chamois or a soft viscose sponge.

Note: Keep temperatures of rinse, fix, and wash close to developer temperature.

Dry in a dust-free place.

Also, see pages 96–99.

DEFINITION

Graininess	Resolving Power	Sharpness	Degree of Enlargement Potential*
Extremely Fine	High 125 lines per mm	Very High	High

*For good-quality negatives.

For Black-and-White Prints

An extremely fine grain panchromatic film with very high resolving power and very high sharpness. PANATOMIC-X Film is an excellent film to select when you want to create prints with a very high degree of enlargement. The film has high definition qualities for reproducing fine detail while providing exquisite tone gradation. The film speed is sufficient when ample illumination is available and picture-taking conditions are not demanding. With special processing, the film in 135 size will produce positive black-and-white slides. A professional version of this film is also available—KODAK PANATOMIC-X Professional Film in 120 size. See page 83.

Film Code Letter Designation: FX.

Film Code Number and Size Available: 5060—size 135-24 exposures, 135-36 exposures.

Storage and Handling: Protect unprocessed film from heat. Have your film processed promptly after exposure.

EXPOSURE

Daylight Exposure Table: For average subjects.

Speed: ISO 32

Shutter Speed 1/125 Second				Shutter Speed 1/60 Second	
Bright or Hazy Sun Distinct Shadows					
On Light Sand or Snow	Average Subjects	Weak Hazy Sun Soft Shadows	Cloudy Bright No Shadows	Heavy Overcast	Open Shade†
f/11	f/8*	f/5.6	f/4	f/4	f/4

*For frontlighted subjects. For backlighted close-up subjects use f/4 at 1/125 second.   †Subject shaded from the sun but lighted by a large area of sky.

Filter Factors: Increase the normal exposure by the filter factor in the table. However, if your camera has a built-in exposure meter that makes the reading through a filter used over the lens, see your camera manual for instructions on exposure with filters. Also, see page 119.

Filter	No. 6	No. 8	No. 15	No. 11	No. 25	No. 58	No. 47	Polarizing Screen
Daylight	1.5	2*	2.5	4	8	6	8	2.5
Tungsten	1.5	1.5	1.5	4*	5	6	16	2.5

*For correct gray-tone rendering of colored objects.

Electronic Flash Guide Numbers: Use this table as a starting point in determining the correct guide number for electronic flash units rated in beam candlepower seconds (BCPS). Divide the proper guide number by the flash-to-subject distance in feet to determine the f-number for average subjects.

Output of Unit—BCPS	350	500	700	1000	1400	2000	2800	4000	5600	8000
Guide Numbers	24	28	32	40	50	55	65	80	95	110

Reciprocity Characteristics: The following table gives the exposure and development compensation for different exposure times.

Exposure Time in Seconds	Either		Change Developing Time by
	Increase Lens Opening by	Or Use Corrected Exposure Time in Seconds	
1/100,000	+1 stop	Use lens opening correction	+20 percent
1/10,000	+½ stop	Use lens opening correction	+15 percent
1/1000	None	No change	+10 percent
1/100	None	No change	None
1/10	None	No change	None
1	+1 stop	2	−10 percent
10	+2 stops	50	−20 percent
100	+3 stops	1200	−30 percent

Note: Make exposure corrections for long or short exposure times as indicated in the table. Make the development correction only if you want the whole roll of film processed for the corrected development time. If correcting the development is not practical because of significantly different exposure times used for different pictures on the roll, develop the film for the normal development time. Usually you can make the contrast correction for reciprocity effect by using higher- or lower-contrast photographic paper as necessary when you make the prints.

Processing Services: You can have your film developed and printed by Kodak or another processing lab by returning the film to your photo dealer. Your dealer can also order enlargements from your negatives from other labs.

Processing the Film Yourself: You can develop your film in your own darkroom by following the steps below.

Safelight: *Total darkness required.* However, when development is half completed, you can use a safelight at 4 feet (1.2 metres) for a *few* seconds. Equip the safelight with a KODAK 3 Safelight Filter (dark green), or equivalent, and a 15-watt bulb.

Developing Times are for small roll-film tanks with agitation for 5 seconds at 30-second intervals throughout development. See page 100 for method of agitation. The most widely used times and temperature are in heavy type. If your negatives are consistently too low in contrast, increase development time; if too high in contrast, decrease development time.

KODAK Packaged Developers	Developing Times in Minutes*				
	65°F (18°C)	68°F (20°C)	70°F (21°C)	72°F (22°C)	75°F (24°C)
D-76	6	**5**	4½	4¼	3¾
D-76 (1:1)†	8	**7**	6½	6	5
MICRODOL-X	8	**7**	6½	6	5
MICRODOL-X (1:3)†	13	**12**	11	10	8½
HC-110 (Dilution B)	4¾	**4¼**	4	3¾	3¼
HOBBY-PAC™ Black-and-White Film Developer	4¾	**4¼**	4	3¾	3¼

*Unsatisfactory uniformity may result with development times shorter than 5 minutes.   †For greater sharpness.

Rinse in KODAK Indicator Stop Bath, KODAK HOBBY-PAC™ Black-and-White Film and Paper Stop Bath, or KODAK Stop Bath SB-5, at 65 to 75°F (18 to 24°C), for 30 seconds with agitation. You can use a running-water rinse if an acid stop bath is not available.

Fix in KODAK Fixer or KODAK Fixing Bath F-5 for 2 to 4 minutes, or KODAK HOBBY-PAC™ Black-and-White Film and Paper Fixer for 5 to 10 minutes, or KODAK Rapid Fixer or KODAFIX Solution for 1 to 2 minutes, at 65 to 75°F (18 to 24°C) with agitation.

Wash the film for 20 to 30 minutes in running water at 65 to 75°F (18 to 24°C). To minimize drying marks, treat the film in KODAK PHOTO-FLO Solution after washing, or wipe the surfaces carefully with a KODAK Photo Chamois or a soft viscose sponge.

Note: Keep temperatures of rinse, fix, and wash close to developer temperature.

Dry in a dust-free place.

Also, see pages 96–99.

DEFINITION	Graininess	Resolving Power	Sharpness	Degree of Enlargement Potential*
	Extremely Fine	Very High 200 lines per mm	Very High	Very High

*For good-quality negatives.

Exposing and Processing: When you use PANATOMIC-X Film, 135 size, as a positive slide film, expose it at a speed of **80** for daylight and **64** for tungsten. Process your film in the KODAK Direct Positive Film Developing Outfit. With the temperature of all the solutions at 68°F (20°C), follow the processing steps below. Agitate continuously during the first 30 seconds in each solution, and for 5 seconds every minute thereafter.

Safelight: *Total darkness is required* until you have completed the bleaching step. For the rest of the process you can use a safelight equipped with a KODAK OA Safelight Filter (greenish yellow), or equivalent, and a 15-watt bulb. Keep the safelight at least 4 feet (1.2 metres) from the film. Do not turn on the normal room lights until the film has been fixed, or the highlights may appear gray.

1. First Developer . . . . 8 minutes
2. Water Rinse . . . . 2 to 5 minutes*
3. Bleach Bath . . . . 1 minute
4. Clearing Bath . . . . 2 minutes
*A 2-minute rinse is sufficient with a running-water wash and good agitation.

5. Redeveloper . . . . 8 minutes
6. Water Rinse . . . . 1 minute
7. Fixing Bath . . . . 5 minutes
8. Wash . . . . 20 minutes

For Black-and-White Prints

A high-speed panchromatic film with fine grain and excellent sharpness. Its high speed makes it especially useful for photographing dimly lighted subjects, such as those in existing light; fast action; subjects requiring good depth of field and high shutter speeds; and for extending the distance range for flash pictures. This is a very versatile film—you can use it to photograph a wide variety of subjects and lighting conditions, and be prepared to photograph unpredictable situations within the capability of your camera.

KODAK TRI-X Pan Professional Film with somewhat different characteristics is sold in 120 and 220 sizes. See description on page 83.

Film Code Letter Designation: TX.

Film Code Numbers and Sizes Available: 5063—size 135-24 exposures, 135-36 exposures; 6043—size 120.

Storage and Handling: Protect unprocessed film from heat. Load and unload camera in subdued light. Have your film processed promptly after exposure.

EXPOSURE

Daylight Exposure Table: For average subjects.

Speed: ISO 400

Shutter Speed 1/1000 Second		Shutter Speed 1/500 Second				
Bright or Hazy Sun Distinct Shadows		Weak Hazy Sun Soft Shadows	Cloudy Bright No Shadows	Heavy Overcast	Open Shade†
On Light Sand or Snow	Average Subjects				
f/16	f/16*	f/11	f/8	f/5.6	f/5.6

*For frontlighted subjects. For backlighted close-up subjects use f/8 at 1/500 second.

†Subject shaded from the sun but lighted by a large area of sky.

Filter Factors: Increase the normal exposure by the filter factor in the table. However, if your camera has a built-in exposure meter that makes the reading through a filter used over the lens, see your camera manual for instructions on exposure with filters. Also, see page 119.

Filter	No. 6	No. 8	No. 15	No. 11	No. 25	No. 58	No. 47	Polarizing Screen
Daylight	1.5	2*	2.5	4	8	6	6	2.5
Tungsten	1.5	1.5	1.5	3*	5	6	12	2.5

*For correct gray-tone rendering of colored objects.

Existing-Light Exposure Table: Use an exposure meter or an automatic camera if you have one. For cameras without working exposure meters, try the settings suggested in the table.

These exposures are *guides*; for more assurance, bracket your exposures 1 or 2 stops on each side of the suggested exposure.

Picture Subject	Shutter Speed	Lens Opening
Home Interiors at Night— Areas with average light Areas with bright light	1/30 1/30	f/2 f/2.8
Candlelighted Close-Ups	1/15*	f/2
Interiors with Bright Fluorescent Light†	1/60	f/4
Indoor, Outdoor Christmas Lighting at Night	1/15*	f/2
Brightly Lighted Downtown Street Scenes at Night	1/60	f/2.8
Brightly Lighted Theatre Districts—Las Vegas or Times Square	1/60	f/4
Neon Signs, Other Lighted Signs	1/125	f/4
Store Windows at Night	1/60	f/4
Floodlighted Buildings, Fountains, Monuments	1/15*	f/2
Distant View of City Skyline at Night	1*	f/2.8
Skylines—10 minutes after sunset	1/60	f/5.6

Picture Subject	Shutter Speed	Lens Opening
Fairs, Amusement Parks	1/30	f/2.8
Aerial Fireworks Displays— Keep camera shutter open on BULB for several bursts	BULB*	f/16
Night Football, Soccer, Baseball, Racetracks	1/125	f/2.8
Basketball, Hockey, Bowling	1/125	f/2
Boxing, Wrestling	1/250	f/2
Stage Shows— Average lighting Bright lighting	1/60 1/125	f/2.8 f/4
Circuses—Floodlighted acts	1/60	f/2.8
Ice Shows—Floodlighted acts	1/125	f/2.8
Ice Shows, Circuses— Spotlighted acts (carbon arc)	1/250	f/2.8
School—Stage and auditorium	1/30	f/2
Swimming Pool—Indoors, tungsten lights above water	1/60	f/2
Church Interiors— Artificial lights	1/30	f/2

*Use a tripod or other firm camera support for exposure times longer than 1/30 second.

†Use exposure times longer than 1/60 second.

Electronic Flash Guide Numbers: Use this table as a starting point in determining the correct guide number for electronic flash units rated in beam candlepower seconds (BCPS).

Divide the proper guide number by the flash-to-subject distance in feet to determine the *f*-number for average subjects.

Output of Unit—BCPS	350	500	700	1000	1400	2000	2800	4000	5600	8000
Guide Numbers	85	100	120	140	170	200	240	280	340	400

Reciprocity Characteristics: The following table gives the exposure and development compensation for different exposure times.

Exposure Time in Seconds	Increase Lens Opening by	Or Use Corrected Exposure Time in Seconds	Change Developing Time By
		Either	
1/100,000	+ 1 stop	Use lens opening correction	+ 20 percent
1/10,000	+ ½ stop	Use lens opening correction	+ 15 percent
1/1000	None	No change	+ 10 percent
1/100	None	No change	None
1/10	None	No change	None
1	+ 1 stop	2	− 10 percent
10	+ 2 stops	50	− 20 percent
100	+ 3 stops	1200	− 30 percent

Note: Make exposure corrections for long or short exposure times as indicated in the table. Make the development correction only if you want the whole roll of film processed for the corrected development time. If correcting the development is not practical because of significantly different exposure times used for different pictures on the roll, develop the film for the normal development time. Usually you can make the contrast correction for reciprocity effect by using higher- or lower-contrast photographic paper as necessary when you make the prints.

PROCESSING

Processing Services: You can have your film developed and printed by Kodak or another processing lab by returning the film to your photo dealer. Your dealer can also order enlargements from your negatives from other labs.

Processing the Film Yourself: You can develop your film in your own darkroom by following the steps below.

Safelight: *Total darkness required.* However, when development is half completed, you can use a safelight at 4 feet (1.2 metres) for a *few* seconds. Equip the safelight with a KODAK 3 Safelight Filter (dark green), or equivalent, and a 15-watt bulb.

Developing Times are for small roll-film tanks with agitation for 5 seconds at 30-second intervals throughout development. See page 100 for method of agitation. The most widely used times and temperature are in heavy type. If your negatives are consistently too low in contrast, increase development time; if too high in contrast, decrease development time.

KODAK Packaged Developers	Developing Times in Minutes*				
	65°F (18°C)	68°F (20°)	70°F (21°C)	72°F (22°C)	75°F (24°C)
D-76	9	**8**	7½	6½	5½
D-76 (1:1)†	11	**10**	9½	9	8
MICRODOL-X	11	**10**	9½	9	8
MICRODOL-X (1:3)†	—	—	15	14	**13**
DK-50 (1:1)	7	**6**	5½	5	4½
HC-110 (Dilution A)	4¼	**3¾**	3¼	3	2½
HC-110 (Dilution B)	8½	**7½**	6½	6	5
HOBBY-PAC™ Black-and-White Film Developer	8½	**7½**	6½	6	5

*Unsatisfactory uniformity may result with development times shorter than 5 minutes.　　†For greater sharpness.

Rinse in KODAK Indicator Stop Bath, KODAK HOBBY-PAC™ Black-and-White Film and Paper Stop Bath, or KODAK Stop Bath SB-5, at 65 to 75°F (18 to 24°C), for 30 seconds with agitation. You can use a running-water rinse if an acid stop bath is not available.

Fix in KODAK Fixer, KODAK HOBBY-PAC™ Black-and-White Film and Paper Fixer, or KODAK Fixing Bath F-5 for 5 to 10 minutes, or KODAK Rapid Fixer or KODAFIX Solution for 2 to 4 minutes, at 65 to 75°F (18 to 24°C) with agitation.

Wash the film for 20 to 30 minutes in running water at 65 to 75°F (18 to 24°C). To minimize drying marks, treat the film in KODAK PHOTO-FLO Solution after washing, or wipe the surfaces carefully with a KODAK Photo Chamois or a soft viscose sponge.

Note: Keep temperatures of rinse, fix, and wash close to developer temperature.

Dry in a dust-free place.

Also, see pages 96–99.

DEFINITION	Graininess	Resolving Power	Sharpness	Degree of Enlargement Potential*
	Fine	High 100 lines per mm	Very High	Moderate

*For good-quality negatives.

For Black-and-White Prints

A panchromatic film for 120-size cameras that has very high speed and medium grain. Use ROYAL-X Pan Film for situations where the highest film speed is essential, such as for taking action photographs by existing light or for obtaining adequate depth of field under poor lighting conditions while handholding your camera. This is a good film to use for photographing sports events outdoors at night or indoors in sports arenas under the existing lighting.

Film Code Letter Designation: RX.

Film Code Number and Size Available: 6046—size 120.

Storage and Handling: Protect unprocessed film from heat. Take special precautions to load and unload camera in subdued light because of the film's very high speed. Have your film processed promptly after exposure.

EXPOSURE

Speed: ISO 1250. For low-contrast scenes, you can obtain good negatives by setting your exposure meter for film-speed numbers up to 2000 with normal development, and up to 4000 if you increase development 50 percent by using the extended times in the development table.

Suggested Exposure Settings:

Lighting Conditions	Average Subject—Normal Development	Low-Contrast Subject—Extended Development
Existing Light Home Interiors at Night— 　Areas with average light 　Areas with bright light	 1/30 sec f/4 1/60 sec f/4	 1/60 sec f/4 1/60 sec f/5.6
Night Football, Baseball, Soccer, 　Racetracks, Boxing, Wrestling	1/250 sec f/4	1/500 sec f/4
Basketball, Hockey, Bowling	1/250 sec f/2.8	1/250 sec f/4
Interiors with Bright Fluorescent Light*	1/60 sec f/8	1/60 sec f/11
School—Stage and auditorium	1/30 sec f/4	1/60 sec f/4
Church Interiors—Artificial light	1/30 sec f/4	1/60 sec f/4
Daylight Heavy Overcast or Open Shade— Subject shaded from the sun but lighted by 　a large area of sky	 1/250 sec f/16	 1/250 sec f/22
Cloudy Bright—No shadows	1/250 sec f/22	1/500 sec f/22
Weak Hazy Sun—Soft shadows	1/500 sec f/22	1/500 sec f/32
Bright or Hazy Sun—Distinct shadows	1/500 sec f/32	—

*Use exposure times longer than 1/60 second.

Electronic Flash Guide Numbers: Use this table as a starting point in determining the correct guide number for electronic flash units rated in beam candlepower seconds (BCPS). Divide the proper guide number by the flash-to-subject distance in feet to determine the f-number for average subjects.

Output of Unit—BCPS	350	500	700	1000	1400	2000	2800	4000	5600	8000
Guide Numbers	150	180	210	250	300	350	420	500	600	700

Filter Factors: Increase the normal exposure by the filter factor in the table. However, if your camera has a built-in exposure meter that makes the reading through a filter used over the lens, see your camera manual for instructions on exposure with filters. Also, see page 119.

Filter	No. 6	No. 8	No. 15	No. 11	No. 25	No. 58	No. 47	Polarizing Screen
Daylight	1.5	2*	2.5	4	8	8	6	2.5
Tungsten	1.5	2	2	4*	5	8	12	2.5

*For correct gray-tone rendering of colored objects.

Reciprocity Characteristics: The following table gives the exposure and development compensation for different exposure times.

| Exposure Time in Seconds | Either | | Change Developing Time by |
	Increase Lens Opening by	Or Use Corrected Exposure Time in Seconds	
1/1000	None	No change	+ 10 percent
1/100	None	No change	None
1/10	None	No change	None
1	+ 1 stop	2	− 10 percent
10	+ 2 stops	50	− 20 percent
100	+ 3 stops	1200	− 30 percent

Note: Make exposure corrections for long exposure times as indicated in the table. Make the development correction only if you want the whole roll of film processed for the corrected development time. If correcting the development is not practical because of significantly different exposure times used for different pictures on the roll, develop the film for the normal development time. Usually you can make the contrast correction for reciprocity effect by using higher- or lower-contrast photographic paper as necessary when you make the prints.

PROCESSING

This film must be processed by using the following procedure. Only the developers listed are recommended. If a photofinisher processes this film, make sure that they can provide the special processing service required.

Processing the Film Yourself: You can develop your film in your own darkroom by following the steps below.

Safelight: *Total darkness required.*

Developing Times are for small roll-film tanks with agitation for 5 seconds at 30-second intervals throughout development. See page 100 for method of agitation. The most widely used times and temperature are in heavy type. If your negatives are consistently too low in contrast, increase development time; if too high in contrast, decrease development time.

| KODAK Packaged Developers | Developing Times in Minutes* | | | | | | | | | |
| | Average Subjects | | | | | Low-Contrast Subjects | | | | |
	65°F (18°C)	**68°F (20°C)**	70°F (21°C)	72°F (22°C)	75°F (24°C)	65°F (18°C)	**68°F (20°C)**	70°F (21°C)	72°F (22°C)	75°F (24°C)
DK-50	5½	**5**	4¾	4¾	4½	8	**7½**	7	—	6½
HC-110 (Dilution A)	6	**5**	4¾	4½	4¼	9	**7½**	7	6½	6
HC-110 (Dilution B)	10	**9**	8	7½	6½	15	**14**	12	11	10
HOBBY-PAC™ Black-and-White Film Developer	10	**9**	8	7½	6½	15	**14**	12	11	10

*Unsatisfactory uniformity may result with development times shorter than 5 minutes.

Note: Use fresh developers, because exhausted developers may produce a deposit of dichroic fog. You can usually swab this off while the film is still wet.

Use an Acid Stop Bath. Rinse in KODAK Indicator Stop Bath, KODAK HOBBY-PAC™ Black-and-White Film and Paper Stop Bath, or KODAK Stop Bath SB-5, at 65 to 75°F (18 to 24°C), for 30 seconds to 1 minute *with continuous agitation.* Drain the film for 2 to 5 seconds before immersing it in the fixing bath. *The use of an acid stop bath is important*—it minimizes the tendency for dichroic stain deposits to form on the film surface.

Fix in KODAK Fixer, KODAK HOBBY-PAC™ Black-and-White Film and Paper Fixer, or KODAK Fixing Bath F-5 for 5 to 10 minutes, or KODAK Rapid

Fixer for 3 to 5 minutes, at 65 to 75°F (18 to 24°C). *Agitate films frequently during fixing.*

Wash the film for 20 to 30 minutes in running water at 65 to 75°F (18 to 24°C). To minimize drying marks, treat the film in KODAK PHOTO-FLO Solution after washing, or wipe the surfaces carefully with a KODAK Photo Chamois or a soft viscose sponge.

Note: Keep temperatures of rinse, fix, and wash close to developer temperature.

Dry in a dust-free place.

Also, see pages 96–99.

DEFINITION	Graininess	Resolving Power	Sharpness	Degree of Enlargement Potential*
	Medium	High 100 lines per mm	High	Moderately Low

*For good-quality negatives.

For Black-and-White Prints

A very high-speed panchromatic film for 35 mm cameras that has extended red sensitivity. Use this film in situations where the highest film speed is essential and fine grain is not important to you, such as for taking action photographs when the light is extremely poor or for obtaining adequate depth of field under poor lighting conditions while handholding your camera. This film's very high speed makes it suitable for photographing sports events under adverse conditions outdoors at night or indoors in sports arenas using the existing lighting and telephoto lenses. Recording Film 2475 has coarse grain.

Film Code Letter Designation: RE.

Film Code Number and Size Available: 2475—size 135-36 exposures.

Storage and Handling: Protect unprocessed film from heat. Take special precautions to load and unload camera in subdued light because of the film's very high speed. After the last exposure, rewind the film *completely* into the magazine before opening your camera to unload the film. Have your film processed promptly after exposure.

EXPOSURE

Speed: EI 1000. For exposure meters marked for ISO/ASA speeds or Exposure Indexes. For low-contrast scenes, you can obtain good negatives by setting your exposure meter for film-speed numbers up to 1600 with normal development, and up to 3200 if you increase development 50 percent by using the extended times in the development table.

Suggested Exposure Settings:

Lighting Conditions	Average Subject—Normal Development	Low-Contrast Subject—Extended Development
Existing Light Home Interiors at Night—		
Areas with average light	1/30 sec f/4	1/60 sec f/4
Areas with bright light	1/60 sec f/4	1/60 sec f/5.6
Night Football, Baseball, Soccer, Racetracks, Boxing, Wrestling	1/250 sec f/4	1/500 sec f/4
Basketball, Hockey, Bowling	1/250 sec f/2.8	1/250 sec f/4
Interiors with Bright Fluorescent Light*	1/60 sec f/8	1/60 sec f/11
School—Stage and auditorium	1/30 sec f/4	1/60 sec f/4
Church Interiors—Artificial light	1/30 sec f/4	1/60 sec f/4
Daylight Heavy Overcast or Open Shade— Subject shaded from the sun but lighted by a large area of sky	1/1000 sec f/5.6	1/1000 sec f/8
Cloudy Bright—No shadows	1/1000 sec f/8	1/1000 sec f/11
Weak Hazy Sun—Soft shadows	1/1000 sec f/11	1/1000 sec f/16
Bright or Hazy Sun—Distinct shadows	1/1000 sec f/16	—

*Use exposure times longer than 1/60 second.

Electronic Flash Guide Numbers: Use this table as a starting point in determining the correct guide number for electronic flash units rated in beam candlepower seconds (BCPS). Divide the proper guide number by the flash-to-subject distance in feet to determine the f-number for average subjects.

Output of Unit—BCPS	350	500	700	1000	1400	2000	2800	4000	5600	8000
Guide Numbers	130	160	190	220	260	320	380	450	530	630

Filter Factors: Increase the normal exposure by the filter factor in the table. However, if your camera has a built-in exposure meter that makes the reading through a filter used over the lens, see your camera manual for instructions on exposure with filters. Also, see page 119.

Filter	No. 6	No. 8	No. 15	No. 11	No. 25	No. 58	No. 47	Polarizing Screen
Daylight	1.5	2*	2	6	3	10	6	2.5
Tungsten	1.2	1.2	1.5	6*	2	12	16	3

*For correct gray-tone rendering of colored objects.

Reciprocity Characteristics: The following table gives the exposure and development compensation for different exposure times.

Exposure Time in Seconds	Either		Change Developing Time by
	Increase Lens Opening by	Or Use Corrected Exposure Time in Seconds	
1/10,000	None	No change	None
1/1000	None	No change	None
1/100	None	No change	None
1/10	None	No change	None
1	+ 1/2 stop	1 1/2	− 10 percent
10	+ 2 stops	40	− 10 percent

Note: Make exposure corrections for long exposure times as indicated in the table. Make the development correction only if you want the whole roll of film processed for the corrected development time. If correcting the development is not practical because of significantly different exposure times used for different pictures on the roll, develop the film for the normal development time. Usually you can make the contrast correction for reciprocity effect by using higher- or lower-contrast photographic paper as necessary when you make the prints.

PROCESSING

You can develop your film in your own darkroom by following the steps below.

Safelight: *Total darkness required.*

Developing Times are for small roll-film tanks with agitation for 5 seconds at 30-second intervals throughout development. See page 100 for method of agitation. The most widely used times and temperature are in heavy type. If your negatives are consistently too low in contrast, increase development time; if too high in contrast, decrease development time.

KODAK Packaged Developers	Developing Times in Minutes*									
	Average Subjects					Low-Contrast Subjects				
	65°F (18°C)	68°F (20°C)	70°F (21°C)	72°F (22°C)	75°F (24°C)	65°F (18°C)	68°F (20°C)	70°F (21°C)	72°F (22°C)	75°F (24°C)
DK-50	7	6	5	4 3/4	4	10 1/2	9	8 1/2	7 1/2	6 1/2
HC-110 (Dilution A)	5 1/2	4 1/2	4	3 1/2	3	9 1/2	8	7 1/2	6 1/2	5
HC-110 (Dilution B)	11	9	8	7	6	17	15	12	11	10

*Unsatisfactory uniformity may result with development times shorter than 5 minutes.

Note: Use fresh developers, because exhausted developers may produce a deposit of dichroic fog. You can usually swab this off while the film is still wet.

Use an Acid Stop Bath. Rinse in KODAK Indicator Stop Bath, or KODAK Stop Bath SB-5, or KODAK Stop Bath SB-1a at 65 to 75°F (18 to 24°C) for 30 seconds to 1 minute *with continuous agitation.* Drain the film for 2 to 5 seconds before immersing it in the fixing bath. *The use of an acid stop bath is important*—it minimizes the tendency for dichroic stain deposits to form on the film surface.

Fix in KODAK Fixer, or KODAFIX Solution, or KODAK Fixing Bath F-5 for 8 to 12 minutes, or KODAK Rapid Fixer for 3 to 5 minutes, at 65 to 75°F (18 to 24°C). *Agitate films frequently during fixing.*

Wash the film for 20 to 30 minutes in running water at 65 to 75°F (18 to 24°C). To minimize drying marks, treat the film in KODAK PHOTO-FLO Solution after washing, or wipe the surfaces carefully with a KODAK Photo Chamois or a soft viscose sponge.

Note: Keep temperatures of rinse, fix, and wash close to developer temperature.

Dry in a dust-free place.

Also, see pages 96—99.

DEFINITION	Graininess	Resolving Power	Sharpness	Degree of Enlargement Potential*
	Coarse	Medium 63 lines per mm	Very High	Low

*For good-quality negatives.

For Black-and-White Prints

A moderately high-contrast, infrared-sensitive film that features abstract tone reproduction. With a red filter, it gives striking and unusual effects. The film is often used for pictorial landscape photographs to create an eerie, dream-like quality with light foliage and dark skies. High Speed Infrared Film is useful to show detail ordinarily obscured by atmospheric haze in distant landscapes. It is also useful in aerial, scientific, medical, industrial, legal, and documentary photography, and in photomicrography.

Film Code Letter Designation: HIE.

Film Code Number and Size Available: 2481—size 135-36 exposures.

Storage and Handling: Film magazines must be handled in *total darkness* when the magazines are outside the film cans. Load and unload your camera only in total darkness. You may want to use a changing bag on location for loading your camera. See your photo dealer for one that's opaque to infrared rays. Store unexposed 135 magazines of this film in a refrigerator at 55°F (13°C) or lower in the original sealed package. It's important to store unexposed film in total darkness, such as the tightly closed film cans. Allow film to warm up to room temperature before opening the package to avoid moisture condensation on film surfaces. Have your film processed promptly after exposure.

If you have to postpone processing of the film, store exposed unprocessed film in the tightly closed film cans under refrigeration below 40°F (4°C). Before opening the film cans and processing exposed film, allow the film to warm up to room temperature.

Do not load or unload your camera or process the film in rooms that have flourescent lighting even with the lights off. Flourescent lamps have an afterglow for a short time after they have been turned off.

EXPOSURE

Focusing: Camera lenses do not focus infrared rays in the same plane as visible light rays. Some camera lenses have index marks on their focusing scales for taking infrared pictures. If your lens has one, use it. Otherwise, set your lens at the smallest opening that conditions permit. If you have to use large lens openings, and your lens has no infrared focusing mark, try to focus on the near side of the main subject or make a focus test. An alternative method is to extend the lens by adding 0.25 percent of the focal length to the lens-film extension for infinity focus.

Filters: To obtain infrared rendition in your pictures, you must use a filter over the lens (or light source) to absorb the blue and green light to which the film is sensitive. For general photography, a No. 25 filter is recommended; or you can use a No. 29 or No. 70 filter. When you want to record only the infrared radiation, use a No. 89B, No. 88A, No. 87, or No. 87C filter.

Speeds: It's not possible to give exact speeds for KODAK High Speed Infrared Film, because the ratio of infrared to visible light is variable, and exposure meters do not respond accurately to infrared radiation. Similar levels of visible light may be vastly different in the amounts of infrared radiation they contain. Make trial exposures to determine the proper exposure for the conditions under which you take your pictures. You can use the following speeds as a basis for determining exposures under average conditions with meters marked for ISO/ASA speeds or Exposure Indexes. With cameras that have a built-in exposure meter that makes the reading through a filter used over the lens, use these film speeds and make the meter reading before you put the filter on the camera. Or, use a handheld exposure meter.

Filter	Film Speed*	
	Daylight	Tungsten
No. 25, 29, 70, or 89B	50	125
No. 87, 88A	25	64
No. 87C	10	25
No Filter	80	200

*Recommmended development in KODAK Developer D-76.

Daylight Exposures: Subjects in bright or hazy sunlight, distinct shadows. Use these recommendations as the basis of trial exposures.

Exposed Through a No. 25 Filter	
Distant Scenes 1/125 second f/11	Nearby Scenes 1/30 second f/11

Photolamps: For use with a No. 25 filter over the camera lens. The following table is based on the use of two 500-watt reflector-type photolamps. Place one lamp on each side of the camera at an angle of 45 degrees to the camera-subject axis.

EXPOSURE TABLE FOR 500-WATT REFLECTOR-TYPE PHOTOLAMPS			
Set Shutter Speed at 1/30 Second			
Lamp-to-Subject Distance	3 ft (0.9 m)	4½ ft (1.4 m)	6½ ft (2 m)
Lens Opening	f/11	f/8	f/5.6

Electronic Flash Guide Numbers: For use with a No. 87 filter. This table is intended as a starting point in determining the correct guide number for electronic flash units rated in beam candlepower seconds (BCPS). Divide the proper guide number by the flash-to-subject distance in feet to determine the *f*-number for trial exposures.

Output of Unit—BCPS	350	500	700	1000	1400	2000	2800	4000	5600	8000
Guide Numbers	20	24	30	35	40	50	60	70	85	100

Flashbulb Guide Numbers: For flash bulbs use a filter such as a No. 25, No. 29, No. 70, or No. 89B with clear flashbulbs. Divide the proper guide number by the flash-to-subject distance in feet to determine the *f*-number. If you use a No. 87 or No. 88A filter, increase exposure by 1 stop. If you use a No. 87C filter, increase exposure by 2 stops.

Synchroni-zation	Shutter Speed	Shallow Cylindrical Reflector	Intermediate Shaped Reflector	Polished Bowl-Shaped Reflector	Intermediate Shaped Reflector		Polished Bowl-Shaped Reflector	
		AG-1	AG-1	AG-1	M3 25	26*	M3 25	26*
X	1/30	90	120	180	200	—	280	—
M	1/30	60	85	120	170	200	240	280
	1/60	60	85	120	170	130	240	180
	1/125	50	70	100	140	90	200	130
	1/250	40	60	80	110	65	160	90
	1/500	32	45	65	85	50	120	65

*Bulbs for focal-plane shutters; use with FP synchronication.

WARNING: Bulbs may shatter when flashed; use a flashguard over your reflector. **Do not use flash in an explosive atmosphere.**

Reciprocity Characteristics: The following table gives the exposure compensation for different exposure times.

			Exposure Time in Seconds		
1/1000	1/100	1/10	1	10	100
+ 1/3 stop	None	None	None	None	+ 2/3 stop or multiply exposure time by 1.6

PROCESSING

You can develop your film in your own darkroom by following the steps below.

Safelight: *Total darkness required.*

Developing Times are for small roll-film tanks with agitation for 5 seconds at 30-second intervals throughout development. See page 100 for method of agitation. The most widely used times and temperature are in heavy type. If your negatives are consistently too low in contrast, increase development time; if too high in contrast, decrease development time.

KODAK Packaged Developers	Developing Times in Minutes*				
	65°F (18°C)	68°F (20°C)	70°F (21°C)	72°F (22°C)	75°F (24°C)
D-76	13	**11**	10	9½	8
HC-110 (Dilution B)	7	**6**	6	5½	5
D-19†	7	**6**	5½	5	4

*Unsatisfactory uniformity may result with development times shorter than 5 minutes.　†For maximum contrast.

Rinse in KODAK Indicator Stop Bath or KODAK Stop Bath SB-5, at 65 to 75°F (18 to 24°C), for 30 seconds with agitation. You can use a running-water rinse if an acid stop bath is not available.

Fix in KODAK Fixer or KODAK Fixing Bath F-5 for 5 to 10 minutes, or KODAK Rapid Fixer for 2 to 4 minutes, at 65 to 75°F (18 to 24°C) with agitation.

Wash the film for 20 to 30 minutes in running water at 65 to 75°F (18 to 24°C). To minimize drying marks, treat the film in KODAK PHOTO-FLO Solution after washing, or wipe the surfaces carefully with a KODAK Photo Chamois or a soft viscose sponge.

Note: Keep temperatures of rinse, fix, and wash close to developer temperature.

Dry in a dust-free place.

Also, see pages 96–99.

DEFINITION	Graininess	Resolving Power	Sharpness	Degree of Enlargement Potential*
	Fine	Medium 80 lines per mm	Medium	Moderately Low

*For good-quality negatives.

For Black-and-White Prints

A variable-contrast panchromatic film with extended red sensitivity and superb definition useful for several applications. Technical Pan Film, when processed in special low-contrast developer, is a superior pictorial film for making giant-size enlargements of 25X and more with little perceptible grain. The film features micro-fine grain and extremely high resolving power and sharpness to obtain its high quality.

For other applications, you can use Technical Pan Film to make reduced copy negatives of printed matter, such as books, newspapers, maps, engineering drawings, documents, and similar originals, and of color and black-and-white continuous-tone originals. The film produces good quality in copies of originals that contain both line and halftone material. You can vary the contrast of the film by choice of developer. The film's moderate to very high contrast combined with excellent definition characteristics meet the requirements for various copying purposes. The film speed varies with development and type of use. See the table below.

Another valuable application for this film is personal microfilming. You can also use the film for making reverse-text title slides with a black background and light type when you photograph white artwork with black type.

Film Code Letter Designation: TP.

Film Code Number and Size Available: 2415—size 135-36 exposures; 6415—size 120.

Storage and Handling: Protect unprocessed film from heat. Load and unload your camera in subdued light. After the last exposure, rewind 135-size film *completely* into the magazine before opening your camera to unload the film. Have your film processed promptly after exposure.

EXPOSURE

Speed: Film speeds are for exposure meters marked for ISO/ASA speeds or Exposure Indexes and recommended development. For copying use the film speeds below for determining trial exposures. For more assurance, bracket the estimated exposure by 1 or 2 stops using half-stop increments.

Use	Contrast Required*	Film Speed	
Pictorial	Low	EI 25	
Copy Applications: Type of Original		Gray Card†	WhiteCard‡
Printed matter; line drawings—good condition.	Maximum—Very High	EI 320	EI 64
Combination of printed matter and half-tone illustrations; hand-written copy; pencil drawings; originals with smudged or broken lines.	High	EI 200	EI 40
Continuouse-tone originals; photographs; artwork; paintings.	Moderate	EI 80	EI 16
Reverse Text Slides§	Maximum—Very High	EI 200	EI 40

*See table on next page for developer and development time to use for required contrast.
†For reflected-light meter readings, including in-camera meter readings, of an 18 percent reflectance gray card, such as the KODAK Gray Card, or incident-light meter readings at the copyboard.

‡For reflected-light exposure meter readings, including readings with in-camera meters, from a matt-white card of 90 percent reflectance at the copyboard.
§After photographing white artwork with black type, mount the processed negatives made on this film in slide mounts for projection.

Illumination: The recommended lighting setup for copying consists of two light sources, one on either side of the copy material, with the lights placed so that they are at an angle of 45 degrees to the material. Use a sheet of clean plate glass to hold the original flat.

Exposure Examples: With two No. 2 photoflood lamps in matt-surfaced reflectors 4 feet (1.2 metres) from the copy, use an exposure of about 1/60 second at f/8. With No. 1 photoflood lamps the same distance from the copy, use about 1/30 second at f/8. These exposures are based on development for maximum contrast in KODAK Developer D-19. See page D 45.

Filter Factors: *Pictorial*—Due to extended red sensitivity of Technical Pan Film, flesh tones and shades of red may reproduce lighter in prints than typical panchromatic black-and-white film. You can compensate for this effect by using a No. 38 light blue filter over the camera lens. Apply the filter factor given in the table below.

Copying—Usually, a filter is not required to achieve the desired contrast between background and subject matter. In special cases, such as in copying old newspapers or books with yellowed paper, use a No. 8 yellow filter or a No. 15 deep-yellow filter. For copying blueprints, use a No. 25 red filter. Increase the normal exposure by the filter factor in the table. However, if your camera has a built-in exposure meter that makes the reading through a filter used over the lens, see your camera instructions for exposure with filters. Also, see page 119.

Filter	No. 8	No. 15	No. 11	No. 13	No. 25	No. 38	No 58	No. 47
Daylight*	1.5	2	—	—	3	3	—	—
Tungsten†	1.2	1.2	5	6	2	—	12	25

*Filter factors are based on a 1/30-second exposure with daylight and normal development in KODAK TECHNIDOL Developer.

†Filter factors are based on a 1-second exposure with tungsten light and development in KODAK HC-110 Developer, Dilution D, for 8 minutes at 68°F (20°C).

Reciprocity Characteristics: The following table gives the exposure and development compensation for different exposure times for development in KODAK TECHNIDOL Developers.

Exposure Time in Seconds	Either		Change Developing Time by
	Increase Lens Opening by	Or Use Corrected Exposure Time in Seconds	
1/10,000	None	No change	+30 percent
1/1000	None	No change	+20 percent
1/100	None	No change	None
1/10	None	No change	None
1	None	No Change	−10 percent
10	+ ½ stop	15 seconds	−10 percent
100	+ 1½ stops	Not recommended	None

Note: Make exposure corrections for long exposure times as indicated in the table. Make the development correction only if you want the whole roll of film processed for the corrected development time. If correcting the development is not practical because of significantly different exposure times used for different pictures on the roll, develop the film for the normal development time. Usually you can make the contrast correction for reciprocity effect by using higher- or lower-contrast photographic paper as necessary when you make the prints.

PROCESSING

You can develop your film in your own darkroom by following the steps below.

Safelight: *Total darkness required.* However, when development is half completed, you can use a safelight at 4 feet (1.2 metres) for a *few* seconds. Equip the safelight with a KODAK 3 Safelight Filter (dark green), or equivalent, and a 15-watt bulb.

Developing Times are for small roll-film tanks with agitation for 5 seconds at 30-second intervals throughout development. See page 100 for method of agitation. For development in KODAK TECHNIDOL Developers, see the recommendations on the next page for agitation interval and method of agitation. If your negatives are consistently too low in contrast, increase development time; if too high in contrast, decrease development time.

Use/Contrast	KODAK Packaged Developers	Developing Times in Minutes 68° (20°C)
Pictorial/Low	TECHNIDOL Liquid* TECHNIDOL LC*	9 15
Copying/Maximum—Very High High Moderate	D-19 HC-110 (Dilution D)† HC-110 (Dilution F)†	4 8 6
Reverse Text Slides/Maximum— Very High	DEKTOL	3

*KODAK TECHNIDOL Liquid Developer is recommended for both 135 and 120 sizes of Technical Pan Film. KODAK TECHNIDOL LC Developer (powder) is recommended only for the 135-size film.
†You can prepare HC-110 Developer, Dilution D, by diluting one part stock solution, mixed according to package instructions, with 9 parts water, and Dilution F by diluting one part stock solution with 19 parts water. Mix both dilutions D and F fresh and discard frequently rather than replenish.

Agitation. The recommended agitation procedures for Technical Pan Film differ from those recommended for other Kodak films. It's important to carefully follow the agitation instructions given below.

Kodak Technidol Liquid Developer. In total darkness, drop the loaded film reel into a full tank of developer solution, smoothly and without hesitation. Attach the top to the tank. Then promptly dislodge any air bubbles from the film or reel by tapping the bottom of the tank on the work surface from a height of about 1 inch. Immediately agitate by using vigorous shaking of 10-12 cycles for two seconds. A cycle being a complete up and down movement of the tank. *Do not rotate the tank.* Let the tank sit for 28 seconds and then start the next 2-second agitation. Repeat every 30 seconds for the remainder of the development time.

Agitation for Technidol Liquid Developer

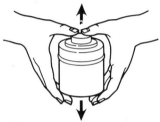

Kodak Technidol LC Developer. In total darkness, drop the loaded film reel into a full tank of developer solution, smoothly and without hesitation. Attach the top to the tank. Then promptly dislodge any air bubbles from the film or reel by tapping the bottom of the tank on the work surface from a height of about 1 inch. Immediately agitate the film tank as follows. Extend your arm and rotate the tank 180° at the wrist with no lateral arm movement. *Do not shake the tank vigorously.* Use an intial agitation of 4 inversion cycles by rotating the tank down and up for each cycle. Let the tank sit for the remainder of the first 30 seconds. After 30 seconds, start 5-second inversion cycles at 30 second intervals for the remainder of the development time. These agitation cycles should consist of 2 to 5 inversion cycles.

Agitation for Technidol LC Developer

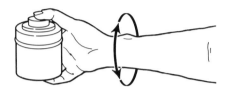

Rinse in Kodak Indicator Stop Bath, Kodak Stop Bath SB-1a, or Kodak Stop Bath SB-5, at 65 to 70°F (18 to 21°C), for 15 to 30 seconds with agitation. You can use a running-water rinse if an acid stop bath is not available.

Fix in Kodak Fixer or Kodak Fixing Bath F-5 for 2 to 4 minutes, or Kodak Rapid Fixer for 1½ to 3 minutes, at 65 to 70°F (18 to 21°C) with agitation.

Wash the film for 15 minutes in running water at 65 to 70°F (18 to 21°C). To minimize drying marks, treat the film in Kodak Photo-Flo Solution after washing. Do not squeegee or sponge the film.

Note: Keep temperatures of rinse, fix, and wash close to developer temperature.

Dry in a dust-free place.

Also, see pages 96–99.

DEFINITION

Graininess	Resolving Power	Sharpness	Degree of Enlargement Potential‡
Micro Fine*	Extremely High* 320 lines per mm	Extremely High*	Extremely High*
Extremely Fine†	Extremely High† 320 lines per mm	Extremely High†	Extremely High†

*For negatives developed in Kodak Technidol Liquid Developer.
†For negatives developed in Kodak Technidol LC Developer, or Kodak HC-110 Developer, Dilution D, for 8 minutes at 68°F (20°C).

‡The degree of enlargement usually will be limited by camera and subject conditions rather than by film characteristics.

Photo on back cover
Kodak Tri-X Pan Film
SCOTT F. LIDDLE, KINSA

D 46

195

PHOTOGRAPHIC PRODUCTS GROUP
Eastman Kodak Company
Rochester, New York 14650

KODAK Films—Color and Black-and-White
KODAK Publication AF-1
CAT 102 6061

M5E075 Major Revision 11-85-CX
Printed in U.S.A.
ISBN 0-87985-365-5

KODAK, INSTAMATIC, EKTRALITE, KODACOLOR, VR, T-GRAIN, KODACHROME, EKTACHROME, SATINLUXE, TRIMPRINT, EKTACHROME-X, VERICOLOR, EKTACOLOR, INSTAGRAPHIC, FLEXICOLOR, HOBBY-PAC, MAGNAPRINT35, SNAP-CAP, PANALURE, VERICHROME, PLUS-X, PANATOMIC-X, TRI-X, ROYAL-X, ESTAR, EKTAGRAPHIC, EASTMAN, GALLERY, KODAFIX, PHOTO-FLO, EKTAFLEX, KODACHROME-X, D-76, D-76R, MICRODOL-X, HC-110, DK-50, DK-50R, D-19, TECHNIDOL, KODALITH, and DEKTOL are trademarks.